CAPITAL MARKETS AND INSTITUTIONS IN BANGLADESH

To the memory of my mother, Fazilatennesa

Capital Markets and Institutions in Bangladesh
Some implications of Japanese experience

M. FARID AHMED
Faculty of Economics
Nagasaki University

LONDON AND NEW YORK

First published 1997 by Ashgate Publishing

Reissued 2018 by Routledge
2 Park Square, Milton Park, Abingdon, Oxon OX14 4RN
711 Third Avenue, New York, NY 10017, USA

Routledge is an imprint of the Taylor & Francis Group, an informa business

Copyright © M. Farid Ahmed 1997

All rights reserved. No part of this book may be reprinted or reproduced or utilised in any form or by any electronic, mechanical, or other means, now known or hereafter invented, including photocopying and recording, or in any information storage or retrieval system, without permission in writing from the publishers.

Notice:
Product or corporate names may be trademarks or registered trademarks, and are used only for identification and explanation without intent to infringe.

Publisher's Note
The publisher has gone to great lengths to ensure the quality of this reprint but points out that some imperfections in the original copies may be apparent.

Disclaimer
The publisher has made every effort to trace copyright holders and welcomes correspondence from those they have been unable to contact.

A Library of Congress record exists under LC control number : 97061066

ISBN 13: 978-1-138-61162-7 (hbk)
ISBN 13: 978-1-138-61166-5 (pbk)
ISBN 13: 978-0-429-44989-5 (ebk)

Contents

Tables and figures	viii
Preface	x
Abbreviations	xii

1 Introduction   1
   Objectives of the study   6
   Scope and methodical approach of the study   7
   Plan of the study   8

2 Private sector, capital market and government policy   10
   Industrial scenario and the state of public sectors   11
   Public to private sectors: policy reversal   18
   Implications for capital market   24
   Capital issue control   30
   Some Japanese experiences   32
   Concluding remarks   38
   Notes   39

3 Financial institutions and corporate financing   42
   Institutional framework   44
   Commercial banks   47
   Performance of Development Finance Institutions (DFIs)   52
   Financial institutions and Japanese experience   60
   Development perspective and selection criteria   67
   Concluding remarks   70

	Notes	71
4	**Securities markets and corporate financing**	73
	Alternative ways of financing	74
	Corporate securities and fund mobilization	77
	New issue market	84
	Secondary market	86
	Regulatory framework	90
	Demand side of the market	92
	Supply side of the market	96
	Policy implications	98
	Concluding remarks	106
	Notes	108
5	**Behavior and structure of stock prices**	110
	DSE trading system	111
	Stock price indexes	114
	Impact of dividend policy	121
	Price earnings ratio (PER)	127
	Dividend policy stabilization	131
	Concluding remarks	136
	Notes	136
6	**Capital market theory and Bangladesh market**	138
	Expected utility and investment decision	139
	Stock market behavior in Bangladesh	141
	Capital Asset Pricing Model (CAPM)	144
	Efficacy of CAPM and the developing market	148
	Testing methods and empirical results	152
	Accounting information and security market	158
	Concluding remarks	165
	Appendix-6.1	166
	Notes	167
7	**Corporate finance and governance structure**	169
	Individual shareholders	171
	Corporate shareholders	173
	Ownership and control	179
	Market segmentation	180
	Capital structure decision	183
	Dividend decision	184

The main bank system	186
Japanese experience in the context of Bangladesh	189
Concluding remarks	199
Notes	200
Bibliography	204

Tables and figures

Table 2.1	Share of different sectors of the economy	12
Table 2.2	Estimates of the SOEs	14
Table 2.3	Contribution of public sectors of Bangladesh	15
Table 2.4	Profit and loss of the major SOEs of Bangladesh	17
Table 2.5	Financial allocations in the plans of Bangladesh	20
Table 2.6	Foreign investment approval	22
Table 2.7	Cumulative foreign direct investment	23
Table 2.8	Capital issues consented	30
Table 3.1	Key financial institutions providing industrial finance in Bangladesh	45
Table 3.2	Banks and their branch offices in Bangladesh	46
Table 3.3	Assets of all banks	48
Table 3.4	Distribution of advances by economic purpose	49
Table 3.5	Liabilities of all banks	50
Table 3.6	Distribution of bank deposits	51
Table 3.7	Loan financing by BSB and BSRS	54
Table 3.8	Classification of ICB shareholders	56
Table 3.9	Performance of ICB unit certificates	58
Table 3.10	Performance of ICB mutual funds	59
Table 3.11	Relative size of banking sector	61
Table 4.1	Growth pattern of listed companies	78
Table 4.2	Funds mobilized by banking system, government saving schemes and stock markets in Bangladesh	79
Table 4.3	Ratio of new equity issues to gross investment and listed securities turnover to GDP	80

Table 4.4	Ratio of saving to GDP and new equity to national saving	81
Table 4.5	Public offering of listed shares	85
Table 4.6	Historical development of DSE	87
Table 4.7	Average monthly turnover of shares on DSE	89
Table 4.8	Laws relating to securities markets in Bangladesh	90
Table 5.1	Equity prices in Bangladesh	114
Table 5.2	Average 'rises' and 'declines' of share price and their deviations	117
Table 5.3	Number of listed companies paying dividends	124
Table 5.4	Changes in time deposit interest rate, dividend yield and average dividend rate	125
Table 5.5	Comparative PER of the listed stocks at year end	129
Table 5.6	Sector wise average PER of the listed stocks on DSE	130
Table 5.7	Average PER of companies and associated cash dividend	133
Figure 5.1	Stock price trend in DSE	115
Table 6.1	Year wise average monthly return from shares and monthly rate of interest on time deposit	143
Table 6.2	Expected return for varying levels of systematic risk	146
Table 6.3	Rates of return, standard deviations and betas for selected stocks	154
Table 6.4	Average return and portfolio beta	155
Table 6.5	Nominal returns on ordinary shares, TBs and risk premium	157
Table 7.1	Comparative position of dividend before and after reciprocal share holding between two corporations	185
Table 7.2	Composition of stock ownership in DSE and TSE	198
Figure 7.1	Structure of prewar business group	175
Figure 7.2	Structure of postwar business group	176

Preface

In the recent past rapid transformations of economic structure, policies and institutions are being observed on a global scale. More so in case of private sectors, financial markets and institutions, perhaps, because they are identified as crucial factors for sustainable economic growth and the achievement of national development goals in a freer market economy. Bangladesh also has witnessed remarkable macroeconomic stability, sweeping deregulation and liberalization over the past few years. Although economic underpinnings consistent with market economy and liberalization appear sufficient in general for the last few years, development of efficient and stable capital markets has not yet been attained. Substantial growth of a robust and vibrant market depends on overall environment, sound policy, legal and structural frameworks, promotional planning, as well as effective execution thereof. Making them all conducive for the rapid growth of the market is not an easy task. This study has made a modest attempt to explore a sensible approach to these issues rather than offer panacea solutions. In pursuing this objective, this study has focussed close attention on the experience of Japanese capital market development that has contributed significantly in the transformation process from a regulated economy to present-day economic superpower status along with the path of market economy. Thus, the implications of the Japanese corporate practices for developing countries are another aspect of this study based on theoretical and empirical analysis of both Bangladesh and Japanese markets. The conventional standard notions developed in Anglo-American countries constitute a strong foundation for the analysis of those markets, but they cannot give adequately convincing explanations of the Japanese financial system. Capital markets in Japan have experienced a radical structural change after World War II as a consequence of reforms introduced by the Occupation Authorities and the need to rebuild. Besides, Japanese capital markets have been evolving continuously since the War. Thus, the traditional practices have been adapted to a much more complex reality. To the extent our arguments are convincing, the results of the study are expected to indicate a somewhat different emphasis in the market development efforts of present-day developing countries like Bangladesh.

The completion of this book reflects the influence, encouragement and support of many individuals. Special mention of selected persons seems to me invidious as well as humiliating for them as that may relate them with my mistakes and naive judgements. However, the following inventory captures only the most obvious and important ones. As a graduate student at Yokohama National University and Nagoya University of Japan for the period from 1983 to 1989 and subsequently as a Professor affiliated jointly with Nagasaki University of Japan and Dhaka University of Bangladesh I had the opportunity to study and teach finance theory, Japanese and Bangladesh capital markets. The analysis and interpretations of this book are the results of my study and teaching on these areas. I have been in close touch with some insightful empirical studies on the recent Bangladesh financial system at Dhaka. Similarly, I have been exposed to a nice academic environment that promotes rigorous research activities at Nagasaki. This book could not have come out without the interactions with students, teachers and colleagues at all these institutions. I am deeply indebted to them for their inspiring discussions and critical comments.

I should record here the name of Professor Tamao Yamada of Chubu University, formerly of Nagoya University, Japan, who kindled my interest in finance theory and development finance and helped me to grow. I owe a great deal to Professor Shigeru Uchida and Professor Takafumi Yoshida who undertook the task of going through the earlier drafts. I am grateful for their advice and encouragement. I must acknowledge the wholehearted cooperation of Professor Akira Shimada who has provided much important information and responded spontaneously to my frequent requests for arranging logistic support necessary to complete this book. None of them, however, is responsible for errors and omissions. I consider it my pleasant duty to express my sincere gratitude to my wife Naherin and to my sons, Navin and Navid for their encouragement and support extended to me for completion of the book. Finally, I acknowledge the partial financial support by the Research Institute of South East Asia, Nagasaki University, for conducting this study.

M. Farid Ahmed
Nagasaki University

Abbreviations

ABSs	Asset-Backed Securities
ADB	Asian Development Bank
AGM	Annual General Meeting
BB	Bangladesh Bank
BCI	Bangladesh Commerce and Investment Ltd.
BCIC	Bangladesh Chemical Industries Corporation
BJMC	Bangladesh Jute Mills Corporation
BKB	Bangladesh Krishi Bank
BMRE	Balancing, Modernization, Replacement and Expansion
BOGMC	Bangladesh Oil, Gas and Minerals Corporation
BOI	Board of Investment of Bangladesh
BOJ	Bank of Japan
BPC	Bangladesh Petroleum Corporation
BPDB	Bangladesh Power Development Board
BSB	Bangladesh Shilpa Bank
BSC	Bangladesh Shipping Corporation
BSEC	Bangladesh Steel and Engineering Corporation
BSFIC	Bangladesh Sugar and Food Industries Corporation
BSRS	Bangladesh Shilpa Rin Sangstha
BTMC	Bangladesh Textile Mills Corporation
BTTB	Bangladesh Telephone and Telegraph Board
CAPM	Capital Asset Pricing Model
CCI	Controller of Capital Issues
CDS	Central Depository System
CSE	Chittagong Stock Exchange
DFIs	Development Finance Institutions

DSE	Dhaka Stock Exchange	
EMH	Efficient Market Hypothesis	
EPF	Equity Participation Fund	
EPIDC	East Pakistan Industrial Development Corporation	
EPZ	Export Processing Zone	
ERA	Economic Research Association of Japan	
FCBs	Foreign Commercial Banks	
FFYP	First Five Year Plan of Bangladesh	
GDP	Gross Domestic Product	
GNP	Gross National Product	
IACB	Industrial Advisory Center of Bangladesh	
ICB	Investment Corporation of Bangladesh	
ICP	Investment Corporation of Pakistan	
IDBP	Industrial Development Bank of Pakistan	
IFC	International Finance Corporation	
IMF	International Monetary Fund	
IPDC	Industrial Promotion and Development Corporation	
IPO	Initial Public Offering	
JBC	Jiban Bima Corporation	
LCs	Local Companies	
MITI	Ministry of International Trade and Industry	
MNCs	Multinational Companies	
MOF	Ministry of Finance	
MOU	Memorandum of Understanding	
NCBs	Nationalized Commercial Banks	
NCL	National Credit Ltd.	
NIP	New Industrial Policy	
NIT	National Investment Trust	
OECD	Organization for Economic Cooperation and Development	
OSE	Osaka Stock Exchange	
PBR	Price Book Value Ratio	
PCBs	Private Commercial Banks	
PER	Price Earnings Ratio	
PICIC	Pakistan Industrial Credit and Investment Corporation	
PIDC	Pakistan Industrial Development Corporation	
RIP	Revised Industrial Policy	
SABINCO	Saudi Bangladesh Agricultural and Industrial Company	
SBC	Shadharan Bima Corporation	
SCAP	Supreme Commander of the Allied Powers	
SEC	Securities and Exchange Commission	
SER	Securities and Exchange Rules	

SFYP	Second Five Year Plan of Bangladesh
SOEs	State Owned Enterprises
TBs	Treasury Bills
TFYP	Third Five Year Plan of Bangladesh
TSE	Tokyo Stock Exchange
TYP	Two Year Plan of Bangladesh

1 Introduction

Capital markets and financial institutions are investment intermediaries linking the savers and users of capital. These intermediaries are interposed between the ultimate borrowers and lenders permitting them efficient transfer of funds. Individuals having surplus funds can lend them for reasonable return to those who need funds to take the advantage of economically and financially viable investment opportunities. The existence of capital markets facilitates such exchange of resources. As a result, both the borrowers and the lenders are better off than they would have been without market intermediaries. Thus, these intermediaries have a positive role in economic growth which is a multidimensional process involving the complexity of many interrelated and interdependent factors of diversified nature. It is difficult to assess the contribution of each factor independently. More so in the case of capital markets and financial institutions whose contribution produces much wider ramification. Of all the factors affecting the rate of growth in any economy, the rate of new capital accumulation plays a role of paramount importance in the process of economic growth. The main function of a capital market along with other financial and non-financial institutions is to assist in the allocation of a nation's limited capital resources among numerous competing alternative uses. The essence of this function is the diversion of a part of society's currently available resources to the purpose of increasing the stock of capital goods so as to make possible an expansion of consumable output in the future (Nurkse, 1952). This process involves three distinct but interdependent activities: a) an increase in the volume of real savings, so that resources that would have been used for consumption purposes, can be released for other purposes; b) a finance and credit mechanism, so that the resources may be claimed by investors; and c) the act of investment itself, so that resources are used for the production of capital goods (Meir & Baldwin, 1964). If capital resources are not provided through such allocative functions to those industries or activities which are capable of increasing production and productivity, the rate of growth of the economy will inevitably suffer. Here lies the importance of finance and credit mechanism. In fact, this is the prime economic role of the financial intermediaries (Gurley & Shaw, 1955). On the subject of the relationship between financial development and economic development, a consensus appeared to have been reached by the mid-1970s, among the leading writers of the subject, that financial development is important and leads to economic development (Patrick, 1966; Porter, 1966; Gurley and Shaw, 1955; McKinnon, 1973; Shaw, 1973; Drake, 1980). This, however, is not to deny the importance of other factors. The economic history of developed countries shows that their periods of expansion have always been characterized by the high rate of capital formation. Shaw's (1973) argument is that the development of financial markets and institutions is a necessary condition for economic growth, and that developing countries typically suffer from a condition of financial repression which keeps finance 'shallow' and restricts economic growth. However, the development experience of Japan demonstrates a different picture which has been analyzed for having an insight of the development problems in the following chapters.

Academic discussion relating to capital markets and institutions of developing countries has not been extensive. Wai and Patrick (1973) are a widely referred paper on this issue who favors its development rather with caution. Drake (1977, 1980, 1985) supports the capital market development. Although Samuels (1981) and Samuels and Yacout (1981) appear to be supportive of capital market development but they have indicated their inefficiency that may result in increasing inequality in income and wealth distribution. Calamanti (1983) and Parkinson (1984) have emphasized the limited role of equity markets in raising new capital in a developing economy. It will be relevant to quote here from Baumol (1965) as:

> All in all, one cannot escape the impression that, at best, the allocative function is performed rather imperfectly as measured by the criteria of the welfare economist. The oligopolistic position of those who operate the market, the brokers, the floor traders and the specialists; the random patterns which characterize the behavior of stock prices; the unresponsiveness of supply to price changes; and management's efforts to avoid the market as a source of funds, all raise some questions about the perfections of the regulatory operations of the market . . .

This remark indicates some of the problems that the capital markets are to encounter. Added to these, developing markets like Bangladesh are likely to face a considerable number of more complicated issues involving structural, institutional and non-economic constraints. There is no easy answer to many of these problems. In this study, an attempt has been directed to explore a sensible approach to the problems of capital markets in a developing country than to offer panacea solutions.

It is generally agreed that capital markets under general equilibrium plays a very important role in an economy in collecting and allocating funds in an efficient manner. In order to ensure these economic activities in developed economies capital markets have or should have a significant link to the overall economy (Baumol, 1965). Capital markets also reflect investors' attempt to forecast economic trends. It is evident that the capital markets and economic activities move in a similar cyclical pattern (Moore, 1975). It is also recognized that the stock price index is a major component of the index of leading indicators of the economy (Zarnowitz and Boschan, 1975). However, it is not an easy task to establish an adequately efficient capital market particularly in an environment of an underdeveloped country. The capital markets are required to meet at least two basic requirements. It should support industrialization through savings mobilization, investment fund allocation and maturity transformation. Besides, it must be safe and efficient in discharging the aforesaid function. In a developing economy such conditions usually do not exist due to prevalence of informal credit markets that tend to limit the capacity to mobilize financial savings, a low degree of ownership-management separation associated with the drawbacks of informational asymmetry and low level of accumulated financial assets making maturity transformation difficult. Of course, these conditions differ widely from country to country.

Many developing economies have attempted to develop capital markets, not only to raise capital but also to diversify ownership of companies. These attempts have produced mixed results. Critics may characterize attempts to develop capital markets in developing economies as misguided efforts to introduce Western institutions into entirely different socioeconomic system or as a naive, if the mere establishment of security markets is expected to have a significant effect on the allocation of resources (Lloyd, 1977). However, they fail to consider that the motives for establishing security markets in developing countries have generally been more political than economic. Security markets in the United States and Western Europe evolved in response to the need for capital generated by the industrial revolution. Security markets in developing countries, however, have typically sprung less from private economic need than government decisions to pursue political and economic goals (Wai and Patrick, 1973), such as financial deepening. Capital markets are considered as an integral part of the developed economies like Japan, U.S.A., U.K. and so forth.

One can hardly escape the impact of activities in capital markets of such economies. On the one hand, these markets are deep, resilient and highly sensitive, and on the other the capital markets of developing countries like Bangladesh are narrow, underdeveloped, shaky and less sensitive. In the middle of the spectrum are the emerging markets such as Korea, Taiwan, Brazil and the like. If the major problem in the process of development is to increase the level of savings and to channel those savings into productive investments, then the mechanism of the capital market is a crucial intermediary element in the process of growth. It becomes a major significance to understand how the existing capital markets operate to assist the accumulation of savings and their allocation in various sectors. Then it may be possible to shape the markets in a manner to provide a more efficient mechanism for channeling increasing savings into productive investment.

Bangladesh markets offer an opportunity to study the development problems of the present day developing markets. With the adoption of a socialistic approach in economic management and nationalization of virtually all large scale industry immediately after liberation of the country in 1971 Dhaka Stock Exchange (DSE), the only bourse of the country at that time, was closed. With the change of government policy it reopened in 1976 after suspension of its activities for about four years. It is still in an early stage of development. In its efforts to design a sound financial system for Bangladesh, the government has had the opportunity to observe the other security markets including the developed security markets and their development experience. However, it is needless to say that security markets do not function in a vacuum; political economic, cultural and institutional constraints affect the development and success of the markets and its institutions.

Stock markets are historically found to be very weak conduits for channelizing investment funds in Indo-Pak-Bangladesh Subcontinent. Investment funds have usually been raised from internal sources or managing agents or from financial institutions as loan. However, with the spree of privatization and success of stock markets in many of the South-East Asian Newly Industrialized Economies (NIEs), Bangladesh presents an optimistic ground for effectively developing and utilizing the capital markets and relevant institutions for industrial financing. With a low saving rate, even lower than South Asian standard, Bangladesh has so far been meeting the resource gap between saving and investment predominantly from external aid. In a more competitive aid environment in recent years, the need for the development of sound and well functioning capital markets have become more urgent than ever before. Recently, with the changing political and economic environment in Bangladesh and elsewhere, the government of Bangladesh emphasized the need for development of capital markets and institutions in the country. Currently, the major institutions working toward development of capital markets are: Dhaka Stock Exchange (DSE), Investment Corporation of Bangladesh (ICB), two long term credit banks - Bangladesh Shilpa Bank (BSB) and Bangladesh Shilpa Rin Sangstha (BSRS), some General Insurance Companies and some Life Insurance Companies, both in private and public sectors. All these are predominantly engaged in long term fund management. Besides, Chittagong Stock Exchange (CSE), the second bourse of the country, started functioning in October 1995. There are commercial banks, both in private and public sectors, for providing short term funds to productive sectors. Bangladesh Bank, Securities and Exchange Commission (SEC) and Registrar of Joint Stock Companies (RJSC) are mainly engaged in regulatory functions. Notably, loan financing through banking system in Bangladesh is facing difficulties due to their unusually low recovery position. They can't recover overdue amounts which are more than 50 percent of total lending. There is some evidence of concern among the aid donors who made significant financial contribution to sustain the lending programs of these financial institutions. But the bank-based financing system has contributed significantly in the successful industrial development of Japan which also eventually paved the way for developing one of the largest well functioning stock markets in the world.

In Bangladesh, the processes of industrialization have suffered in the past due to a lot of factors, such as, lack of entrepreneurs, low levels of productivity, lack of capital, lack of discipline in the financial sectors in general and banking sectors in particular and the like. The industrial sector accounts for about 15 percent of the GDP and absorbs about 8 percent of the total labor force. Since the first industrial policy announced in 1976 it has undergone revision several times toward liberalization and market economy up to 1995. Bangladesh has a vast labor force unemployed. Only industrial development can facilitate their employment. Thus, the need for rapid industrialization can hardly be overemphasized in the context of Bangladesh. Only the process of rapid industrialization of the country can bring about desired upliftment of the country from a traditional economy to a modern economy. In this process the role of the capital markets and institutions in providing finance for new upcoming industrial and servicing units as well as for the existing ones is predominantly important.

Historically, public issues by the private companies are small both in Bangladesh and Japan. Government of Bangladesh has been making efforts to develop the capital markets through different policy measures and tax concessions. Various measures have been directed toward fostering privatization and equity segments of the capital markets. These measures are likely to encourage mobilization of domestic resources and development of industrial sectors. The country has achieved remarkable macroeconomic stability, sweeping deregulations and liberalizations over the last few years although some sporadic and spurious impediments have been observed here and there. In fact, the country seems to be on the right track in respect of privatization and capital market development, still their progress could not be attained at a desired level. It is encouraging to note that the private sectors have come of an age and equity markets displayed an upward growth in terms of number of the companies listed in the stock exchanges, investors' response to public offerings of securities and market capitalizations. Nevertheless, cautious observers tend to believe that the progress so far achieved is below expectation and appears to be experiencing some strangulation. The market capitalizations, average trading volume, average company size etc. are smaller than those of other South Asian nations. Speculative elements along with the investors' expectations bring abnormally sharp fluctuations in the stock market, sometimes rather irrationally.

It is believed by many scholars and policy makers that the Japanese experience in the post-Meiji Restoration period is relevant and useful in the context of Bangladesh (Farouk, 1974). The security market in Japan has experienced an unprecedented expansion in the past decades and has established itself as one of the leading markets in the world. It was primarily a regulated market during its growth period. It has been undergoing liberalization gradually but steadily since the late 1970s. Subsequently it has become one of the world's largest security markets. The processes of this development through times have drawn the attention of researchers and practitioners at home and abroad. The way in which Japanese markets have been governed and the nature of market structure supported by government is fundamental to the understanding of Japanese market development. In the backdrop of the scenario portrayed above, this study is a modest attempt to identify the actual deterrents attributable to the underdeveloped condition of the capital markets of Bangladesh and to see whether any relevance can be drawn from the experience of Japanese capital market development processes. Simultaneously, the analysis has been extended in the light of relevant text book models.

Objectives of the study

The primary aim of the proposed study is to assess and analyze the development processes of capital markets in Bangladesh and Japan in terms of finance theory. The focus will be given mainly in mobilization and promotion of savings, meeting the financial needs of the industrial sectors of the economy. In this context we do not merely review the overall growth and their quantitative performance but also critically evaluate their qualitative functional performance in general. The impact of the policy/structural changes introduced in the development process of both Bangladesh and Japan will be examined from the standpoint of growth requirements. In this connection the successful use of different structural/policy change will be analyzed and evaluated. Attention will be given on useful relevances that may be drawn from the experiences of Japanese capital market development processes for having suitable market structure and operational efficiency in the capital markets of developing countries in general and Bangladesh in particular. The study of the Japanese markets separated from the Western world by distance, institutional arrangement and culture, is likely to deepen our insight about the development processes and problems of developing markets like Bangladesh. Thus, the Japanese experience in capital market development seems to be more useful than that of other developed market of the West. To the extent the arguments are convincing, the results of the study are expected to present a different direction and emphasis to the academics, policy-makers in the government, entrepreneurs, concerned authorities and institutions including stock exchanges, regulatory bodies like Securities and Exchange Commission (SEC), Central Bank, and others who are interested in it. Accordingly, the specific motivations of this study are as follows:

1 To analyze and evaluate the development processes of capital markets and institutions in Bangladesh and Japan.

2 To examine the trends in the equity prices with a view to discovering their behavioral pattern and also to locate the main factors, both economic and noneconomic, which influence the course of equity price behavior.

3 To investigate whether the rate of return on the stocks in Bangladesh can be explained in terms of finance theory.

4 To evaluate the existing institutional framework and their performance in the capital markets of Bangladesh.

5 To assess the implications of the experience of Japanese capital market development processes for Bangladesh.

Scope and methodical approach of the study

In this study we cover the role, actual and potential, of most of the important financial intermediaries forming capital markets of Bangladesh and Japan. While examining the overall importance of capital markets and relevant institutions, we attempt to assess the role which they should be called upon to play in the context of the emerging needs of Bangladesh. In these efforts assessment of Japanese experience has been taken into account.

In order to attain the objectives of the study various methods for data collection and analysis has been used. For collecting basic data relating to Bangladesh markets, we have largely relied on various publications of Bangladesh Bank, Dhaka Stock Exchange, Securities and Exchange Commission of Bangladesh, various government publications and so forth. Similarly, for collecting basic data on Japanese markets we have mainly depended on the various publications of Bank of Japan, Tokyo Stock Exchange and Japan Securities Research Institute, Government publications, research output of individual researchers connected with different segments of our study and so on.

Moreover, we have tried to remove some of the gaps in our study by visiting important institutions working in the area of our research. Accordingly, we have discussions bearing on important problems and issues with different top executives of relevant institutions/agencies. We had the privilege of exchanging views with some of the top ranking academic economists of Bangladesh and Japan or drawing direct impetus and inspiration from the learned articles and books of such scholars. Relevant data and statistical results have been analyzed and interpreted in the light of the finance theories. In this effort suitable statistical tools and techniques have been used.

Plan of the study

The study is divided into seven chapters where:

Chapter 1 gives an introduction containing a broad overview of the study, research design and coverage of the study.

Chapter 2 examines the privatization process of industries, its implications for capital markets, the role of the regulatory authorities and the changing dimension of the government policies.

Chapter 3 elaborates the present structure of financial markets and evaluates the role of financial institutions.

Chapter 4 deals with the corporate securities markets, barriers in their development processes and an assessment of market participants.

Chapter 5 evaluates the securities pricing mechanism with reference to the macroeconomic, microeconomic and non-economic variables.

Chapter 6 presents an empirical analysis of risk-return relationship of an emerging market like Bangladesh by using Capital Asset Pricing Model (CAPM).

Chapter 7 investigates the Japanese corporate finance, capital market structure and their development. An effort has been made to see the implications of

Japanese corporate finance for the efficient development of emerging markets like Bangladesh.

2 Private sector, capital market and government policy

Almost all countries of the world, embarking upon the path of industrial and economic development, have shown a tendency to resort to economic planning, though its extent, form and degree have varied from country to country. In socialist planned economy, state leadership and control dominate in economic activities. In capitalist market economies state intervention in private business was extended during the 1930s, but since World War II a 'mixed economy' has become common among the industrial nations. In the developing countries, too, no matter how capitalistic or socialistic their approaches to economic development, it is hardly possible to embark upon industrialization without an active state policy. While taking recourse to economic planning, the government is required, inter alia, to decide the role of the public and private sector in the industrialization program of a country. 'The extent of the public sector, its mode of organization, its relationship with the private sector, the permanence or transience of its contribution to the economy - these are matters which are dictated, upon a point, by 'objective circumstances'; beyond that point, they depend on what way of life, what kind of society the government has chosen to promote'(Hanson, 1959).

Decades of experience with the dominance of public sectors convincingly demonstrate that it had retarded development of the concerned countries (World Bank, 1991). This study conducted on 70 countries for the period of 1970-88 shows that private investment, not public investment, tends to be positively and unambiguously related to higher economic growth. Besides, SOEs cause increasing inefficiency due to ready availability of budgeting support (IMF, 1986). Persistent inefficiencies, mounting losses, widespread corruptions and neglecting national interest are some of the most important factors that militate against the public sector ownership and management of economic agents.

Accordingly, disenchantment toward public sectors has become a global phenomenon. Private sectors, on the other hand, have got momentum as a symbol of growth, dynamism and industrialization.

Bangladesh has been striving for higher levels of economic growth and rapid industrialization. But the saving rate in Bangladesh is very low averaging 6-7 percent per annum while its investment rate exceeds 12percent per annum creating a perennial gap which has so far been met predominantly through external aid. However, curtailing the government sector in the economy can minimize this gap to a large extent. Most State Owned Enterprises have been incurring losses and, thereby, pressuring on the government exchequer, public finance, banking sector, private sectors and on the overall growth prospects of the nation. Thus, fostering the private sector to play a dynamic role under a freer and robust economic system is becoming indispensable for economic growth. As the engine of economic growth, private sectors need to play its due role for alleviating widespread poverty, enhancing productivity and efficiency levels and for curbing rampant wastage of the scarce resources by the public sectors. In this situation the need for a structural reform emphasizing privatization for ensuring the balanced growth of domestic economy and the reduction of the financial burdens of the government is direly felt by all concerned. Simultaneously, a well-developed capital market is recognized as an obvious corollary of the private sector. Neither of these has attained a desired level of development in Bangladesh till now. In the backdrop of this scenario it is aimed to address the development of private sectors and capital markets in Bangladesh and to see any relevance to that of Japan.

Industrial scenario and the state of public sectors

Present day Bangladesh was the erstwhile East Bengal under British rule for about 200 years till 1947. The then 'muslin' of Dhaka was very popular and exported to Europe and other parts of the world. Besides, handwoven jute goods were a very important industry. During British rule East Bengal was not given equitable shares in the economic infrastructure whatever they constructed. In fact, agriculture was the only occupation as a result of British policies. The then East Pakistan now Bangladesh had hardly any industrial base under the British Tutelage till 1947. There were only some cotton mills in addition to about 150 tea gardens, medium or small size, in this part of the subcontinent. In 1949-50, contribution of the manufacturing sector to the GDP was only about 3percent, large scale enterprises being contributed just over half a per cent (Alamgir and Berlage, 1974). There were only 252 (2 percent) industrial units located in East Bengal out of 13,163 in the whole of undivided India. After partition of India in 1947 Pakistan government established Pakistan Industrial Development Corporation (PIDC) in 1952 for development of industry and in 1962 East Pakistan Industrial Development Corporation (EPIDC) was created with the responsibility of industrial development in the then East Pakistan. EPIDC started joint venture projects with the private sector with a debt equity ratio of 70:30. However, sometimes the equity ratio was relaxed as low as 7.5 percent. It helped in establishing 74 manufacturing units, the major investment of which was in the jute sector (BOI, 1995). It also took the leading role in creating a new class of local entrepreneurs in 1960s with the financial support from the then Industrial Development Bank of Pakistan (IDBP) and Pakistan Industrial Credit and Investment Corporation (PICIC). The finance was controlled from West Pakistan where the head offices of all financial institutions including State Bank of Pakistan, National Bank of Pakistan and other commercial banks were located excepting the Eastern Banking Corporation and the Eastern Mercantile Bank which were set up on the initiative of local entrepreneurs. The head office of IDBP[1], PICIC, National Investment Trust (NIT), the Equity Participation Fund (EPF) and Investment Corporation of Pakistan (ICP) were also located there.

Bangladesh had a colossal destruction during liberation war in 1971. The rate of development in the industrial sector has been unexpectedly low. Presently, the industrial base of Bangladesh is very narrow since the economy maintains a strong agrarian economic base. The industrial sectors, both large and small, accounts for about 15 percent of the GDP and absorb about 9 percent of the total labor force. The proportional contribution of agriculture, industry and services to GDP as calculated for the past years is presented in Table-2.1. During the 1970s, 1980s, and early 1990s the contribution to GDP from agricultural sectors decreased noticeably while the contribution by the industrial

Table-2.1
Share of different sectors of the economy *(Figures in % of total)*

Sectors	1973-76	1977-80	1985-88	1992-95
Agriculture	58.3	52.2	40.0	30.3
Industry	11.4	14.5	14.4	15.6
Services	30.4	33.4	45.6	54.1

Source: Estimated from various issues of Economic Trends, Bangladesh Bank.

sector increased only by smaller increments. The remaining contribution came from the service sector with an increasing trend. In spite of its paramount importance for absorbing surplus manpower and economic development, industrial sectors have not flourished at its desired level. There was change of government policy associated with discernible redirection and emphasis toward industrial structure. Accordingly, an intertemporal watershed has some analytical relevance.

The then Pakistan government started industrialization through private sectors with active support from government. The private entrepreneurs were mainly responsible for the rapid industrialization in Pakistan and according to Papaneck 'the rate of increase in manufacturing remained among the highest in the world, with a much larger base, its effect was great'(Papaneck, 1967). But lack of initiative from local entrepreneurs a non-Bengali entrepreneurial class entered the industrialization process until 1960s when a nascent local Bangladeshi entrepreneurial class began to emerge under active state sponsorship. In large scale production, Bangladeshi entrepreneurs remained mainly confined to jute manufacturing and cotton textiles. And at the time of liberation, they owned about 34 percent and 53 percent of fixed assets in jute and cotton textiles respectively. The newly developing entrepreneurs, it appears, were more interested in small and medium industries. However, even here their ownership accounted for about 20 percent of fixed assets by the time of liberation (Ahmed, 1978). As of 1969-70, public ownership accounted for about 36 percent of the fixed assets in the modern industrial sector (Sobhan, 1974). The number of registered factories in 1968-69 was 3,130. Of this, 791 units were in textiles, 576 in chemicals and 406 in food manufacturing - the three major industries (Ministry of Planning (TYP), 1978-80). In addition, there were a large number of small non-registered enterprises, and a much larger number of cottage manufacturing units. There were 330,400 industrial units in rural areas with assets worth below Tk. 0.5 million, of which, about 82 percent was classified as cottage industries[2]. The above facts suggest that Bangladesh inherited a very little industrial base from the past regimes.

The development philosophy of the government of Bangladesh was to give the state the lead role in the industrialization process after liberation of the country in 1971 which continued up to 1975. A shift in this policy came into effect with the change of government in that year. There was hasty and wholesale nationalization, particularly of every important sector of industry, without any preparedness and without considering whether there would be a necessary modicum of know-how, expertise and personnel available. The share of government control of the manufacturing sector rose from 34 to 92 percent followed by a rigid control and restrictions on new enterprises to be set up by the private sector (BOI, 1995). As a matter of fact, 85 percent of capacities and 70 percent of fixed investment were placed in the nationalized sector under 11 sector corporations (Ministry of planning (FFYP), 1973-78). In the FFYP (1973-78) of Bangladesh it was resolved to establish a socialistic pattern of society and a large and growing public sector was thought to be instrumental for this purpose. As a result the public sectors had a phenomenal growth in Bangladesh economy immediately after liberation. In an order it was stated that 'it is expedient to provide for the nationalization of certain industrial enterprises' and vested in the government 'all the shares in each of the scheduled industrial enterprises . . .' The same order established various industrial corporations 'to supervise and coordinate, subject to any regulation that may be made in this behalf, the activities, business and affairs of the scheduled industrial enterprises placed under it' (Government of Bangladesh, P.O. No.27, 1972). Stating that 'it is expedient to provide for the taking over of the undertaking of certain banks in Bangladesh . . . ,' the government dissolved 12 existing banking institutions and replaced them with six banks (Sonali, Agrani, Janata, Rupali, Pubali and Uttara), all of whose capital 'shall stand vested in and allotted to the government' (Government of Bangladesh, P.O. No. 26, 1972). Besides, all insurance companies and all abandoned properties were placed at the disposal of the government. Placing a further clamp on the private sectors, the government placed a low ceiling of Tk.2.5 million on private investment, abolished the Investment Corporation of Bangla-

Table - 2.2
Estimates of the SOEs *(In million taka)*

Sector	No. of Firms	Assets	Net worth
Manufacturing	151	205,012	11,100
Energy & telecommunication	14	215,525	69,329
Transport	7	33,313	13,669
Trading	9	25,630	5,268
Agriculture	18	4,979	1,511
Construction	4	6,544	4,179
Financial institutions and insurance companies	11	-	4,400
Services & others	15	32,587	11,170
Total	229	523,590	120,626

Notes: i) Negative net worth has been valued at zero. ii) About 40 firms have been transferred or in the process of transfer during the period 1993 to 1995. iii) Net worth figures for Bangladesh Railway and Bangladesh Water Development Board were not available.
Source: Derived from World Bank, SOE Financial Statements.

desh (ICB) and closed down the Dhaka Stock Exchange (DSE). Accordingly, the private sectors' share in the fixed investment of modern industrial sectors came down from 64 percent to only 10 percent. In terms of the number of units, however, the private sector still remained predominant. Nearly 90 percent of the registered factories numbering more than three thousand was in the private sector (Ahmed, 1978). They were mostly of small scale. Besides, there were a large number of small scale and cottage industrial units in private hands which were not registered.

The most fundamental implication of nationalization of industries for private capitalism in Bangladesh was its virtual elimination from large scale industrial ownership. However, most of these nationalized industries suffered losses subsequently. A World Bank study (1981) supports privatization on the ground that rapid expansion of the SOEs has stretched its managerial capacity to the extent that there will be serious inefficiencies. Private enterprises have demonstrated better performances even in the utility sectors where regulation is essential and there are 'natural monopolies.' Governments in many countries cannot afford to provide external financing of losses or the capital required for necessary investment projects. It is becoming increasingly difficult to raise other sources of financing government projects like commercial bank lending (IFC, 1992). In Bangladesh SOEs dominate many important sectors: in the utility sector they represent 71 percent of value added, nearly 100 percent of railway and communication and 83 percent in banking and insurance (World Bank, 1994b). According to the estimate at Table-2.2 net worth of the SOEs appears to be about Taka 120,626 million which is about 15 percent of GDP. It is also noticeable from the Table that utility and infrastructure sectors dominate in total SOEs assets. Only energy and telecommunication sector accounts for more than 57 percent of the total net worth of all SOEs. Table-2.3 indicates that with a net worth of about 15 percent of GDP, it contributes only about 6 percent to it (For details see World Bank, 1992 & 1994a). Bangladesh's

Table - 2.3
Contribution of public sectors of Bangladesh *(In million taka)*

Sector	Contribution to GDP	Public sector contribution	Contribution in %
Agriculture	316,723	294	0.1
Industry	150,168	21,505	14.3
Services	436,396	33,170	7.6
GDP at market prices	903,287	54,969	6.1

Source: Derived from World Bank, 1994a.

public sector is not large. This is mainly because agriculture, trade and services, which account for over two-thirds of GDP, are predominantly in the private sector. Overall about 85 percent of total GDP is in the hands of private sectors, the remaining about 15 percent being the public sector contribution to GDP. On a global scale, public enterprises accounted for around 10 percent of GDP and in the developing countries they typically produce between 10 and 20 percent (Killick and Commander, 1988 and Berg, 1985). In Malaysia, India and Sri Lanka, Government accounts for one third of GDP; public expenditure in Thailand, Pakistan and Indonesia is one quarter of GDP (Kohli, 1987 and Tanbi, 1987). Problems of measurement and the reliability of statistics do exist, and there is certainly no reason to believe in the existence of an optimal level of involvement by the government in GDP.

The financial performance of the public sector industrial corporation over the successive plans of Bangladesh shows the domination of loss figures during the FFYP and SFYP (Ministry of Planning (TFYP), 1990-95). Although originally planned to operate on commercial principles, the annual loss of the SOEs stood at US$500 million in 1992 representing about 2 percent of GDP and 45 percent of the country's annual aid disbursement (World Bank, 1992). The profit and loss position of the major SOEs for the period 1982-83 to 1992-93 is presented at Table-2.4. It appears from this Table that the volume of loss is increasing year after year and the combined loss of only 10 state owned corporations stands at about Taka10.5 billion in 1992-93.

Some enterprises borrowed from financial institutions and failed to repay their loans and interest thereon. Others received subsidies to meet their current expenditures. A number of important actions were purporting to improve the performance of the public sector concerns. These actions, to sum up, included a reorganization of public sector corporations and units thereunder, allowing increased flexibility in pricing, capital restructuring, and improved system for monitoring of performance, but with no tangible improvement. The World bank, the IMF and other international agencies are interested in privatization as an integral part of structural adjustment. Behind the policy prescription for developing or for centrally planned economies, there lies the belief in the neoclassical market-oriented view of the development process and policy (Cook and Kirkpatric, 1988). It has also been argued that the market mechanism provides a pragmatic alternative to redress the perceived failure of government planning systems and SOEs (Vernon-Wortzel and Wortzel, 1989). However, it has not been proven that private ownership could have performed better given the circumstances under which the SOEs operated (Nankani, 1990 and Lesser, 1991). There are two mechanisms by which government investment may affect economic growth. These are the externality effect of government size and the intersectoral productivity differentials between the private and government sectors' investment spending. The comparison of direct effect of government and private investment on growth is hardly the right approach. At best, it provides only a partial indication of the impact of government investment spending on growth (Nyong, 1994). The issue is not one of comparing direct impacts on growth of public and private investments. More crucial is the recognition of the indirect effects of public investments via raising the profitability of private investments and the absorptive capacity (Khan and Reihard, 1990 and Ndulu, 1991). Public enterprises theoretically fulfil important functions that are necessary for the development of the private sectors. These are similar to those discussed in neoclassical theory, including the provision of infrastructure, linkage generation, technological development, research and development, education, social amenities like health services, housing and the like. For Bangladesh the SOEs demonstrate continuously an increasing trend in loss figures as shown in Table-2.4. Most of these SOEs were profitable before nationalization. It is unlikely for the private sectors to swallow such huge loss year after year.

Table -2.4
Profit and loss of the major SOEs of Bangladesh *(In million taka)*

corpora-tions	1982-1983	1983-1984	1984-1985	1985-1986	1986-1987	1987-1988	1988-1989	1989-1990	1990-1991	1991-1992	1992-1993
BSEC	-273	-202	-135	-85	-49	-62	-78	-365	-861	-1069	-1000
BSFIC	218	189	-234	-336	-315	-95	-255	164	-129	-692	-924
BCIC	158	121	131	105	-86	198	374	455	343	-548	-66
BTMC	23	112	42	-566	-245	-354	-22	-175	-574	-434	-959
BJMC	134	-310	-1462	-1583	-420	-1431	-1882	-3709	-2473	-3122	-3679
Total	260	-90	-1658	-2465	-1114	-1744	-1863	-3630	-3694	-5865	-6628
BPC	597	1600	1817	1051	1473	938	1273	369	2492	3512	3134
BOGMC	72	136	101	-29	-71	95	-191	-272	302	533	648
BSC	24	4	6	-117	-101	37	-245	-244	-627	-383	38
Biman	123	163	-23	-57	-352	-266	30	117	-400	263	194
BPDB	417	453	199	-285	172	-89	652	-3375	-2802	-7749	-7848
Total	1493	2266	442	-1902	7	-1029	-344	-7035	-4729	-9689	-10462

Source: Derived from World Bank, 1992.

The efficiency argument states that private ownership is likely to produce better results and higher profits. It also argues that private sectors are more inclined to introduce improved production techniques whereas the public sectors may rely on obsolete production techniques and suffer from large wastage (Wilson, 1984; Yoder et al., 1991). The property rights argument stresses that managers of SOEs neither have a stake in their performance, nor do they have equivalent incentives to operate efficiently as opposed to private owners (Hanke, 1987; Van De Walle, 1989). This means private ownership of enterprises can bring more efficiency even with market imperfections. The distortion argument emphasizes the allocative aspect indicating government intervention in resource allocation causes widespread distortion. Consequently, performance of the public sectors is not comparable to that of the private sectors (Lal, 1983). All these suggest that privatization can perform a major role in economic development principally determined by the market forces and private enterprises. Accordingly, public sector enterprises were being transferred to private sectors as an unpreventive measure. One of the major areas of the reform agenda of the government of Bangladesh is promotion of private sectors. Although a wide range of measures has already been undertaken to that end, the micro response of the macroeconomic measures of the government is yet to take off. The remarkably poor progress has drawn the attention of the policy makers. However, privatization itself is not a sufficient condition to efficiency improvement in the industrial sector. It is reported by IFC (1992) that the experience of different countries indicates that the process of successful privatization should be a part of a broader macroeconomic reform program. Prior to the implementation of the privatization process, there should exist a positive macroeconomic framework in the concerned economy. This framework will make the investment attractive through fostering competitive and free markets. Private sectors thus will be encouraged to invest in the productive sector. In case of Bangladesh, substantial economic, financial, fiscal and other reforms conducive for a market economy have been undertaken in the recent past, yet more need to be done. Above all, there is a need to transform public and political commitment to that end. In this connection one should note that since government investment is positively related to private investment government needs to continue investment in areas which are not attractive to private sectors (von Furstenberg and Malkiel, 1977). This is because in a country like Bangladesh an increase in government investment would increase income directly and indirectly through the multiplier effect when resources are yet to be fully utilized and infrastructural facilities like transport, communication, electric power, irrigation etc. appear to be not attractive for private investment. However, these sectors can be transferred to private hands at a later stage of development.

Public to private sectors: policy reversal

Between 1975 and 1981, a number of major policy changes were made to encourage participation of private sectors which included, among others, the following:
1 Elimination of ceilings on private investment.
2 Relaxation of investment sanctioning procedures.
3 Amendment of the constitution to allow denationalization.
4 Reopening of stock exchange and establishment of Investment Corporation

of Bangladesh (ICB).
5   Introduction of a number of export promotion measures.

With the change of government in 1982, New Industrial Policy (NIP) was announced in June 1982. The policy reflected a rapid acceleration of the measures that were initiated by the earlier regime. In 1986 a Revised Industrial Policy (RIP) was adopted which aimed at expanding and strengthening the measures undertaken in 1982. Some further measures for reform were undertaken in late 1980s. These included putting public sector enterprises at par with private sector enterprises with regard to various policy issues, further incentives to foreign investment and financial sectors reform together with replacement of subsidized refinancing by a more general rediscounting facility. Government has also carried out major reforms in trade policy and rationalized taxation policy in the light of the industrial policy. To provide a package service under one roof government established a Board of Investment (BOI) on 1 January 1989. The purpose of BOI is smooth sanctioning of investment projects proposed by domestic and foreign investors without unnecessary bureaucratic interference. It can indeed play a very useful role to private investors by simplifying, processing and coordinating functions of several erstwhile government agencies providing support services and helping to obtain access to necessary infrastructures.

According to World Bank estimate private investment in manufacturing rose from Tk.0.5 billion in 1979-80 to Tk.1.1 billion in 1984-85, both at 1973-74 prices. Since 1985-86, private investments (actual)and manufacturing growth has, however, considerably slowed down (Rahman, 1990). This decline has been due to both demand and supply factors. On the demand side, the stagnation of the economy and weak demand for domestic manufacturers and the rapid capacity expansion in ready-made garments industry and some other subsectors in the mid-1980s had a dampening demand on new investment. On the supply side, weak financial institutions, credit recovery problems have mainly been due to the inept portfolio management, wrong choice of 'entrepreneurs' etc. The denial of credit to borrowers with poor repayment records etc. might have reduced investment financing to some extent. Despite certain constraints in the manufacturing sector, the manufacturing capability of the industries in Bangladesh particularly its private sector, has otherwise shown signs of improvement. This explains the fact that the share of industrial sectors in GDP of the country rose to about 11 percent in 1993-94 from about 8.4 percent in 1987-88.

The last industrial policy was announced in July 1991. Major elements of this policy were as follows: (i) developing the industrial sector in order to increase its contribution to the GNP, income, resources and employment, (ii) expansion of industries by putting more emphasis on development of private sectors, (iii) withdrawal of disparity between foreign and local entrepreneurs in providing different facilities, (iv) developing export-oriented, export-linkage and efficient import substitute industries, (v) encouraging development of labor intensive industries through acquisition and improvement of appropriate technology, (vi) contraction of government authority over the industrial arena and confine it particularly in establishing strategic industries and improve efficiency of public sectors, (vii) developing agro-based and agro-supportive industries, and (viii) creating possible opportunities for revitalizing and rehabilitating sick industries.

The industrial policy of 1991 spells out the following major policies with regard to privatization: '(i) abandoned, vested and taken over industrial enterprises and shares and other proprietary interests will continue to be disinvested; (ii) except industries in the reserved sector, capital will continue to be withdrawn gradually from industries under corporations; (iii) if required, 100 percent shares of public enterprises will be sold; (iv) industries in the public sector will be sold through floating of tenders; (v) in order to ensure widest possible distribution of shares and securities among the general public, and associate them in the management, shares will be unloaded mainly through

Table -2.5
Financial allocations in the plans of Bangladesh   (In million taka)

Plans	Public Sector		Private Sector		Total	
	Amount	%	Amount	%	Amount	%
First Five Year Plan(1973-78)	7,552	84.41	1,395	15.59	8,947	100
Two Year Plan (1978-80)	5,700	69.85	2,460	29.15	8,160	100
Second Five Year Plan(1980-85)	32,750	74.69	11,100	25.31	43,850	100
Third Five Year Plan(1985-90)	26,000	44.83	32,000	55.17	58,000	100
Fourth Five Year Plan (1990-95)	419,300	60.83	270,000	39.17	689,300	100

Source: Compiled from First Five Year Plan, Second Five Year plan, Third Five Year Plan and Fourth Five Year Plan, Planning Commission, Government of Bangladesh.

public subscriptions; and (vi) Bangladeshis working abroad will be encouraged to purchase these industrial units or shares in foreign currencies.' However, the privatization proposals of the government have been inviting the wrath of the labor union and some political parties that make its proper implementation doubtful.

Although this policy does not reflect much qualitative change over its predecessor, it reiterates strong commitment for further deregulation, privatization, trade policy reforms and export promotion. Proper implementation of these policies may broaden the industrial base of the country but it is possible that these policies may have to face difficulties in their implementation process due to various uncertainties usually associated with a developing country. If we look to the past industrial policies of Bangladesh we will find liberalizations have been done several times and many incentives and policy supports have been envisaged for industrialization of the country but so far very little tangible results could be achieved.

Government's increasing reliance on private sectors also reflects in the allocation of funds in different plans of Bangladesh as it appears in Table-2.5. The major share of public sector industries can be clearly seen in the earlier plans. The share of this sector is declining from 84.41 percent in the First Five Year Plan to 74.69 percent in the Second Five Year Plan and to 44.83 percent in the Third Five Year Plan with a rise in allocation of resources in the Fourth Five Year Plan. However, the private sector is becoming increasingly dominant in the total industrial investment.

In the 1960s it was generally believed that external capital could perform a significant role in both resource mobilization and structural transformation which were needed for the acceleration of capital formation and growth in developing countries (Chenery and Strout, 1966). However, some studies have indicated that a substantial part of the increase in external resources has gone into increased consumption although these are subject to different interpretations[3]. Wai and Wong (1982) have indicated that the inflows of foreign funds to the private sector, be it a trade credit or other forms of loans or equities, constitute a source of capital to this sector. Under a pegged exchange rate system, foreign capital inflow contributes positively to the capital account of the balance of payments and helps overcome the savings constraint in the financing of investment. However, the resultant increases in imports, foreign investment income, and debt service on the current account should not be neglected.

Foreign Private Investment (Promotion and Protection) Act 1980 ensures legal protection to foreign investment in Bangladesh against expropriation and nationalization and to ensure equal treatment. Repatriation of capital invested including capital gains, remittances of all post tax-dividend profit and foreign capital, remittances of royalty and technical fees and reinvestment of repatriation dividends is treated as new foreign investment. Bangladesh also established Export Processing Zones (EPZs) - one is at Chittagong and another is at Dhaka. Besides, two more EPZs are in the process of implementation. The industries in EPZs enjoy special fiscal incentives and other infrastructural facilities. Hundred percent of foreign investment is allowed in the EPZ. Tax-free import beyond National Import Policy restrictions, offshore banking facilities, relocation of existing industries from abroad, availability of foodstuff and beverage on payment of nominal tax for foreigners working in EPZs etc. are permissible for these zones.

The important tax concessions and other measures adopted by government are: (i) tax-holiday for five years for developed areas, seven years for less developed area, nine years for least developed areas and 12 years for the special economic zone, (ii) 15 percent import duty on capital machinery for industries

Table-2.6
Foreign investment approval (100% and joint venture)

Period	Total number of units	Total investment (in million)	
		Taka	US Dollar
Pre-Liberation	21	390	40
After Liberation (i) Up to February 1991	139	15,593	389
(ii) From March 1991 to December 1994	253	44,277	1,107
KAFCO	1	9,000	225
Total	414	69,260	1,761

Source: Board of Investment (BOI), 1995.

in developed areas, 7.5 percent duty for less developed areas and 2.5 percent for least developed areas, (iii) accelerated depreciation from 80 percent to 100 percent is allowed, depreciation allowance can be carried forward if the unit sustains loss, (iv) exemption of tax on interest on foreign loans, (v) exemption of tax on royalty, technical know-how and technical assistance fees, (vi) relief from double taxation for foreign investors, and (vii) tariff protection unto four years to the deserving industries.

It is gathered that the Board of Investment (BOI) and its predecessor Department of Industries approved/registered about 8,600 investment projects up to December 1994 including 414 joint venture/100 percent foreign investment projects. Period-wise and sector-wise position of the foreign investment (100 percent and Joint Venture) projects under BOI are presented in Table-2.6. This Table indicates that during the period from March 1991 to December 1994, the flow of foreign investment increased significantly compared to the past. The figure for the period from March 1991 to December 1994 shows almost three times increase in the flow of foreign investment. Investors from 38 countries have registered their investment projects with BOI. Table-2.7 shows the cumulative foreign direct investment of major investing countries as on December 1995. Although the foreign investment is increasing gradually in quantitative terms, qualitative aspects also deserve consideration. Some empirical findings indicate that qualitative differences are far more important than quantitative differences in explaining

Table-2.7
Cumulative foreign direct investment *(In million US $)*

Serial number	Country	Foreign direct investment
1	Malaysia	963
2	Japan	754
3	UK	294
4	Singapore	240
5	Hongkong	134
6	Germany	129
7	USA	110
8	South Korea	76
9	China	66
10	India	47
11	The Netherlands	44
12	Canada	34
13	Pakistan	31
14	Thailand	29
15	Italy	22
16	Switzerland	20
17	Greece	20
18	Sweden	13
Total		3,026

Source: Board of Investment, Dhaka, Bangladesh, 1995.

different rates of growth across countries (see for example; Fry, 1995, King and Levine, 1993). It has also been pointed out by the World Bank (1989b) that 'historically the quality of investment has been at least as important for growth as the quantity. Although the fast growing countries had higher rates of investment than the others, empirical studies generally find that less than half the growth in output is attributable to increases in labor and capital. Higher productivity explains the rest. Faster growth, more investment, and greater financial depth all come partly from higher saving. In its own right, however, greater financial depth also contributes to growth by improving the productivity of investment.' Endogenous growth models, on the one hand, suggest that capital flows from the capital-rich countries to capital-poor countries can influence only a small and transient effect on capital-poor countries' growth rates. On the other hand, these models imply a more important role for capital in the growth process. However, without diminishing marginal productivity of capital, there is no incentive to transfer it from capital-rich countries to poor countries (Krugman, 1993).

In spite of the government commitment the overall investment environment is yet to be free from constraints and blemishes. No doubt the official policy has supported investment activities but among others, the political unrest and strain labor-management relationship have emerged as important factors in deterring the expected result. New industrial investments in the country are also hampered by lack of infrastructures - power connections, gas, telephones etc. It is observed that the policy supports initiated by the government have not affected the inertia from which local investors and their foreign collaborators have suffered for so long. Unless adequate investments along effective lines are made to expand the infrastructural support facilities, the objective of the industrial policy for creating a favorable investment climate will hardly make any sense. The political leaders must create confidence among investors to invest their resources for economic development of the country. In this regard important issues need to be given attention are:

1. There must be ensured political stability in the country in which democratic institutions would perform their respective duties free from fear or favor.
2. The neutrality of law and supremacy of the judiciary must not only be ensured but seen to be rigidly administered.
3. Legal remedies and citizens' rights should be free from bureaucratic rigidities and made available to the citizens without discrimination.
4. Political, social and professional institutions should be encouraged to do their duties independently.

Implications for capital market

As one after another control regimes are relaxed under the onslaught of liberalization, businesses become busy in calculating gains and losses, the threats and the opportunities. On the other hand, capital markets respond to these changes rather quickly. This is because the liberalized industrial policy will yield results in the product markets only with a lag of one or two years, while the impact on the financial markets will be more immediate. So today capital market watchers are trying to figure out what will be the impact of new industrial policy on the capital markets.

The structure of industrial base has always been an important factor for capital market development. Saving of a country can be channeled into productive investments either by government or private sector. In the private sector, the role of government is minimal. Deregulations of various sectors, particularly of financial markets, induce the private sector to rely on the capital markets for investment funds to implement their projects. Privatization permits entry of the private sector into all productive sectors and thereby allows establishment of enterprises in growing numbers who look to capital markets to meet their capital needs. It is argued that if financial repression is absent, it raises the return on investment which in turn, increases the level of saving. Moreover, privatization provides opportunity for working of financial intermediaries to match the demand for and supply of funds. In a centrally planned economy where the public sector enjoys state patronage and where a number of areas are exclusively reserved for the public sector, the private sector growth is severely limited, which naturally restricts the need for capital markets. Like other developing countries, government of Bangladesh played a predominant role in the development of industrial sectors. Consequently, the large and medium scale industrial enterprises in Bangladesh have generally been public enterprises. These enterprises have not been encouraged to raise funds of their own. Instead, they have received funding directly from the government and/or have benefitted from low interest loans from state-owned banks, or from borrowing abroad with government guarantees. Listing in the stock exchanges and share issues have been made redundant by these easy sources of funds.

The industrial scene of Bangladesh is dominated by a relatively small number of large enterprises which coexist with large number of small units. About 65 percent of the public limited companies registered with the Registrar of Joint Stock Companies have paid up capital below Tk. 5 million and about 21 percent have paid up capital over Tk. 10 million (Khan et al., 1995). A relatively extensive industrial foundation is a necessary condition (although not sufficient one) to an increased supply of shares, *ceteris paribus*. If we look at the comparative picture of listed stocks of the Asian emerging markets, we find that the total market capitalization of Dhaka Stock Exchange (DSE) was $1.04 billion compared to $127.51 billion in India, $12.26 billion in Pakistan, $191.78 billion in South Korea and $199.28 billion in Malaysia (IFC, 1995). Besides, the average size of the companies was the smallest among the emerging markets listed by International Finance Corporation (IFC). The average company size, as estimated by IFC (1995), is US $ 6 million for Bangladesh while this is US $ 13 million for Sri Lanka, US $ 17 million for Pakistan, US $ 29 million for India, US $ 338 million for Thailand, US $ 274 million for South Korea and US $ 219 million for Indonesia. The markets appear to be less liquid than others if it is considered in terms of the share of annual transaction volume to market capitalization. The turnover ratio in case of Bangladesh is 14.3 against 25.9 in Sri Lanka, 26.9 in Pakistan, 24.1 in India, 60.9 in Thailand, 174.1 in South Korea and 29.4 in Indonesia (IFC, 1995). The supply of equities is restricted by the paucity of large private concerns in various industries. Unless the existing industrial structure of the country undergoes a transformation, desirable flow of equities may not be forthcoming. This is a weakness which, by its very nature, can't be remedied in the short run. The enlargement of the industrial base and the size distribution thereof can come about only with the gradual development of the country. Until the transformation process is successful, other things being equal, the necessary flow of equities to sustain an efficient market can't be expected.

With privatization, capital markets tend to become active, expansive and competitive in resource mobilization activities. Large private sectors thus help to accelerate the development of capital markets. Capital markets are equally essential to the success of a privatization program. Without a well-developed capital market, the pace of privatization would slow down and the urge for privatization might diminish. Moreover, growing importance is attached to public floatation of equity as a method of privatization. In this connection, not only the primary market but also the secondary market plays a critical role. As the privatization wave touched Bangladesh during the recent past, inflow of equity capital began to give a rising trend to stock markets. Presence of large primary markets and vibrant and liquid secondary markets are vital for the development of private sectors. Some macroeconomic and institutional environments are prerequisites for successful privatization. These relate to the need for macroeconomic stability, deregulation and the development of capital markets to precede privatization (Nyong, 1994). In most developing countries, a main drawback to privatization has been the absence of a developed primary market (Asian Development Bank, 1992). An IMF report on privatization in developing countries states that 'the thinness of domestic capital markets necessarily places limits on the ability to finance privatization from domestic resources' (Hemming et al., 1987). Bank credit facilities needed to be made available for the private investors in view of the absence of developed and efficient security markets and limited financial capabilities of entrepreneurs in developing countries. Although the enterprises are small in relation to developed countries, the investment for them generally exceeds the financial capabilities of the entrepreneurs from his own resources. Since capital markets in a developing country like Bangladesh are still underdeveloped and not adequately efficient in resource mobilization, any short term or medium term loans for financing business operations would relieve the pressures on entrepreneurs for the day-to-day operations and enable them in total to finance a larger amount of capital formation. This is more relevant for those countries that are in the process of rapid economic growth. In the emerging markets business firms tend to increase rapidly. This may necessitate a substantial amount of resources from the financial system unlike the well-established firms in developed countries whose investment activities tend to depend more on retained earnings. The impact of squeezing credit for the private sector tends to reduce the level of private investment. In the short run this would alleviate inflationary pressures but in the long run, growth in productive capacity of this sector would be adversely affected.

The number of companies privatized in the past years, has gone a long way to broaden the capital market structure in Bangladesh (Asian Development Bank, 1989). The privatization program was extended to financial sectors as commercial banks, insurance companies and investment companies were allowed to operate in the private sector. This opportunity was quickly availed of and a good number of banks and insurance companies were established. By 1989-90, eight new private banks were set up; out of which all but one has floated shares for public subscriptions and enlisted with the Dhaka Stock Exchange (DSE).

The essential purpose of privatization is to make the society more competitive. This helps to create more investment, more wealth and more employment in the economy. Privatization can create dynamic activities and opportunities. Its impact has been pronounced in the securities markets of Bangladesh. Increased and expanded roles of the private sectors have induced a number of companies to go public and obtain stock exchange listing. The number of companies listed with DSE rose to more than 200 in 1996 from nine in 1976. This has led to increased turnover and hence increased liquidity. It was remarked in a study that privatization 'has not only given a boost to the stock exchange activities, but has also helped in creating confidence in the minds of the investing class' (Asian Development Bank, 1989). The role of the capital markets within an economy is closely related with finding a positive and constructive role for private investment within the economy. Accordingly, both private investment and the capital markets must somehow be integrated into the development program of the economy. It is important for the government to set regulations, designed to ensure competition for the newly privatized entity so that it does not become a monopoly and allow inefficiency to continue. Besides, government should have to play an active role to maintain stable economic condition, price level, inflationary rate and efficient capital markets.

Divestment operations under which the shares or securities of public sector enterprises are offered for a public subscription can help strengthen the process of promoting an industrial democracy. Such moves in Bangladesh are necessary to develop confidence and investment habits among small investors and relieve the pressure on public resources. In the second half of the 1980s, the divestment operation and the Holding Company Scheme began. The scheme has a direct bearing on the equity markets. It permits public sector enterprises, as public limited companies, floating of shares in these companies for a public subscription. This scheme allows the retention of government equity ownership at 51 percent with 49 percent of its equity made available for a public subscription. Of the 49 percent, 15 percent is kept reserved for the employees and remaining 34 percent is available to the general public. Divestment of 49 percent of shares was responded by the general investors as manifested in the fact that all but two of the 11 public issues (excepting the portion of employees) by public industrial enterprises were oversubscribed. This was mainly because most of the enterprises divested were reputed and profitable ones and the issues were made at par[4]. However, divestment of 49 percent of shares of public industrial enterprises slowed down considerably in 1988-89. The main reasons attributable to this fact are: (i) some enterprises under divestment programs were not perceived attractive and rewarding by the investors which resulted in undersubscription of some issues, (ii) damages and disruptions caused by the unprecedented floods and drought resulted in losses or sharp decline in profit by some enterprises, and (iii) relatively smaller stock markets were overcrowded by simultaneous public offering (reverse crowding out effect) (World Bank, 1989a). In order to accelerate the process of privatization the government is considering the sale of government owned 51 percent shares in various enterprises in recent years. It is expected this will have its positive impact on the capital markets of Bangladesh. The key factors affecting capital markets are equity earnings. The lowering interest rates and convertibility of Taka are likely to have a favorable impact on domestic and foreign investment and earnings thereon. This will encourage the savers to put their money in the stock markets instead of banks and government bonds. The new norm is likely to entail larger equity financing and prod companies to raise more funds directly from the capital markets. To the extent greater equity financing will mean more competitive mobilization of public savings, it could make companies more accountable in their use of funds over a period of time. It can also be argued that high equity and lower debt will insulate companies more effectively from financial burdens during difficult times and thereby provide protection to investors. Moreover, greater recourse to equity finance should also help augment the floating stock of shares in the markets and impart greater stability to share prices. In case of privatization through public floatation, valuation of the firm and pricing the shares are crucial. Undervaluation may cause private investors over benefitted and oversubscription resulting in instability in the capital markets. Overvaluation, on the contrary, may cause undersubscription. More accuracy in the valuation may be attained if it is based on the future performance of the firm rather than the past, and the future performance may be measured in terms of price earnings ratio (PER), price-book value ratio (PBR), average net income before interest and depreciation, expected growth rate etc. of similar industries.

The inflows of foreign direct investment in private sector-oriented developing countries produce favorable effects on the domestic economy particularly through linkage effect in domestic industries (van Loo, 1977). From the standpoint of domestic private investors, it would appear to be not very much different whether foreign capital is in the form of direct investment or portfolio investment. Accordingly, the inflow of foreign capital to the private sector as a whole is considered as determinant of private investment (Wai and Wong, 1983). In case of Bangladesh significant impact of foreign portfolio investment is observed in the stock prices of DSE.

It has been mentioned by Bouin (1992) that issue of a large volume of securities for public subscriptions is often constrained by limited absorption capacity of developing markets. A study (Ahmed et al., 1993) also reveals that a great majority of private investors of Bangladesh are not adequately aware of the opportunities in stock markets and not investing in company shares. This may be due to lack of developed and efficient stock markets and lack of confidence in investing in company shares. There is a strong preference among private investors to invest in bank deposits and government bonds and a reluctance to invest in equity markets. This indicates the need for inculcating 'equity-culture' among private investors and making them aware of the investment opportunities in company equities and its high returns with moderate risk. Since all the issues are oversubscribed by Taka 6,936.6 million or 454 percent[5] in 1995, it indicates the absorption capacity of the market. However, government may adopt a policy of off-loading limited number of shares of SOEs each year through public floatation or prearrangement with local and foreign investors. Widespread retail (public) participation of individuals as well as employees allowing maximum diffusion of share holding will lead to popular acceptance of privatization. Competition from the private sectors may be encouraged and budgetary transfers to the public sectors reduced progressively.

Capital issue control

When a company either public or private wants to raise funds through issue of shares or debentures, it approaches the capital markets by advertisement in daily newspapers or financial journals or through broker or underwriter. But proper consent must be taken from the Securities and Exchange Commission (SEC)[6] before any public offer. In Bangladesh, capital issues have been controlled under Capital Issues Act 1947. All issues of shares, bonds, debentures and other instruments creating a charge (or a lien) on the assets of the company are governed by this Act. Previously all issues above Tk. 0.5 million for public companies and above Tk. 2.0 million for private companies required the consent of SEC but now exemption limit has been increased to Tk.2.0 million and Tk. 5.0 million respectively due to increase in capital cost. The control on capital issues was imposed with a view to make best use of capital which is short in supply. The activities of the DSE and all industrial investment in the country are governed by the Capital Issue Act of 1947 which was first formulated by the British during World War II to channelize investment into war related industries. However, some changes have been brought into it particularly in relation to bonus issue and right issue to suit the current needs of the investors. Former CCI laid down strict conditions with regard to the ratio of bonus shares

Table - 2.8
Capital issues consented
(In million taka)

Year	No. Of companies		Total		Average Amount per Company	No. of Prospectus Issue
	Public	Private	Number	Amount		
1983-84	106	45	151	1303.9	8.6	12 public limited companies
1984-85	60	20	80	1490.0	18.6	16 public limited companies
1985-86	48	15	63	2710.0	43.0	17 public limited companies
1986-87	59	15	74	2639.4	35.7	12 public limited companies (2 companies issued debentures)
1987-88	71	2	73	2859.5	39.2	15 public limited companies (2 companies issued debentures)
1988-89	56	20	76	5859.9	77.1	17 public limited companies
1993-94	89	-	89	5968.0	67.1	14 public limited companies (2 companies issued debentures)
1994-95	48	-	48	8167.0	170.1	27 public limited companies (2 companied issued debentures)
1995-96	63	-	63	9079.1	144.1	26 public limited companies (2 companies issued debentures)

Source: Prepared from various Annual Reports, Quarterly Reviews of Securities and Exchange Commission of Bangladesh (SEC) and Ahmed (1992).

to capital and reserves etc. and right issues which resulted in various difficulties for the companies. However, SEC has introduced certain regulations to simplify the conditions. There is a feeling among the investors and other interested parties that SEC should come forward with more positive actions for streamlining the market which has so far been not getting due attention.

Consent of capital issues given since 1983-84 has been presented in Table-2.8. It appears that in 1983-84 highest number of companies was given consent for capital issue. During the period 151 consents were given for Tk. 1303.9 million, which works out to Tk. 8.6 million per consent. This was apparently due to the New Industrial Policy (NIP) declared by Government in 1982 emphasizing the private sectors. This was initial period after declaring the NIP when investors felt encouraged to invest considering good prospects in industrial investment. In this period though the total number of issues was large, the average issue was small. Thereafter, the total number of companies given consent was, by and large, stable but the average was gradually increasing. This indicates an increasing trend of the cost involved for establishing industries in an inflationary situation. Besides, the increasing number of companies given consent is believed to be due to more liberal industrial policy and other fiscal measures declared subsequently. However, the number of companies issued the prospectus is very small every year relative to the number of companies given consent for capital issue throughout the period. Debenture issues were also very limited.

The Capital Issue (Continuance of Control) Act of 1947 requires that the prospectus or other documents offering the security for sale must contain a statement that this consent has been obtained from the government which, however, does not take any responsibility for the financial soundness of any scheme or for the correctness of any of the statements made or opinion expressed with regard to them. Most companies still have to solve financing, production and operating problems after having obtained the consent of the SEC.

In order to obtain the approval of the SEC, a company files an application that provides such information as its business, capital structure, value of the offering, categories of ownership, objective of the issue, costs of projects, financing arrangements, dividends and market prices. The SEC reviews the application to determine, among other things, that the project is an approved investment, sound and that the sponsors have sufficient stake in it. It is reported that the high officials of the companies considered SEC's evaluation as a formality to check such things as the public distribution of the required percentage of shares. The overall debt/equity ratio is formulated by the government but it is not sacrosanct, and in particular cases, may be established by the development banks where the SEC may help in determining the policies by using its official capacity.

Some Japanese experiences

Many of the watchers of Japanese development process think that Japanese experience offers a good deal of relevance for the present day developing countries while others are skeptical about its usefulness in a different environment. It is difficult to find the extent of contribution of Japanese industrial policy to its economic growth. There have been many favorable factors - economic and noneconomic - contributed to Japan's growth. Among them industrial policy is one of them. It is not feasible to isolate the contribution of any single factor. It is, however, conceivable that mere emulating the industrial policy of any country cannot produce a desirable outcome rather the particular situation prevailing in a country determines the rationality and effectiveness of the policy.

In the early stage of Japan's industrialization the government played an important role in stimulating and promoting modern industries. 'The enrichment and strengthening of the country' and 'the encouragement of productive industries' became national slogans in the period after the Meiji Restoration of 1868. In order to achieve its national objective the Meiji government played an active role as a regulator of private business activities. It is said that the Meiji government went into the new world with a sword in one hand and iron in the other. Needless to say, the former symbolized military industry and the latter modern industry for market.

Government measures for industrialization included the establishment of Western-type industrial organization and the introduction of Western technology. Following occasional similar activities in the closing decade of the Tokugawa regime, foreign experts were employed and Japanese sent abroad to study. The government's active financial participation in the early industrialization of Japan[7] began with the restoration. The government invested, it has been calculated, 135 million yens in Government enterprises. About equally divided between the 1868-74 and 1875-80 periods (Emi, 1971), these investments represented about two-fifths of the government's total nonmilitary capital expenditures from 1868 through 1880 and were equal to about 5 percent of its total expenditures. Most of the investments were financed out of ordinary revenue or it might be argued, during the first period out of the receipts from paper currency issues.

After a decade of direct government investment in mines, railroads, arsenals and factories, the Meiji leaders found the side effects of their policies. These were in the form of inflation, trade deficits, corruptions and looming bankruptcies. Consequently, on 5 November 1880 a famous deflationary policy 'Outline Regulation for the Sale of Government-Operated Factories' was issued. As an alternative to the state investment, the government began helping private entrepreneurs to accumulate capital and to invest it in ways that seemed to promote Japan's needs for military security and economic development.

Beginning in 1880, government disposed of the enterprises which it had promoted, owned and managed, to private business usually at bargain rates which is considerably less than its original price. Consequently, the purchasers were given a good head-start as industrialist. For thirteen enterprises, for example, about one-eighth of the government total investment, sales receipts were slightly below one-half of the original investment (Smith, 1955). Although the reasons for the disposal seem to have been primarily financial - the need to raise cash (Smith, 1955) and the avoidance of continuous deficits - by that the government felt that it had fulfilled its role as an industrial pioneer, and that private business was in a position, both administratively and financially, to operate and expand the enterprises.

The beneficiaries of this policy were the big merchant houses of Mitsui, Mitsubishi, Sumitomo, Yasuda, Okura and so on which later came to be known as *zaibatsu*. They purchased the previously government-run enterprises and received generous financial aid from the government. They also raised capital by incorporation of such privileged sectors like transportation and banking. In the case of *zaibatsu*, however, it was not necessary to use the capital raising function of incorporation because they received the privilege of government-aid and they had accumulated sufficient capital internally.

The Meiji government did not sell out all of its government establishments, but retained strategical industries and factories like iron, machinery, ship-building, chemical, railways etc. According to a study of capital formation in Japan, government investment (construction and durable equipment) was much more in sum total than private investment(residential and nonresidential construction) in the period before World War I - to some extent until World War II - and the share of government investment was more than half of the total investment including agriculture and inventories during the whole period of 1887-1940 (Rosovsky, 1962). The role of the government in the early stage of Japanese industrialization was to create a modern industrial state with strong military power. As a result, the Japanese economy in the inter-war period might be described as a 'sustained growth into maturity'(Rostow), or as 'the second stage of industrial growth' (Moffman).

In sum, Japan's industrialization did not come directly out of transfer of government enterprises to private entrepreneurs. Just as the government continued to be an entrepreneur in some industries, private business also grew by their own efforts. The fact that the industrial revolution in Japan took place in two leading sectors of the economy, the railways and cotton textile industry, is evidence supporting this contention. However, the *zaibatsu* had been so powerful in economic and political affairs during the period of the 1920s and early 1930s that people thought the *zaibatsu* controlled Japan. 'Probably no other modern industrial society organized on the basis of private property,' Professor Lockwood has said, 'has offered a comparable display of the unrestrained 'power of business', employing all the devices of monopolistic control' (Lockwood, 1954). Moreover, the role of government policy had a great bearing on the industrialization of Japan. Five policy instruments which the Japanese government might have used to directly promote favored industries are (i) protection from foreign competition, (ii) direct subsidies, (iii) subsidies through the tax code, (iv) preferential access to credit, and (v) special aid through government procurement. These policy tools are not exhaustive but a convenient way of focusing the key issues[8]. However, it is one thing to demonstrate the theoretical possibility of welfare-enhancing industrial policies, it is another to implement them in reality. Implementation, at a minimum, would require that policy makers identify the correct sectors for targeting and design the proper instruments to execute the policy.

The industrial policy of Bangladesh faces all the bottlenecks that Japan had to face in its initial stages of industrialization. That is, efforts for industrialization in Bangladesh are lacked in:
1 Industrial tradition through evolutionary process of gradual development.
2 Finance ready to be invested in the industries.
3 Enterprise in the people to take up hazardous tasks of industrialization without the successful pioneers, and in spite of difficulties in the way of finance.

But the political and social changes that had taken place with the inception of a new state - again like Japan after Meiji Restoration - necessitated economic reorientation which called for the industrialization of the country at a rapid pace.

There has been a set of arguments behind the policy of assigning a major role to the public sector in Bangladesh which seem to be not unquestionable. To begin with, economic planning rests upon a very strong assumption that since the private sector is guided by profit and other considerations, it cannot be entrusted with the task of achieving the targets set in the plans. Hence planned rapid economic development can be possible only if the basic and key industries are in the public sector. Hanson has also expressed that ' . . . economic planning is always liable to be hit-or-miss game when private enterprise accounts for a large sector of the economy and the aims of the state have to be sought through the mediation of the profit-seeker'(Hanson, 1959). The assumption, implicit in this line of reasoning has, however, been falsified by the experience in Japan where most of the industries so far belonged to the reserve list and concurrent list in Bangladesh have been developed in the private sectors. Moreover, the actual achievements of these industries, instead of falling short of the proposed targets in various plans, have mostly exceeded them.

Secondly, it is also argued that the industries requiring huge investments can be developed only in the public sector as the state has a better ability to mobilize internal and external resources. The better ability to mobilize resources, however, does not necessarily imply that the government must utilize those resources itself. In fact there are ways and means by which the resources mobilized by government can be made available to the private entrepreneurs for industrial investment. In Japan also the industries requiring massive investments have not necessarily been developed in the public sector. Calder (1993) argues that Japan's remarkable industrial development is mainly due to the strategies planned and pursued by the private corporate sector based on the banking system. He examines the mechanisms of industrial fund allocation during the two decades from the 1930s to the early 1950s which could be regarded as a preparatory period for rapid development in Japan. During this period, the most remarkable fact was the establishment of the indirect financial system centered on the Bank of Japan (BOJ). Accordingly, the Japanese economy in the postwar period could be characterized not by state-led strategic capitalism but by 'corporate-led strategic capitalism.' He also argues that the intricate relationships among different key agencies like the MOF and the BOJ secured a strong position over the control of industrial fund allocation after World War II. But the policy stance of these monetary authorities was 'regulatory' in the sense that their priority was to recover and preserve the stability of the Japanese economy and financial system rather than to be 'strategic' in promoting industrial development. While the Japanese government intensively intervened in the process of industrial fund allocation, it does not necessarily imply the existence of state-led strategic capitalism. Rather, the private sector based on private banks played a leading role with respect to industrial development.

A great deal of controversy has also raised in the past as to the desirability of public sector management of such industry in Bangladesh. Experiences indicate that public sector management proved to be less responsive to accountability and as such oblivious of profitability of individual operations within an industry. The so-called policy support led to what may be called underwriting inefficient management of different industrial units in the public sector. Financial support extended to the otherwise morbid units proved to be sunk-costs for the banks that extended such support. The inability of the public sector to generate enough surplus for reinvestment does not seem to be the story of Bangladesh alone. Even in Japan, where efficiency is high everywhere, one of the biggest public sector enterprises - the Japan National Railways (JNR) - was not a source of surplus for reinvestment and consequently it has been transferred to a private sector in recent times. Of course the transfer is accomplished at the mature stage of the economy.

The obvious corollary of placing greater reliance on the public sector in Bangladesh, had been a lesser reliance on the private sector. Moreover, the ideological obsession that concentration of economic power is bad, has led to frequent attempts to curtail the scope for the large business in the private sector in the past. In sharp contrast, in Japan, the private sector has been recognized as the engine of economic growth and within the private sector a very heavy reliance has been placed on the prewar *zaibatsu* and later on the postwar *keiretsu/kigyoshudan*[9]. It is also commonly agreed that the largeness of the size has contributed to the efficiency of industrial production and has been an important factor behind the international competitive power of the Japanese industries. In the past, the big business has been considered undesirable on ideological grounds in Bangladesh and a better capacity to produce on a large scale, associated with it, has not been given the weight that it deserved.

The industrial policy of Bangladesh, until recently, characterized by placing major reliance on the public sector and curtailing the scope for operation of the private sector, if seen in the light of the Japanese experience - achievement of a rapid rate of growth through relying on the private sector, in general, and the *zaibatsu/keiretsu/kigyoshudan*, in particular - brings forth an important question: whether one of the significant factors responsible for economic malaise in Bangladesh stems from the fact that it had 'more' reliance on the 'less' efficient sector and 'less' on the 'more' efficient sector.

In connection with sale of public enterprises, one of the enlightened bureaucrats who pushed forward the establishment of the Ministry of Industries in Japan, commented, 'To keep profitable enterprises under government management would contradict the very purpose of encouragement of private business. Furthermore, enterprises with large deficits are some heavy drains on the treasury and no time should be lost in selling them to the public disregarding the sunk-costs, so as to stop the bothersome losses' (Tokyo University *Henshu linkai*, 1971). Bangladesh government has been preserving and protecting nationalized sectors even today with heavy burdens of loss and thereby discouraging private capital and entrepreneurs. Japanese experience suggests immediate transfer of these enterprises to private sectors irrespective of their profitability. But there is, however, one danger that the economic history of Japan has to offer us. Sudden transfer of industries in large scale created a sort of 'financial oligarchy' in Japan from which the economy could never emerge. Even the SCAP of McArthur proved too weak to break the *zaibatsu*. In view of this grave lesson from Japan, we have to lay down a definite and clear program of this 'transfer back' process so as to avoid the undesirable possibilities in the long run.

East Asia's unprecedented economic success during last three decades has been termed 'the East Asian Miracle' in a recent World Bank publication (World Bank, 1993). Among the East Asian countries Japan played a leading role by setting the example of high growth at the beginning and then followed by others. This phenomenon has profound implications on theories and strategies of economic development. Although these countries have similarity in terms of economic growth, geographical proximity and export promotion, but they are significantly different in size, factor endowments, history, ethnic composition, political systems and culture. Their success fundamentally originated not to economic liberalism rather to selective industrial policies[10]. They used different instruments to implement their policies. Control over the formal capital markets in terms of rates, allocation of funds, protection of industry through differential exchange rates, import restrictions and the fiscal regime were pursued consistent with industrial policies. Besides, they adopted highly selective foreign investment policy.

Japanese experience demonstrates that not only the formulation of a policy rather the competence of the relevant authorities to implement it, acceptability of the policy to the interest groups and emphasizing the long term national interest instead of self interest are of paramount importance. In this regard the efforts of the Ministry of Trade and Industry (MITI) are comprehensive and far reaching. It is responsible for shaping the Japanese industrial structure, guiding the development of specific industries, managing foreign trade and business relations, ensuring sufficient supply of energy and raw materials. MITI resorts to many actions covering a wide range from broad policy making to ad hoc working-level problem solving, formal regulation as well as informal administrative guidance. It also works to develop a consensus between government and business on long term national issues and minimizes confrontation and distrust among different interest groups. In this effort MITI has attached to it many deliberation councils (*shingi kai*), Industrial Structure Council is considered most important among them. The membership is extensive representing different businesses, government, consumers, academics, mass media, labor and local interest groups. This council and its subcommittees are responsible for examining diverse industry related issues, particularly identifying the implications thereof.

MITI has played a very significant role in devising Japan's industrial policy. The OECD's Industrial Committee has produced a comprehensive account of past Japanese industrial policy, as given by MITI itself. The Administrative Vice-Minister Yoshida Ojima furnished an authoritative statement of MITI's performance:

The Ministry of International Trade and Industry (after the war) decided to establish in Japan industries which require extensive employment of capital and technology, industries that in consideration of comparative cost of production should be the most appropriate for Japan, industries such as steel, oil refining, petrochemical, automobiles, aircraft, industrial machinery of all sorts, and electronics, including electronic computers. From a short run, static viewpoint, encouragement of such industries would seem to conflict with economic rationalism. But, from a long range viewpoint, these are precisely the industries where income elasticity of demand is high, technological progress is rapid, and labor productivity rises fast . . . According to Napoleon and Clausewitz, the secret of successful strategy is the concentration of fighting power on the main battle grounds; fortunately . . . Japan has been able to concentrate its scant capital in strategic industries (OECD, 1972).

Obviously, official influence is not lacking in this statement. Ultimately MITI's policies succeeded to bring Japan to the present state of one of the economic superpowers of the world with its scanty natural resources, capital and technology. In these efforts Japan emphasized the role of private sectors as it appears from the following statement:

MITI did, of course, engage in an extraordinary amount of legal and extralegal guidance, assistance, and intervention in the Japanese private sector during a period in which the economy's growth performance was exceptionally strong. The policies espoused by the MITI - import protection, controls on foreign investment and on purchases of foreign technology, financial aid to selected industries through government lending institutions, selective tax incentives, and administrative leadership to prevent excesses in investment and production - did not in any case prevent the economy from going forward at a rapid pace (Trezise and Suzuki, 1976).

Japan provides a version of economic planning not of dictatorial or coercive type but rather is meant to add an element of certainty, continuity and consistency to the nation's economic policy. Bangladesh suffers from inconsistency in its policies during the past 25 years. Bangladesh economic policy is perceivably susceptible as ad hoc and is subject to changes with the change of government.

Concluding remarks

Much has been written about the success of Japanese industrial policy by the Westerners and the Japanese. Most of the explanations come from one of the two basic theories: One is known as benign conspiracy. The Japanese are believed to have some traits of homogeneity of the society, a nonconfrontational mode of decision making and a national sense of purpose[11].

On the contrary, a view that is increasing in popularity, is that the success of Japanese industrial policy is the result of a sinister conspiracy. Advocates of this attitude argue that the Japanese government, corporations and groups cooperate closely to further their shared interests. The participants, managed by the MITI, target segments of industry and subsidize the efforts of companies with grants, tax relief, tariff protection, and market sharing agreements, then press forward into Western markets until all effective oppositions have been destroyed[12]. Both of these approaches seem to be followed by the Japanese depending on their suitability.

As an Asian country with many similarities with Japan, Bangladesh has many things to learn from their policy. Standard of living of the common people of Bangladesh needs to be improved at a rapid pace. That implies an urgent need for economic development. This can be accelerated through undertaking pragmatic steps deserved by different sectors of the economy. Since the public sector of Bangladesh has been a drag on the economy for decades without any sign of improvement, privatization provides the alternative to get rid of this burden. But the privatization process also is facing difficulties. The major problems include lack of proper understanding of its merits, lack of strong political commitment, lack of developed, adequate and efficient capital markets, existence of monopolies of SOEs in certain sectors and bureaucracy. Our natural resources are yet to be tapped for optimum use. This is a difficult task for either public or private sector alone. It would be desirable to make optimum use of the potentiality of the public sector for undertaking the national infrastructural activity and performing the role of promoting the private sectors. Private sectors, on the other hand, should be allowed to play its due role making full use of the initiative, skill, imagination and financial resources of this sector. In this effort conducive environment needs to be developed with appropriate macroeconomic policy supports, political commitment and stressing the growth potential of this sector. It is important to note that privatization itself is not a sufficient condition for efficiency improvement in industrial sector. Healthy competition, effective regulation and restructuring of industrial sectors need to be ensured for reaping its benefits. In this regard successful privatization programs of Japan appear to be instructive for Bangladesh.

Notes

1 The head office of IDBP was transferred to Dhaka only two years before independence of Bangladesh in 1971.

2 According to an unpublished survey report carried out by the Bangladesh (the then East Pakistan) Bureau of Statistics.

3   For example, Weisskopf (1972) and Chenery and Syrquin (1975) have supported the view that the ratio of savings to GNP is adversely affected by foreign capital. Wai (1972) also found a negative relationship between national savings and capital inflows, but pointed out the possibility of a two-way causation. In some cases, foreign borrowings are induced by large government budget deficits which imply lower national savings.

4   Although the intrinsic value of a share was higher than the par value in case of a number of enterprises, public issues were made at par due to legal binding, implying that the share offer had inherent prospect of capital gain. This rule was withdrawn in November 1991 and fresh issues can now be made at a premium.

5   Calculated from SEC Quarterly Review - various issues.

6   Previously, Controller of Capital Issues (CCI) had the responsibility of regulating the capital markets of Bangladesh but in 1993 SEC has been constituted to foster a well functioning securities markets including taking over the responsibilities of CCI.

7   The main source of information is Smith (1955).

8   These policy tools are described in more detail in Noland (1990).

9   *Zaibatsu* or big business corporates, which originated in Japan during the second half of the Meiji period, had their nucleus in certain wealthy merchant families. They played a significant role in the development of Japanese industries during the 1920s and 1930s. They were dissolved by t he SCAP authorities at the end of the World War II. During the post war period, however, they have reemerged as *keiretsu/ kigyoshudan*. Today, they occupy a very important position in Japanese industrial economy in general and in case of Japaneseleading industries, in particular. The main difference between the *zaibatsu* and *kigyoshudan* is that while in the case of the former, the focal position was occupied by a particular family, in case of the latter, the central position is occupied by a particular bank.

10 For details see Amsden (1989), Johnson (1982), and Wade (1992).

11 Representative of this idea are Ouchi (1982), Vogel (1979) and Gibney (1982).

12 Books representative of this idea are Wolf (1983), Taylor (1983) and Bandon (1983).

3 Financial institutions and corporate financing

Literatures on economic development (Christian and Pagoulatos, 1973; McKinnon, 1973; Shaw, 1973; Bhatia and Khatkhate, 1975; Fry, 1980, 1982) have focused considerable attentions on the established hypothesis (Goldsmith, 1966, 1969; Gurley and Shaw, 1955, 1967; Patrick 1966; Porter, 1966) that the financial intermediation process is a precondition of economic growth. Schumpeter (1983) considers credit as 'a phenomenon of development' and regarded the banking system, along with entrepreneurship as key agent in the process of development. Banks are, therefore, considered as one of the most important segments amongst financial intermediaries.

In developing economies state plays a pioneering role, a promotional role and also a stimulating role for promoting private enterprises. Shortage of initial capital for starting new industries and of funds for rehabilitation and expansion of the existing industries is common in these economies. Even in the developed countries it has not always been possible to raise necessary funds from the stock market as and when required. In such a situation states have been playing some constructive roles through providing the financial support to intending entrepreneurs coupled with management counseling services. This necessitates the establishment of such institutions which may fill the gap between the demand and supply of capital and related services. Institutions established with the specific purpose to pioneer industries, to subscribe shares and debentures, to guarantee and grant long term loans, to underwrite issues or to help in filling the 'gap' in some other way may be called Special Financial Institutions or Development Finance Institutions (DFIs). The role of DFIs in fostering economic growth has attracted wide attention. Government directed credit has some positive contribution in some high performing Asian countries (World Bank, 1993). Thus, organized financial institutions are found in all countries of the world for supporting investment activities through efficient allocation of capital funds. Although DFIs tend to be associated now-a-days with developing countries, this has not always been the case. To start with, they tend to be based historically on French Credit Mobilier established in 1852, generally considered as the pioneer in the field. Industrialized countries have their DFIs in this century, notably the Reconstruction Finance Corporation of the U.S.A. established by the Roosevelt government in the early 1930s to counteract the slump but dissolved at the end of the 1939-45 war. The Industrial Bank of Japan (IBJ) was established in 1902 and many more institutions were established after the First World War. The Industrial and Commercial Finance Corporation and the Finance Corporation for Industry were set up in the U.K. in 1945 by the commercial banks and the Bank of England (which was then also private). Japan passed through a transition process from a war time command economy to a market oriented economy. During this transition process public financial institutions particularly, the Reconstruction Finance Bank (RFB) (*Fukko Kinyu Kinko*) and Japan Development Bank (JDB) played a very notable role. The RFB worked as a provider of industrial funds during 1947-49. Then its functions were taken over by the Counterpart Fund (*Mikaeri Shikin*), the JDB and other public financial institutions. RFB and JDB depended heavily on the IBJ, the most powerful bank during the war.

The present third world nations are mostly characterized with DFIs. The important reasons for such institutions are as follows (Kitchen, 1993):

1. The private sector does not provide adequate institutions or finance to provide long term capital for investment purposes. The lack of institutions in many countries is aggravated by the lack of a securities market.
2. The central roles in economic development which governments take on forces them to set up such institutions to identify, appraise, promote, finance and implement investment projects.

A DFI can play twin role in the realm of economic development viz., financing and promotion. It is true that while lack of finance might inhibit investment, cheap or plentiful credit cannot *per se* be an instrument for successful investment. Careful and expert investment decision is essential taking the prevailing economic condition into consideration. Financing of a project would depend on the viability of the project which is determined through scrutiny of its economic, financial, technical and management aspects. The provision for various kinds of technical and managerial assistance, undertaking economic and technical research, conducting of survey works and feasibility studies, pursuing the potential investors, fostering of the capital markets etc. should be ensured. Moreover, as an institution tends to have 'institutional conscience' it becomes 'a less comfortable sleeping partner than the private person'. All these constitute the main features of promotional roles of DFIs. The creation of such an institution is aimed at solving this twofold problem at one stroke. In Bangladesh, DFIs appear to be necessary because financial institutions are limited in number and entrepreneurial activities are largely concentrated on activities that may yield quick returns, such as trading. Besides, shortage of funds in the capital markets, technical knowledge and facilities to promote industries and investors indicates the great need of such institutions. However, institutional finance generally begins with banks although it may differ in form and practice in different countries. The difference between banks of the credit mobilier type and commercial banks in the advanced industrial country (England) was absolute. Between the English bank essentially designed to serve as a source of short term capital and a bank designed to finance the long term investment needs of the economy there was a complete gulf. The German banks, which may be taken as a paragon of the type of the universal bank, successfully combined the basic idea of credit mobilier with short term activities of commercial banks (Gerschenkron, 1965). Basically, Bangladesh has been following the British type financial system. It has pursued a 'supply leading'[1] finance strategy as is seen in other developing economies (Patrick, 1966) to widen the industrial base through establishing DFIs, and commercial banks in public and private sectors.

Institutional framework

Comprising three layers, the banking system of Bangladesh has been designed in such a way that different types of banks specialize in different types of lending. The layers consist of (a) the regulatory authorities, (b) public finance and (c) private finance. At the top of the system the Central Bank of Bangladesh, the Bangladesh Bank (BB), and the Ministry of Finance form the key regulatory authorities. Government financial institutions are mostly owned and controlled by government. These include Bangladesh Krishi (agricultural) Bank (BKB), Grameen (rural) Bank, Rajshahi Krishi (agricultural) Bank (RKB), Bangladesh Shilpa Bank (BSB), Bangladesh Shilpa Rin Sangstha (BSRS), Investment Corporation of Bangladesh (ICB)[2], Bank of Small Industries and Commerce Bangladesh Ltd., Post Office Savings Scheme, three Nationalized Commercial Banks (NCBs) and three life and non-life insurance organizations. As regards private finance, the financial institutions so far developed are in the category of commercial banks, some life and non-life insurance companies. There are fifteen private commercial banks (PCBs) owned by Bangladeshis and ten foreign commercial banks (FCBs) owned by foreigners as on June 1996. In the private sector there are two Islamic Banks based on the principle of profit sharing instead of traditional charging of interest on deposits[3]. Side by side, twenty life and non-life insurance companies are working in the private sector including one foreign life insurance company. Most of the private sector

Table - 3.1
Key financial institutions providing industrial finance in Bangladesh

Ownership	Long term Fund	Short term Fund
Public	BSB, BSRS, ICB, NCBs, Life and Non-life Insurance Organizations	NCBs and BSB*
Private	PCBs, FCBs, Life and Non-life Insurance Companies, DSE, CSE, Leasing Companies,** Investment Companies** and others.	PCBs and FCBs

*Notes: *Occasionally this institution provides short term finance to the projects for which long term finance was provided earlier. **Their role is very limited and not much visible.*

insurance companies were established in 1985 and 1986. Table-3.1 shows the major dichotomy of key financial institutions in Bangladesh capital markets.

The banking system underwent structural changes with the creation of six nationalized commercial banks (NCBs) through nationalization of all commercial banks in 1972. Before nationalization there were twelve commercial banks in the private sector and two DFIs - one for industrial finance and the other for agricultural finance - in the public sector. With the change of government policy toward privatization two commercial banks were denationalized in 1984 and one in December 1986. However, with the government liberalization policy, applications seeking permission for setting up more private banks and insurance companies are under consideration of the authorities concerned.

An obvious indication of the size of the financial structure and the level of banking activity is the number of bank branches. The number of branches of all commercial banks rose from 4,719 in 1983 to 7,112 in 1993 as it is seen from Table-3.2. Higher rate of increase in the number of bank branches is observed for PCBs than those of NCBs. This reflects the government policy emphasizing the private sector. The branches of FCBs are not too many and they are more or less stable. In case of specialized banks the increasing number of branches is mainly attributable to agricultural banks which are in the public sector. The figure for industrial banks (ICB and BSRS) has not been shown in this Table because they have only a few branches.

The capital markets of Bangladesh are broadly divided into two segments, e.g., the non-security segment and the security segment. The non-security segment comprises two development finance institutions - BSB and BSRS and the security segment comprises the Dhaka Stock Exchange (DSE), recently established Chittagong Stock Exchange (CSE), ICB and its co-underwriters, e.g., BSB, BSRS, Sonali Bank, Rupali Bank, Pubali Bank, Uttara Bank and Shadharan Bima Corporation (General Insurance Corporation). BSB and BSRS mainly provide long term and medium term loans to entrepreneurs while ICB and its co-underwriters primarily support equity finance either through direct underwriting or through bridge finance. Bangladesh does not have a structured money market. The money markets in Bangladesh revolve primarily around BB, NCBs, PCBs and FCBs. One of the recent developments is an interbank market. According to the Governor of BB, 'It was slow at first. But when we increased our dealing spread, banks found that if they went to the market, it

Table - 3.2
Banks and their branch offices in Bangladesh

Year	NCBs	PCBs	FCBs	Specialized Banks	Total (All Banks)
1983	2,817	1,049	21	832	4,719
1984	2,854	1,102	21	950	4,927
1985	2,900	1,116	21	955	4,993
1986	2,810	1,153	21	1,024	5,008
1987	2,945	1,189	22	1,068	5,224
1988	2,982	1,237	22	1,105	5,346
1989	3,010	1,314	22	1,145	5,491
1990	3,106	2,165	22	1,148	6,441
1991	3,235	2,382	22	1,167	6,806
1992	3,131	2,488	25	1,176	6,820
1993	3,202	2,652	29	1,229	7,112

Note: ICB, BSRS and BB are not included in this Table.
Source: Prepared from Bangladesh Bank, Scheduled Bank Statistics, 1994.

might be cheaper . . . We do not participate in the interbank market. If they have a surplus they can sell it to us. The market is now quite active' (Euromoney, 1995). However, money market instruments like commercial papers, banker's acceptances, treasury bills, certificates of deposits etc. are not traded in the marketplace owing to the nonexistence of any secondary market.

The financial institutions play a dominant role in the industrialization process of Bangladesh. Industries in this country rely heavily on debt financing. The DFIs provide loans to the enterprises at a very high debt-equity ratio. In most cases the ratio is 70:30 and sometimes is higher depending on the location and type of industry. DFIs, viz., ICB, BSB and BSRS also provide venture capital mainly in the form of bridge finance and underwriting. They sanctioned venture capital to 749 companies from the fiscal year 1076-77 to 1992-93. Although the borrowing companies are required to make public issue of shares and debentures in return, only 71 out of 749 companies have made public issue of securities during the period from 1976 to 1994 (Khan et al., 1995). This indicates that mere preparing some rules is not sufficient condition to bring the companies for public floatation. Congenial environment and effective mechanisms need to be devised for this purpose. Some NCBs participate in venture capital financing through the consortium. In addition, some private financial institutions viz., Saudi Bangladesh Agricultural and Investment Company (SABINCO) and Industrial Promotion and Development Corporation (IPDC) take part in these activities.

Commercial banks

In many developing countries commercial banks are dominant among all financial institutions. Commercial banks account for 65 percent of financial savings in developing countries compared to 55 percent in industrialized countries (Kitchen, 1993). These banks, of course, are financial intermediaries, and therefore they play a large role in the provision of credit and investment funds. Historically British type banking in the developing countries is eminent. It is hardly surprising because of the fact that most of the present day developing countries including Bangladesh were British colonies. In Bangladesh short term finance in the form of trade credit, working capital and personal credit are mainly provided by the British type commercial banks. They provide little in the form of long term loans relative to their total assets, and seldom take an equity stake in business. The increase in the number of banks and branches provides only one dimension of banking growth in Bangladesh. Much more important than this indicator are the changes in assets and liabilities that reflect the direction and magnitude of growth of the financial sector.

Growth of assets

Table-3.3 shows the basic categories of bank assets and their distribution for a period of 19 years from 1975-76 to 1993-94. The item 'cash in hand and at bank' increased about 43 times or 21.93[4] percent annually and as a proportion of total assets it increased from 5.2 percent in 1975-76 to 9.8 percent in 1993-94. 'Money at call and short notice' increased more than five times or 9.44 percent annually but as a proportion of total assets it declined from 1.5 percent to 0.4 percent. These two items together reflect a general rise both in absolute and relative terms indicating more liquidity in recent years than before. Foreign currency balance has increased from 0.6 percent in 1975-76 to 2.8 percent in 1993-94 as a share of total assets. It grew at an annual rate of 27.86 percent reflecting increased flow of foreign exchange and also their increased use both as earning assets and as liquid assets. Asset items like bills and advances represent the bulk of the finance used by current business operations. These two items together increased from Tk. 11,313.5 million in 1975-76 to Tk. 253,305.3 million in 1993-94 representing an annual growth rate of 17.77 percent. Although the relative share of advances in total assets rose from 33.9 percent to 37.1 percent, which peaked in 1989-90 with 45.7 percent but the relative

Table - 3.3
Assets of all banks (In million taka)

Year	Cash in hand & at Banks	Money at Call & Short Notice	Foreign Currency Balance	Bills	Advances	Investments	Other Assets	Total
1975-76	1,457.2 (5.2)	421.7 (1.5)	171.3 (0.6)	1,318.7 (4.7)	9,494.8 (33.9)	2,558.1 (9.2)	12,572.9 (44.9)	27,994.7 (100.0)
1977-78	2,070.6 (4.9)	512.9 (1.2)	373.9 (0.9)	1,789.6 (4.2)	14,485.3 (34.0)	3,858.8 (9.1)	19,441.8 (45.7)	42,532.9 (100.0)
1979-80	4,062.1 (5.6)	442.9 (1.2)	537.1 (0.7)	2,929.9 (4.1)	25,420.8 (35.3)	4,745.7 (6.6)	33,903.3 (47.1)	72,044.8 (100.0)
1981-82	4,440.3 (4.0)	188.3 (0.2)	2,707.7 (2.5)	3,658.9 (3.3)	41,188.9 (37.3)	7,251.7 (6.5)	51,080.3 (46.2)	110,516.1 (100.0)
1983-84	7,842.9 (4.0)	1,333.5 (0.7)	3,041.4 (1.5)	5,222.3 (2.7)	64,565.9 (32.8)	15,050.6 (7.7)	99,672.7 (50.6)	196,729.3 (100.0)
1985-86	12,200.8 (3.4)	1,829.8 (0.6)	5,964.7 (1.6)	5,443.2 (1.5)	104,728.6 (28.9)	18,554.1 (5.1)	213,290.8 (58.9)	362,012.0 (100.0)
1987-88	24,539.2 (7.6)	5,266.8 (1.6)	9,667.4 (3.0)	7,774.8 (2.4)	133,427.9 (41.2)	21,232.7 (6.6)	122,023.6 (37.7)	323,932.4 (100.0)
1989-90	29,831.0 (7.2)	2,516.6 (0.6)	15,858.6 (3.8)	10,078.2 (2.4)	190,324.8 (45.7)	22,667.0 (5.4)	145,198.5 (34.9)	416,474.7 (100.0)
1991-92	28,377.1 (5.4)	2,216.6 (0.4)	16,179.0 (3.1)	11,832.0 (2.2)	215,858.4 (41.0)	49,725.0 (9.5)	201,984.1 (38.4)	526,172.2 (100.0)
1993-94	63,028.6 (9.8)	2,348.0 (0.4)	18,263.4 (2.8)	14,078.3 (2.2)	239,227.7 (37.1)	61,384.9 (9.5)	246,257.1 (38.2)	644,587.3 (100.0)

Note: Figures in parentheses indicate percentage of the totals.
Source: Calculated from Bangladesh Bank, Bangladesh Bank Bulletin, July-September, 1994.

share of bills almost consistently dropped from 4.7 percent to 2.2 percent. Relative shares of investments did not grow much which was 9.2 percent in 1975-76 and 9.5 percent in 1993-94 while from the beginning of 1980s up to the beginning of 1990s this share dropped considerably with the lowest being 5.1 percent in 1985-86. However, the share of other assets shows a declining trend almost steadily during this period. Table-3.4 provides a detailed breakdown of the types of advances extended by banks to customers for six years from 1988 to 1993. More than 67 percent of total comprised advances for non trade financing in almost all the years under consideration. The share of agricultural sectors declined from 24.5 percent in 1988 to 18.2 percent in 1993 of the total advances while that of the industrial sectors rose from 22.3 percent in 1988 to 28.2 percent in 1993. Advances for working capital financing showed an upward trend during the period. This appears to be in line with the increasing share of industrial sectors and decreasing share of agricultural sectors in GDP. The relative share of all other sectors except construction declined.

Table - 3.4
Distribution of advances by economic purpose

(Figures in % of total)

Economic Purposes	Dec. 1988	Dec. 1989	Dec. 1990	Dec. 1991	Dec. 1992	Dec. 1993
Agriculture, Fishing & Forestry	24.5	22.9	22.7	18.2	18.7	18.2
Industry (exclude working Capital)	22.3	27.1	26.5	27.8	27.2	28.2
Working Capital Financing	4.8	7.8	9.7	9.9	9.1	9.1
Construction	3.3	3.9	3.9	4.9	5.1	5.2
Electricity, Gas, Water & Sewerage	0.4	0.5	0.2	0.3	0.1	0.1
Transport & Communication	1.6	1.7	1.5	1.6	1.5	1.3
Storage	0.8	0.9	0.7	0.9	0.8	0.8
Trade	37.4	30.8	31.0	31.8	32.7	32.2
Miscellaneous	4.9	4.5	3.7	4.6	4.8	4.9
Total	100.0	100.0	100.0	100.0	100.0	100.0

Source: Calculated from Bangladesh Bank, Bangladesh Bank Bulletin, July-September, 1994.

Growth of liabilities

On the liabilities side, remarkable growth is observed in items like paid up capital, deposits and borrowings (Table-3.5). Borrowings have grown in absolute and relative terms in almost all years except 1993-94, highest being 14.6 percent of total liabilities in 1981-82. During the period of 19 years paid up capital of banks increased about 44 times or at an annual rate of about 22 percent. Their relative share also increased from 1.2 percent in 1975-76 to 2.4 percent in 1993-94 implying a declining trend of leverage in the capital structure of the banking system.

Table - 3.5
Liabilities of all banks *(In million taka)*

Year	Paid up Capital	Reserve	Deposits	Borrowings	Foreign Liabilities	Other Liabilities	Total
1975-76	353.5 (1.2)	363.5 (1.3)	11,957.4 (42.7)	1,736.8 (6.2)	260.5 (0.9)	13,326.5 (47.7)	27,994.7 (100.0)
1977-78	458.5 (1.0)	467.7 (1.1)	17,521.6 (41.3)	3,854.3 (9.1)	408.8 (0.9)	19,822.0 (46.6)	42,532.9 (100.0)
1979-80	471.8 (0.7)	660.8 (0.9)	28,216.5 (39.2)	9,003.0 (12.5)	321.6 (0.4)	33,368.1 (46.3)	72,041.8 (100.0)
1981-82	842.2 (0.8)	611.8 (0.6)	39,140.5 (35.4)	16,104.8 (14.6)	1,802.2 (1.6)	52,014.6 (47.0)	110,516.1 (100.0)
1983-84	1,714.9 (0.9)	1,389.6 (0.7)	73,749.5 (37.5)	18,231.9 (9.3)	836.0 (0.4)	100,807.4 (51.2)	196,729.3 (100.0)
1985-86	2,322.7 (0.7)	1,499.7 (0.4)	111,365.7 (30.8)	31,512.1 (8.7)	2,312.8 (0.6)	212,999.0 (58.8)	362,012.0 (100.0)
1987-88	2,998.0 (0.9)	2,200.4 (0.7)	156,160.1 (48.2)	33,240.4 (10.3)	5,790.5 (1.8)	123,543.0 (38.1)	323,932.4 (100.0)
1989-90	3,635.5 (0.9)	2,830.0 (0.7)	208,410.9 (50.0)	47,410.5 (11.4)	7,495.8 (1.8)	146,692.0 (35.2)	416,474.7 (100.0)
1991-92	8,614.4 (1.6)	3,874.4 (0.7)	270,089.9 (51.3)	42,375.9 (8.1)	12,371.8 (2.4)	188,845.8 (35.9)	526,172.2 (100.0)
1993-94	15,413.5 (2.4)	4,851.8 (0.8)	347,962.7 (54.0)	35,490.1 (5.5)	11,994.8 (1.9)	228,874.4 (35.4)	644,587.3 (100.0)

Note: Figures in parentheses indicate percentages.
Source: Calculated from Bangladesh Bank, Bangladesh Bank Bulletin, July-September, 1994.

Deposits as a source of funds have demonstrated a phenomenal growth in the past two decades. They increased from Tk.11,957.4 million in 1975-76 to

Tk.347,962.7 million in 1993-94 representing an annual growth of 19.4 percent. It is, therefore, desirable to have a brief understanding of the changing composition of bank deposits. Despite the fact that there is an upward trend in the growth of bank deposits in Bangladesh, the trend has not been uniform. Growth was slow in relative terms during the early part of 1980s compared to other times. The general rising trend indicates a better intermediation performed by the banking system supported by higher interest rates.

As we come to the recent period, time deposits have increased more rapidly than have demand deposits, thus altering the composition of bank deposits. In 1975-76 demand deposits accounted for 51.75 percent of total deposits and time deposits for 48.25 percent, while in 1993-94 these percentages were 18.56 and 81.44 respectively (Table-3.6). This suggests that deposits are regarded more

Table - 3.6
Distribution of bank deposits

(Figures in % of total)

Year	Demand Deposits	Time Deposits	Total Deposits
1975-76	51.75	48.25	100.00
1977-78	43.96	56.04	100.00
1979-80	40.69	59.31	100.00
1981-82	30.90	69.10	100.00
1983-84	29.18	70.82	100.00
1985-86	28.64	71.36	100.00
1987-88	18.81	81.19	100.00
1989-90	16.64	83.36	100.00
1991-92	17.11	82.89	100.00
1993-94	18.56	81.44	100.00

Note: *Demand portions of Savings Bank Accounts has been included in Demand Deposits while the time portions have been included in Time Deposits.*
Source: *Computed from Bangladesh Bank, Bangladesh Bank Bulletin, July-September, 1994.*

as a store of value than as a medium of payment. Relatively higher interest rates partially account for this development. Since demand deposits are more volatile form of bank deposit, the structural shift even in the face of falling interest rates in recent years may reflect, *inter alia*, the growing confidence of savers in the banking system. Drake (1980) notes that the general public has come to appreciate better the opportunity costs attached to idle current accounts, as financial understanding deepens in the course of development and is spurred by the experience of inflation. Besides, the spread of bank branches undoubtedly promotes monetization and willingness of people to hold bank deposits. However, the private banks in Bangladesh are not going to open branches to remoter areas where incomes are low. In such cases, they may be persuaded through direct government participation in the cost involved in advertising for promoting and collecting small savings; or by means of bribing the banks through offering them government deposit and account business ...' (Maynard, 1970). In view of the need for increasing reliance on domestic resources, banks need to be encouraged for domestic resource mobilization.

Performance of Development Finance Institutions (DFIs)

Both BSB and BSRS were established in 1972 and wholly owned by government. They provide loan finance in foreign and local currency to both public and private sectors. While the ICB has provided significant financial support over the past years in the development of entrepreneurship, it is primarily engaged in the provision of venture capital and hence is not immediately involved in recovering payments against their investment in particular enterprise. BSRS's role as a development financing institution has been changed consequent upon a Memorandum of Understanding (MOU) reached between the government of Bangladesh and the donor agencies on 2 March 1985. On 16 March 1987, the Industrial Advisory Center of Bangladesh (IACB) was merged with BSRS. Consequently, BSRS has been functioning primarily as a financier of Balancing, Modernization, Replacement and Expansion (BMRE) projects in its own portfolio and recovering the loans.

Generally, DFIs in Bangladesh go by the industrial policy declared by government time to time in catering the financial needs of the industries. They formulate their own operating policies keeping in view the government industrial policy. DFIs would require to pursue the lending policies designed to improve the quality of its portfolio and reduce its risk exposure[5]. Finances are made available to projects which are in line with government development plans. DFIs encourage those projects that utilize local raw materials, save foreign exchange, use labor intensive technology and have favorable linkage effects. Adequate security consistent with normal business is obtained to cover the loans. Of course, emphasis is given on sound management and financial position and projected profitability of the respective projects to cover repayments. In selecting projects they are guided by commercial considerations within the overall government policy framework and socioeconomic priorities. Narrow private profitability should not be the only consideration for DFIs, rather such issues as the creation of new employment, foreign exchange earnings, development of external economies accruing to other firms and individuals, and supporting the development of indigenous entrepreneurs in certain sectors of the economy in spite of their less efficient use than likely to accrue from others deserve due attention. The DFIs in Bangladesh has some positive contribution in these regards. With a cash recovery of Tk. 9,971.45 million against cash disbursement of Tk. 8,540.22 million since their inception up to 30 June 1991, the two DFIs are likely to make significant contribution to the economy of Bangladesh. The other important elements in specific terms include gross investment mobilized-Tk.36,243.15 million, net foreign exchange earnings-Tk.9,345.94 million, net foreign exchange savings-Tk.17,351.54 million and number of employment opportunity created-122,052. As many as 580 units out of BSB's portfolio of total 1,284 units liquidated their debts to BSB and 142 units out of BSRS's portfolio of total 397 units liquidated their debts to BSRS despite the poor collection performance, 722 projects having liquidated their debt liabilities with the DFIs are now operating satisfactorily with positive contribution to the economy (Haque, 1992). However, their overall loan recovery position is remarkably poor. Table-3.7 presents data on the volume and structure of resources committed by BSB and BSRS. In order to provide a clearer perspective on the flow of term financing from public financial institutions, it has shown their resource commitments in the aggregate of financial resources extended toward industrial and entrepreneurial development. This brings out that a total of Tk. 20,394.9 million was sanctioned by these two institutions for financing investment between 1972 and 1994. Out of this amount 78.23 percent was provided by BSB and 21.77 percent by BSRS. Of the aggregate of public funds made available, 96.0 percent was sanctioned to the private sector, and 4.0 percent to the public sector. The disbursement represents Tk.11,454.0 million or 56.16 percent from the sanctioned amount by the end of March 1994. Of the disbursed funds 95.2 percent went to the private sectors and 4.8 percent to the public sectors.

While it is evident that during the last two decades the term lending institutions have primarily served the private sector, this was not always the case. Table-3.7 has offered the data for four separate periods, i.e., 1972-75, 1975-82, 1982-89, and 1989 - 94 as well as the aggregate thereof. There was change of government in 1975, 1982 and 1990 associated with discernible redirection and emphasis of public policy toward the private sector. Accordingly, some issues involving important policy implications appear to be relevant from this intertemporal analysis.

The data shows that up to June 1975, about 78 percent of total resources sanctioned and disbursed went to the public sectors and the other 22 percent to the private sectors. In sharp contrast, the periods of 1975-82, 1982-89, and 1989-94 accounted for 96.8 percent, 98.6 percent and 98.1 percent respectively of funds made available to the private sectors and 92.6 percent, 99.2 percent and 95.9 percent respectively of disbursed amounts went to these sectors. Obviously, the private sector was getting increasing importance in later

Table - 3.7
Loan financing by BSB and BSRS   *(In million taka)*

Period	Sanction			Disbursements		
	Public	Private	Total	Public	Private	Total
A. *Amount*						
1972/73 - 1974/75@	362.9	99.4	462.3	82.1	23.2	105.3
1975/76 - 1981/82	243.0	7,303.2	7,546.2	285.0	3,561.8	3,846.8
1982/83 - 1988/89	72.4	5,134.2	5,206.6	30.6	3,723.1	3,753.6
1989/90 - 1993/94*	137.0	7,042.7	7,179.7	153.3	3,593.0	3,748.3
1972/73 - 1993/94*	815.3	19,579.5	20,394.9	553.0	10,901.1	11,454.0
B. *Percentages*						
1972/73 - 1974/75	78.5	21.5	100.0	78.0	22.0	100.0
	(44.5)	(0.5)	(2.3)	(14.8)	(0.2)	(0.9)
1975/76 - 1981/82	3.2	96.8	100.0	7.4	92.6	100.0
	(29.8)	(37.3)	(37.0)	(51.5)	(32.6)	(33.6)
1982/83 - 1988/89	1.4	98.6	100.0	0.8	99.2	100.0
	(8.9)	(26.2)	(25.5)	(5.6)	(34.2)	(32.8)
1989/90 - 1993/94	1.9	98.1	100.0	4.1	95.9	100.0
	(16.8)	(36.0)	(35.2)	(28.1)	(33.0)	(32.7)
1972/73 - 1993/94	4.0	96.0	100.0	4.8	95.2	100.0
	(100.0)	(100.0)	(100.0)	(100.0)	(100.0)	(100.0)

Note: *Figures are up to 31st March 1994. @ Figures cover from December 1971.
**Percentage figures within the parenthesis are column percentages, those outside the parenthesis are row percentages.
Source: Computed from various issues of Resume of Activities of the Financial Institutions in Bangladesh, Ministry of Finance, Government of Bangladesh.

periods. The redirection of public policy led to a progressive rise in the ceiling imposed on private investment till it was finally eliminated in the Investment Policy of 1978. However, the period of 1990-94 shows a relatively smaller amount of funds sanctioned and disbursed to the private sector reflecting the government declared policy of emphasizing financial sector reform and discipline which was badly needed due to unusually large volume of non-performing loans.

The dramatic reverse direction of public financial resource transfers after

1975 explains the larger weight of loan financing to the private sectors. There was some acceleration in this policy during the period 1982-94 which is consistent with the Industrial Policy of 1982, 1986 and 1991 emphasizing the private sectors. These figures reasonably imply that public financial institutions were primarily meant for servicing the public sectors up to mid-1975 while the share of the private sectors reflected their diminished state of the economy due to policy issues and resource constraints during that period. As already pointed out in Chapter 2, following the nationalization policy of March 1972, only 10 percent of fixed investment in the modern industrial sectors was left in the private hands. This weight in asset ownership was thus reflected in the lending programs of these financial institutions.

The role of DFIs is not confined within the function of sanctioning, disbursement and collection of loans. Rather, they should go beyond these functions. Long term financing, usually provided by DFIs, is exposed to more risk than the usual conventional commercial lending institutions and less amenable to cost-benefit analysis. On the other hand, success of an industrial project is related to various factors which may be either internal or external. Only physical security with fixed assets and bank guarantee can hardly be a matter for such type of risk. Although there is a legal relationship between DFIs and the client, DFIs can't escape from the responsibility of supporting and main-taining good health of the projects financed by them. In addition to supplying finance, these institutions very often need to extend technical and other advisory assistance side by side monitor and supervise the borrowing firms. 'Given the unconventional nature of development banking, the generally undercapitalized position of loan applicants and their inability to provide adequate collateral security, it is necessary for development bank loan assessments to be very thorough and to require much information from applicant firms; nevertheless, development banks would do well to avoid the difficulties created in Malaysia at one stage where the process of obtaining a development loan was so searching and difficult as to tax impossibly the liabilities of all but the best managed local enterprises'(Drake, 1980).

The Industrial Policies of 1982, 1986 and 1991 necessitated public resources to finance more ambitious investment projects sponsored by the private entrepreneurs with limited equity base in most cases. The rising commitment of loanable funds for investment needed to be supplemented by the public commitments of risk capital. This was the rationale for the establishment of ICB in 1976. It has a share capital of 2,000,000 shares, each with Tk. 100 par value, outstanding and distributed as on 30 June 1995 shown at Table-3.8.

ICB's concern with the securities market is clearly set forth in its governing ordinance which states that the Corporation was established to encourage and broaden the base of investments, develop the capital markets, mobilize savings and provide support for ancillary matters thereto. Reflecting this strong mandate, ICB is given extensive authority to carry on activities pertaining to the securities markets including: underwriting, managing and distributing securities;

Table - 3.8
Classification of ICB shareholders

Sl. no.	Shareholder	No. of shareholders	No. of shares	Percentage
1.	Government of Bangladesh	1	540,000	27
2.	Nationalized Commercial Banks	3	318,320	16
3.	Development Finance Institutions	2	269,480	13
4.	Insurance Companies	2	267,558	13
5.	Bangladesh Bank	1	240,000	12
6.	Denationalized Private Commercial Banks	3	238,840	12
7.	Private Commercial Banks	4	48,004	3
8.	Foreign Commercial Banks	2	42,830	2
9.	General Public	526	34,968	2
	Total	544	2,000,000	100

Source: ICB Annual Report, 1994-95.

promoting, organizing, and managing trusts or funds of any type; opening and maintaining investors' deposit accounts and other term deposit accounts; purchasing and selling shares over-the-counter to holders of investors' accounts, making advances for the purchase of shares, engaging in investment, reinvestment and holding securities, merchandizing securities as principal or agent, managing investment portfolios; providing professional counsel regarding investments, becoming a member of the stock exchange in Bangladesh; and taking part in the formation, management, supervision or control of a company. It has been gathered that with accumulated non-performing loans, ICB's debt finance has come to almost zero in recent years and its operation has been declining gradually. Although ICB primarily engaged in the provision of venture capital and hence not immediately involved in recovering payments against their investment, its dues/overdues in respect of interest on bridge loan, debenture loan and debenture principals stood at about Tk.2,790.2 million and that of the not due amount at about Tk. 104.7 million on 30 June 1994 (Ministry of Finance, 1993-94a) representing more than 96 percent of the total becomes either due or overdue.

ICB's investors' scheme represents a typical margin transaction wherein an investor makes a margin deposit with a securities firm in the form of cash or cash-equivalents, on the basis of which the firm grants a loan. The investor then uses the combined balance of his deposit and the loan to buy securities which the firm keeps as collateral. In order to increase the demand of securities in the market 'Investors Scheme' was introduced in June 1977. As on 30 June 1995 the number of net operative accounts was 44,192 through which about Tk. 506.7 million was invested. Of these account holders government and non-government employees account for 55 percent, retired personnel 4 percent, engineers, doctors and lawyers 4 percent, businessmen and agriculturists 14 percent, housewives and working woman 14 percent, laborers 6 percent and others 3 percent. Under this scheme, the account holders are financed at 1:2 ratio subject to a maximum limit of Tk. 200,000 at an interest rate of 11 percent. This low ratio encourages entrance of investors into the market. Approximately 83 percent of the account holders' deposits ranged from Tk. 1,000 to Tk. 5,000 (ICB, 1994-95). That probably indicates the dominance of small savers in the scheme. Account holders can buy and sell shares according to their own choice. It is observed that for any transaction it takes about six/seven days, or more. Securities markets offer different price every day. With the frequently changing prices, account holders' choices may not remain consistent for such long time. Withdrawal of shares also takes long time. This time lag may be related with organizational inefficiency. It is reported by the local press that due to discriminatory policy of the Corporation about 40 percent of the accounts has been closed down and about 10 percent of the accounts are owned by the higher officers of the Corporation. Almost all privileges of the Corporation go to 10 percent of the account holders.

Selling of Unit Certificates is another program of ICB. Table-3.9 reveals that although the gross sale of units during 1994-95 increased by about 146 percent of the previous year, the repurchase being remained almost at the same level. This is the maximum sales volume since its inception that reflects the increasing popularity of the Fund. The net cumulative investment of the Fund stood at Tk. 2,244.36 million in 182 securities of 171 companies as on 30 June 1995. The market value of the securities stood at Tk. 4,114.21 million on that date representing an appreciation of Tk. 1,869.8 million or more than 83 percent. The cumulative investment of the fund as on 31 March, 1994 stood at Tk. 1,393.3 million at cost in 147 securities of 141 companies. The intrinsic value of a unit certificate of Tk.100 each has been shown more than Tk. 200 (Ministry of Finance, 1993-94b). But ICB avoids the process of trading of unit certificates in the stock exchanges. This allows unrealistic return estimation not confirmed by 'market' valuations. It is gathered that out of the total sale of unit certificates, 69.47 percent were sold over the counter of the Corporation during the year 1994-95, 27.66 percent with the assistance of DSE members and the rest through commercial banks. It has been reported in the local press that out of Tk. 1,170 million accumulated from the sale of unit certificates on 30 June

1990, ICB could invest only Tk. 730 million and the balance was transferred to money markets. It seems to be not congenial for the capital market development in Bangladesh as it shows diversions of funds for other purposes.

Table - 3.9
Performance of ICB unit certificates   (In million taka)

Items	1990-91	1991-92	1992-93	1993-94	1994-95
1. Gross Sales					
Units	4.94	2.08	1.43	2.65	6.18
Amount	587.20	237.24	162.73	307.74	756.62
2. Repurchase					
Units	0.93	3.38	1.86	0.72	0.73
Amount	115.12	374.17	203.19	81.19	88.86
3. Net Sales					
Units	4.01	(1.30)	(0.42)	1.93	5.46
Amount	472.08	(136.93)	(40.46)	226.55	667.76
4. Investments (on June 30)					
At cost	987.03	1,086.85	1,070.93	1,396.95	2,244.36
At market price	1,519.98	1,607.68	1,590.12	3,446.35	4,114.21
5. Dividend Per Unit	18.00	16.70	17.00	17.40	17.50

Source: ICB Unit Fund Annual Report, 1994-95.

The mutual fund operations of ICB are intended to generate some interest in the stock markets in general. It is observed from Table-3.10 that each of the six Mutual Funds was oversubscribed and the market value was much higher than the respective cost price of the portfolio as on 30 June 1995. Market capitalizations of the six Funds amounted to Tk. 357.5 million as on that date against the issued capital of Tk. 95.0 million. Since the stocks included in the Mutual Funds all appear to be sound, dividend paying issues, these Funds may well serve the purpose. This permitted very high dividend rates (in most cases it varies from 20 percent to 40 percent) frequently quoted on ICB Mutual Funds on their par value. In 1987, the market price of Tk. 100 certificate of the First Mutual Fund rose to Tk. 1500 but the market price of the same came down to Tk. 450 in 1991. ICB failed to protect its investors from such unusual loss. ICB could not play its due role in stabilizing stock prices at the desired level. Although the number of enlisted companies has increased, market capitalization dropped to Tk. 11,798 million on 30 June 1990 from Tk. 15,431 million on 30 June 1989. Again, the worst downswing took place in the share markets in November 1996. These caused a huge loss to the general investors. All these have brought the role of ICB into question.

Table - 3.10
Performance of ICB mutual funds[6]   *(In million taka)*

Mutual funds	Floatation date	Fund size	Amount subscribed	Cost price	Market price	Dividend per certificate(Tk.)	No. of certificateholders
First Mutual Fund	April 25, '80	5.0	8.2	12.0	117.2	50.00	1,249
Second Mutual Fund	June 17, '84	5.0	13.4	7.6	23.7	40.00	1,392
Third Mutual Fund	May 19, '85	10.0	14.0	16.1	44.7	27.00	5,975
Fourth Mutual Fund	June 6, '86	10.0	14.4	14.4	46.6	41.00	5,722
Fifth Mutual Fund	June 8, '87	15.0	81.8	21.2	47.1	28.00	6,192
Sixth Mutual Fund	May 16, '88	50.0	185.0	57.2	78.2	18.00	17,785
Total		90.0	316.8	128.5	357.5	-	38,315

Source: *ICB Annual Reports.*

Indeed, ICB is overburdened with its diversified programs. The responsibility of varied programs currently undertaken by ICB can be entrusted with more than one institution. However, ICB needs to be more assertive to realize its objectives. In the immediate future ICB, DSE and CSE need to extend more efforts in matching the supply of and demand for securities. ICB functions both as a development finance company and as an underwriter. It performs the former role when it provides either bridge or debenture financing to new companies. In this capacity, it competes with the two much larger development banks - BSB and BSRS - already in the field. In its capacity as an underwriter, it renders investment banking function that is essential for the securities markets. ICB is the only institution engaged in the activities like Investors' Scheme, Unit Fund and Mutual Fund in Bangladesh till the end of 1996 when BSRS initiated Mutual Fund activities. Without having no other alternative, investors are coming to it at an increasing rate in spite of allegations against ICB activities. Since it is not facing any competition, it is difficult to evaluate its activities. In the meantime government has formulated policy for introducing such institutions in the private sector. Merchant banks are expected to come into the market in the private sector very soon. Then ICB is likely to face competition and a more meaningful comparative assessment can be made. Gordon (1983) makes some interesting comparisons between private sector and government-owned DFIs. Private sector DFIs were found to be generally more vigorous, efficient and profitable than government-owned equivalents. They have been more effective in mobilizing domestic resources, and more active in the development of capital market institutions and instruments. However, ICB should be more effective in its activities and aggressive participant in the capital markets. With those objectives it should:

1   conduct trading in such a way that speculative trading cannot dominate the market;

2. do trading on shares effectively on behalf of their clients;
3. acquaint its activities with the general public through newspapers, journals, radio, television and open branches throughout the country in order to popularize its scheme; and
4. inform its account holders of the shares it purchases and sells on behalf of them regularly.

Financial institutions and Japanese experience

In the process of a financial development, a money market generally precedes the capital markets and within the capital markets the non-security segment is likely to precede the security segment. Access to a variety of financial instruments for both money and capital markets enables economic agents to pool, price and trade risk satisfying the varying tastes of investor. In order to establish a modern financial system, the Meiji government introduced British commercial banking system, limiting ordinary banks' primary business to short term financing. Since the Japanese stock market was underdeveloped and thinly traded before World War II, it could not play a dominant role as a source of long term funds for the industrial sectors. Thus 'special banks' (which were authorized to issue bank bonds), viz., Nippon Kangyo Bank, the Industrial Bank of Japan (IBJ), and the Agricultural and Industrial Banks were set up around 1900 to fill up this gap. The current long term credit banks, trust banks and financial institutions for small and medium sized enterprises and for the agriculture and forestry originates from the prewar financial system.

To develop a sound security market, supply and demand must be integrated and the institutions operating in between need to be set in proper perspective. In the developed countries, institutions are major buyers and sellers of securities. Reflecting, at least in part, the underdeveloped condition of the securities markets, institutions have been minor participants in Bangladesh. As regards commercial bank loans, World Bank estimated that about 37 percent of the loan of the then six nationalized commercial banks[7] annually passed due dates of repayment. The big borrowers of the commercial banks, mainly constitute industrialists, traders, importers and exporters, who have taken loans as working capital, import or export financing and other types of business. Even a good number of defaulting borrowers of BSB and BSRS have been receiving working capital from commercial banks. The government of Bangladesh has shown its seriousness about realizing the outstanding industrial loans through adopting various measures. These have resulted in a low level of key operations by these institutions over the recent years. This may adversely affect the efforts for a viable and diversified industrial development in a balanced way.

Without long term credits by these institutions, investments in heavy and many other related industries needed a solid and diversified base for sustained industrial growth, are bound to suffer. The role of the banking system in Japan, particularly in the capacity of a main bank, is very significant in contrast to the limited role of Bangladeshi banking system. Table-3.11 presents a comparative picture of banking systems. The Japanese banking sector displays as the largest representing 167 percent of GNP followed by German representing 146 percent while Bangladeshi banking sector represents the smallest share, only 56 percent. American banking sector is also far behind that of Japan and German. This reflects the weakness of Bangladeshi banking sector while that of Japan has strong financial base and influence on the Japanese corporate structure with shared authority at the top. Large financial intermediaries hold concentrated blocks of stocks and provide relatively large volume of loans. The JDB used to examine investment projects proposed by potential borrowers, and as a rule supplied its loans in the form of syndicated loans with private banks. It regularly monitors the performance of the borrowers during the loan commitment by

Table - 3.11
Relative size of banking sector

Country	Ratio between Assets of Banking Sector and GNP
Japan	Assets of Banking Sector/GNP = ¥ 728,577bill./¥436,927bill.= 167%
German	Assets of Banking Sector/ GNP= $1,900bill./$1,300bill. = 146%
America	Assets of Banking Sector/ GNP= $3,399bill./$5,465bill. = 62%
Bangladesh	Assets of Banking Sector/ GNP= Tk.526,172mill./Tk.940,353mill.= 56%

Source: Prepared from Roe, (1993) and Bangladesh Bureau of Statistics, (1993).

requiring regular business operation reports from them. Sometimes it consults the main bank of a borrowing company to obtain inside information about the borrower, because the main bank may be better informed than the JDB. Bangladeshi commercial banks hold a relatively modest amount of investments in non-government securities. An examination of the statements of the individual banks reveals very small holdings of shares. In general such holdings amounted less than 1 percent of the total deposits (Robbins, 1980). The internal policy of the banks clearly does not favor the acquisition of securities of companies in the private sector. This attitude represents a combination of factors including a reluctance to hold long term investments in the face of short term obligations, the modest amount of securities available, lack of their liquidity and lack of confidence in the stock markets of Bangladesh. Even granted these factors, however, the virtual abstinence is extreme. The commercial banks of Bangladesh, as in most less developed countries, are so dominant in the nation's financial structure that their help in the creation of securities markets becomes very important. There is reason to believe that banks are not performing their due role in this regard. Japanese experience suggests banks along with DFIs will not only involve them in loan giving but also in regular monitoring activities. Then the bank fund is likely to be used in a better way and the possibility of blocking of funds be reduced.

It has been widely held that the JDB was an effective instrument by which the Japanese government stimulated industrial development after World War II and it can be considered as a model for many developing countries of today. RFB provided funds to key industries such as coal and steel which contributed to the reconstruction of the economy. It is indicated by Okazaki et al., (1995) that RFB funds were meant for relatively poor performing firms in 1948-49. This is consistent with the general view that RFB was a political institution and was subject to the rentseeking activities of politicians and other influential parties. However, with the change of loan policy in 1949 better performances of the loan receiving firms were observed. It is also said JDB loans promoted development of key industries without serious negative effects. Ogura and Yoshino (1984) have indicated that the majority of JDB loans went to basic industries such as electricity, shipping and coal rather than high tech industries. Horiuchi and Otaki (1987) have shown that JDB loans, even if small in size, were important as a signaling device; i.e., they transmitted information concerning the government's industrial policy and extracted loans from other banks. In a more recent study Horiuchi and Sui (1993) have observed JDB loans led to an increase in lending by private banks and to increase in investment by loan receiving firms. More specially, initiation of JDB funding led to significant increases in investment and a total borrowing by the JDB loan receiving firms increased in two years following the start of JDB funding. They also find that the effects are larger for those firms without a private main bank. It is needless to say that in Japan private banks play an important role by monitoring firms in the capacity of a main bank. Such close relation between a bank and industrial firms does not exist in Bangladesh. The important aspect of this relationship need not be reiterated. We will find more detail discussion on this issue in Chapter 7. The study of Horiuchi and Sui has also confirmed the existence of signaling effect of JDB loans in general and emphasized that its most essential function was not only to provide funds but also to exchange information between policy makers and industrial companies. Simultaneously, it monitored the managerial behavior of borrowing companies from various angles. Thus, it reduced the agency costs for the borrowing firms.

The main philosophy behind setting up the financial institutions in Bangladesh like BSB and BSRS was to ensure optimum development of the industrial sectors through providing financial support and promotional activities. But they have directed very limited efforts to vitalize the securities markets relative to their financial strength. According to Cameron (1967), banks' role was inadequate as a supplier of funds. Securities markets were complements rather than substitutes for banks. Consortia of banks were useful to underwrite the shares and bank like Credit Mobilier was acting as intermediaries between small shareholders and the firms. The limited role of Bangladeshi financial institutions with regard to securities markets is sometimes explained by the underdeveloped condition of securities markets. It is also likely to reflect a belief that their primary role is one of development financing rather than of investing in the securities markets. The relatively large equity investments inherited by BSRS indicate that its predecessors, Pakistan Industrial Credit and Investment Corporation (PICIC), Investment Corporation of Pakistan (ICP) and National Investment Trust (NIT) were reasonably active in the securities market. In Germany the financial institutions not only played a key role in the industrialization process, but also promote the development of financial instruments like stocks. Kemp (1978) has pointed out:

> Credit banks on similar principles were founded in . . . Germany during the following decade . . . These banks also undertook the usual banking services for customers and they were less interested in holding large stock of industrial shares than in encouraging the sale of such shares over their own counters. This was increasingly possible as railways were floated and industrial firms adopted the joint stock form of organization.
>
> German investment banking . . . provided an alternative model to that of Britain . . . It obviated the need for the slow build-up of capital by small firms, and by making it possible to raise large amounts of capital, enabled big plants embodying the latest techniques to be established from the start.

All these suggest that in the process of securities market development, both BSB and BSRS need to become buyers, sellers and underwriters of the securities of the publicly traded companies along with their loan financing. Besides, a portion of their loan may be granted in the form of a debenture that can later be distributed directly or through ICB.

There was a time when loan sanction and loan disbursement were the main criteria for evaluating the performance of these institutions in Bangladesh. But now, the recovery of disbursed loans has become an important element of their performance evaluation. Lower recovery of loans is at present a great problem faced by these financial institutions. BSB has recovered only 19 percent of its overdue amount and 37 percent of its current dues whereas BSRS has recovered only 8 percent of the overdue amount (Ministry of Industries, 1985). The overdue loan of BSB stands at Tk. 3,225.9 million or 39 percent of total loan amounting to Tk. 8,146.4 million on 30 June 1990. The overdue loan of BSRS stands at Tk.4,432.1 million or 51.7 percent of total loans on 30 June 1990. As on 31 March 1994, BSB had the total outstanding term loans of Tk. 13,420.0 million of which Tk. 6,870.0 million was overdue. This accounted for about 51 percent of total outstanding loans. Similarly, BSRS had total outstanding loans of Tk. 9,275.4 million of which Tk. 5,305.5 million or about 51 percent was overdue on the same date (Ministry of Finance, 1993-94b). These figures indicate an unsatisfactory performance associated with increasing accumulation of overdue loans. Since the government policy is directed toward building up private entrepreneurship through fiscal concessions, liberal provision of public resources and disinvestment of nationalized enterprises, it is desirable to appraise the efficacy with which the private sectors have handled publicly provided resources. The lower recovery rate indicates that the major portion of the fund disbursed is blocked in the hands of borrowers. This blocking of funds is a serious problem for the overall industrialization process of the country. Shortfalls in the SFYP were partly due to the fact that the loan recovery problem forced suspension of credit lines of these lending agencies. 'As the SFYP was coming to a close, industrial finance grew into a serious crisis. Due to accumulation of overdue debts the credit lines from the development finance institutions to private sectors were frozen . . . Freezing of the credit lines of the development finance institutions poses a serious problem to finance private industries under TFYP'(TFYP, 1985-90). However, with some stringent measures taken by the government in recent years, the situation is improving although at a slow pace. The recovery target of 100 largest defaulter borrowers of NCBs and new loans of Tk. 10 million and above disbursed after June 1990 was achieved. The NCBs achieved 197.23 percent of their collection target from their 100 largest borrowers at the end of June 1994. In case of new loan collection, 77.48 percent of the target was achieved at the end of March 1994 (Ministry of Finance, 1993-94b). Some provisions of the Financial Loan Court and Bank Company Act 1991 were amended to strengthen legal provision for recovery and ensure more discipline in the financial sector. Bank Company Act (Amended) 1993 was promulgated. The credit information Bureau set up in Bangladesh Bank has been providing necessary information promptly as required by commercial banks. All these efforts are aimed to reduce in 'default culture'. A substantial part of RFB loans, specially RFB operating funds loans, were deficit financing loans *(akaji yushi)*. Deficit-financing loans were defined by the RFB as the loans for compensating deficits of an enterprise to enable its operation (MOF, 1976; *Fukku Kinyu Kinko* (RFB), 1950). The BOJ pointed out that 'deficit financing loans created the lack of serious managerial efforts on the part of the borrowing firms to reduce costs by rationalization and increasing production and aggravated the inclination of the firms to depend on the government' (BOJ, 1962). Financial support to cope with deficit financing of the enterprise is sometimes desirable, but it is the usual tendency of the borrowers not to repay the loan money in the current situation in Bangladesh.

Both BSB and BSRS have been examined and evaluated by various agencies including the World Bank which observed 'These institutions have faced difficulties, particularly with respect to their capital structure, foreign exchange availability, staffing, financial policies and project appraisal procedures'(World Bank, 1978). It is gathered that the continuing problems of lack of skilled professionals and high employee turnover because of limited salary scales were very much dominant in these institutions. These banks have been suffering from severe liquidity constraints because of their low loan recovery rate and misallocation of resources (Sobhan, 1990). Low recovery rate is related to the misappraisal of projects, errors in assumptions about market behavior, demand and supply and long time taken for project approval. Again, misappraisal and the errors in the underlying assumptions of the projects were closely associated with the extraction of premiums by the relevant bank employees (Nabi, 1992). Specialized financial institutions viz., IDBP, PICIC, ICP and the NIT of pre-independence period have been subsequently converted to BSB and BSRS did not experience such a grave situation in those days. Apparently, political influence and inefficiency in management are partially attributed to such problems. In case of Japan, necessary skilled personnel for credit analysis were supplied to both RFB and JDB by IBJ which had these resources. The experience of RFB and JDB suggests that public financial institutions must be free from political forces. It need not be confused with government industrial policy which must be a sound one and the individual loan policies required to be left in the hands of banks rather than politicians. Fry (1978) has noted that under repression, 'nonprice rationing of investable funds must occur. This typically takes place on the basis of quality of collateral, political pressures, 'name', loan size, and convert benefits to responsible officers. These criteria can be counted on to discriminate inefficiently between investment opportunities.' Accordingly, companies take unusually high volume of loans compared to their equity and thereby become highly risky. This implies shifting of a major burden to the bank in case of a loss. With high degree of leverage, the entrepreneurs could recover their equity by overvaluing equity inputs (e.g., land and buildings), overinvoicing equipments and raw materials and distributing earnings (Varley, 1992). They are tempted to lose their creditworthy entity as their lack of creditworthiness does not affect their attempt to take further loans. In contrast, businesses with relatively reduced exposure to risk resort to either sharing the ownership with shareholders or use internal fund for expansion purposes. The interest rates charged by the DFIs were not consistent either with the risk associated with the project, or the equity and repayment schedule (Khan et al., 1995). The soft lending policy of the government made borrowing preferable because of ease of mobilizing funds, no necessity to repay in time, shifting of the major burden of risk, deductibility of interest expense for tax purposes and greater control over the company. Of course, most companies need not pay taxes at their initial years of operation due to tax holiday applicable at that stage.

The financial institutions in Bangladesh cannot work independently due to political pressures. Most of the project loans were given on political considerations without examining the project profiles (Economic Times, Dec. 1990). This is also one of the important reasons for overdue loans and undue delay in repayment. Reflecting a qualitative difference from RFB, JDB's unique role enabled it to be useful in ensuring smooth communication between the policy makers and the business, and helped the JDB obtain valuable information that would not be available to private banks. After pointing out that the amount of the JDB credit was a small share of the total amount of funds raised by private business, Ueno (1978) has argued that JDB credit was important because it announced the names of specific firms which would be prosperous under the industrial policy. According to Ueno once a firm obtained credit from the JDB, private banks and financial institutions competed with each other to supply loans to the firm 'virtually without credit examinations.' Similarly, Sato (1990) argues that 'if the JDB decides to make a loan to an industry private banks interpret it as an indication that the government considers that industry as a growth industry worthy of being financed by public funds, and is willing to back up the industry if it falls into financial difficulties. Knowing this stance of the government, private banks are induced to extend credit to that industry.' The DFIs in Japan have played a very important role different from those of Bangladesh DFIs. In addition to political considerations, failure to repay loans to these institutions has been related to two points in a research study (Sobhan et al., 1981). The first relates to the long term gestation period as between the sanction of the loan and the commissioning of a project. This incapacitates the firm to generate revenues leading to an inevitable build up of arrears. This would imply that borrowers tend to financially in poorer shape than they projected themselves when applying for the loan. In this regard one should not forget the basic difference between a short term commercial bank loan and a long term industrial credit. Whereas a short term commercial bank loan is usually granted against pledge or hypothecation of readily marketable stocks, a long term credit is sanctioned against assets yet to be created and its repayment is expected to come out of profits to be generated by such assets. The time lags between submission of loan application and commercial production depend on the size of the project, availability of machinery and raw materials, shipping facilities etc. (Ahmed, 1978). However, if proper steps are taken there is scope for reducing the time gap to some extent. Secondly, in many cases the enterprises become sick and non-operational. Even when made operational still fail to maintain a satisfactory debt service record. It suggests that there is a tendency of intentional non-repayment of debt on the part of borrowers. Besides, the borrowers are allegedly not using their borrowed money for which they borrowed. Instead, they divert the money to other purposes. Consequently, the enterprises cannot run efficiently and the authorities responsible for improving repayment performance are faced with a more intractable problem relating to the character of the entrepreneurial class and the socioeconomic environment within which they operate.

Development perspective and selection criteria

The perspective of a DFI differs from that of an ordinary financial institution. Development institution seeks to promote such industrial development as is consistent with overall national development strategy. The objectives may not be clear, and some of them may be such as can't be quantified and measured. It is needless to say that the relative significance of the various objectives changes with time and circumstances. Besides, the objectives may be dependent of the extent of information with regard to the alternative courses of action, and the information can never be perfect; not only is the future uncertain and unknowable, but also information relating to the present as well as the past is always incomplete (Arrow, 1974).

It may be noted that capital market theory has considerable relevance to DFIs. The recognition that some sectors carry more risk than others should enable them to use a higher discount rate in the higher-risk business. Also DFIs need a well-diversified portfolio of loans and equity stakes so that they can diversify away specific risk. The principle of diversification is an argument against establishing institutions which were too specialized. Such institutions have limited scope for risk diversification. DFIs by their objectives are obliged to finance projects associated with high financial and commercial risks. Thus, these institutions require high expected return according to capital market theory. However, the requirement to meet the government's national objectives implies that it may be required to finance projects whose financial return is expected to be lower than if it is considered on commercial grounds. It seems difficult to reconcile the financial and national objectives of DFIs. In Japan, JDB successfully applies two types of interest rates. One is the standard interest rate *(kijun kinri)* and another is the special interest rate *(tokubetsu kinri)*. The latter has been substantially lower than the former. The margin between these two rates was from 2.5 to 3.5 percent during the 1950s, but it became narrower as the Japanese economy grew. As of October 1992, it was only from 0.6 to 0.05 percent (Horiuchi and Sui, 1993).

Each lending institution has developed its own selection criteria consistent with its requirements. For example, Asian Development Bank (ADB), World Bank and Islamic Development Bank (IDB) have their own guidelines of project appraisals. Although such guidelines differ from each other in format, no major difference is observed in terms of contents. Bangladeshi DFIs broadly consider the following aspects in the process of the appraisal: technical, market, financial, economic and management[8]. However, the appraisal work is beset with various problems. As Bangladesh has hardly any indigenous technology base, industries have to depend largely on borrowed technologies which are likely to be found not always suitable in the context of country's socio-economic condition[9]. If technology is imported, an attempt should be there to adapt and modify technology to suit the resource structure and environment of the country. This requires technological competence. Moreover, adequate and updated primary or secondary data are not readily available. These reflect on the forecast of actual scenarios. A considerable number of sponsors are first generation entrepreneurs lacking experience of running any industrial enterprise. These factors cause unreliable and incomplete information in the feasibility report and project proposal. On the other hand, the lending agencies are found badly equipped with less competent personnel and less effective organizational structure involving lengthy and cumbersome procedure for approval of the project appraisal.

A DFI has no *raison d'etre* for its existence unless it seeks to promote industrial development that is consistent with country's development objectives. Hence it can't judge the soundness of a project merely on the basis of its ability to service its debt to the DFI. Of course, a project needs to be financially sound *vis-a-vis* it should be compatible with the development objectives of the country. If financially and economically sound projects are not available, DFIs should facilitate the identification and formulation of such projects. They should also take the initiative, in cooperation with other relevant agencies, in devising changes in institutional and other policies that would make economically (a term for the soundness of a project from the point of view of development objectives) sound projects financially viable.

The major emphasis of a DFI has to be on the efficient use of scarce resources. For many countries, the scarcest resources relate to saving, foreign exchange, skilled manpower and entrepreneurial-managerial talents. From an economy's point of view, it is thus essential to concentrate on initiating a process of efficient allocation and creation of these scarce resources (Kaldor, 1972). In a developing country like Bangladesh major resources like skilled manpower, foreign exchange and entrepreneurial-managerial talents are scarce. In such a situation it is quite likely that there may arise a conflict between the requirements of efficient resource allocation and efficient resource creation. Import controls and high tariff rates are in essence a reflection of this conflict. Since resource creation is of paramount importance for generating self-sustaining process of development and since it depends on critically on-the-job learning and experience, these external economies of projects need to be taken into consideration in devising a choice criterion. These benefits are real and substantial, even though not quantifiable. Although these benefits are broadly common to all industrial projects, there are cases particularly in terms of technology and management where these may be specific to some projects. These should be taken into consideration in project evaluation.

However, once costs and benefits of a project are derived over a period of time - for years inclusive of the gestation lag and project life - the yield can be obtained in terms of its internal rate of return (IRR). This IRR, usually called the economic rate of return, can then be compared with the cutoff rate of return. This rate would usually be considered around 15 - 20 percent per annum. The cutoff rate can be determined on the basis of actual rates of return realized from the existing viable projects. It can also be derived from the estimated growth target for industrial output under certain assumptions with regard to saving (plow back) in relation to gross benefits. Let λ = industrial output, α = gross return, C = total capital, s = proportion of gross return plowed back into investment, I = investment and g = rates of growth of industrial output, then $\Delta\lambda = I. \lambda/C$. Here λ/C is the inverse of the capital coefficient. This can be expressed as

$$\Delta\lambda = s\alpha . \frac{\lambda}{C}$$

$$\therefore \Delta\frac{\lambda}{\lambda} = s.\frac{\alpha}{\lambda}.\frac{\lambda}{C}$$

$$\therefore g = sr$$

$$\text{Thus, } g = s.\frac{\alpha}{C}$$

Where r is the rate of return, α/C. If $s = 0.5$ and $g = 0.10$, $r = 0.10/0.50$ or 20 percent. Taxes and subsidies are ignored in this process since they are considered as mere transfer payments. Also, financing pattern is of no significance from the economy's point of view. However, the economic appraisal of a DFI must necessarily be based on the detailed project analysis from the standpoint of organization, management, technical as well as financial soundness. The fundamental issues where cross checks are necessary, relate to demand estimation, gestation lag, capital and input structure and the structure of returns. The gestation lag and capital costs of projects are generally underestimated in Bangladesh resulting higher than estimated cost at the operational stage of the project.

The difficulties of these institutions are further aggravated by the fact that most of its prospective borrowers do not provide all the data required for examination of their schemes. Many projects financed by DFIs are reportedly not running economically due to poor planning. The main cause of poor planning in the industrial sector is the lack of general business information, non-availability of accurate statistical data etc. The entrepreneurs, in submitting their project proposals and progress report to these institutions in most cases dress up their figures to make them agree with the schedules. The DFIs with a little care can find out this malpractice which has demoralizing effects on prospective investors. Since entrepreneurial talent is deficient in Bangladesh, it is likely that they will not be as efficient as the already developed and experienced entrepreneurs of developed countries. DFIs need to be well equipped to provide with the necessary accurate information to the prospective investors for preparing plans. In order to reduce the management deficiency and encourage the emergence of the new entrepreneurs likely to come from the ranks of traders, civil servants, landlords, technicians and professional people, training facilities should be made available by these institutions during postinvestment period in addition to existing technical and advisory services and perform their promotional role.

Concluding remarks

In Bangladesh formal financial institutions are still underdeveloped, limited in number and not competitive. Thus, the market does not experience saving vehicles of diversified nature in large volume for adequate saving mobilization. It is, therefore, difficult to avail these opportunities for a substantial part of the population and thereby paved the way for development of informal financial markets associated with their inherent drawbacks. Japanese government industrial policy measures were implemented through JDB loans. A particular firm could borrow from the JDB gives an important signal to private banks and thereby promotes the firm's investment expenditure. This explains the well-known information effect. Here lies one of the important weaknesses of Bangladesh DFIs. The banking sector becomes more efficient in the process of economic development, the less important the DFIs become as a promoter of industrial development. This is also observed in case of Japan. Government policy has been aimed at providing encouragement to the private financial institutions in Bangladesh. Government efforts for providing more incentives to the private sector financial institutions and developing close relation between banks and firms appear to have become increasingly relevant. At the present stage financial institutions are needed to be equipped with skilled manpower and made them free from political influences. This may help in curbing the 'default culture' of Bangladeshi entrepreneurs. New institutions particularly in the form of securities companies, investment banks need to be encouraged in the private sector which can indeed play an important role in market development.

Notes

1. In contrast to *demand-following* finance, *supply-leading* has two functions: to transfer resources from traditional (nongrowth) sectors to modern sectors, and to promote and stimulate an entrepreneurial response in these modern sectors.

2. BSB, BSRS and ICB are DFIs working for the development of industrial sector and BKB and RKB for agricultural sector of Bangladesh while Grameen (rural) Bank is specially designed to extend credit for landless, unemployed and under employed people for undertaking income generating activities.

3. The main tenet of Islamic Bank is that interest should not be paid on deposits, nor charged on loans. This has led to deposits being treated as a form of equity in the bank, and rewarded with a dividend or a share of the profits. Similarly, traditional loans are replaced by a form of equity investment in the borrower's activity. For details see Ahmed et al. (1983).

4. Annual growth rate is calculated using the following formula: $x(1+r)^t = x^*$ where r is annual growth rate, x is the initial amount, x^* is the terminal amount and t is the number of years.

5   In this effort Bangladesh DFIs largely focus their attention on such areas like investment policy, financing criteria, policy on lending and investment limits, repayment period of loans, security for loans, foreign exchange risk, project implementation, follow-up and recovery of loans, loan loss provisions etc.

6   During the year 1994-95 Seventh Mutual Fund amounting Tk. 30.0 million was issued to the public against which an amount of Tk.423.9 million was received representing more than 14 times higher than the issued amount. In 1996 Eighth Mutual Fund of Tk. 50.0 million has been offered to the public against which applications received are for more than Tk.1,230 million representing about 23 times of the offer. Besides, recently BSRS has offered Mutual Fund in addition to its own functions.

7   After denationalization of three, only three commercial banks remain in the nationalized sector at present.

8   Technical aspects mainly include project purpose and design, production capacity, technology and manufacturing process, machinery and other equipment, repair and maintenance, safety provision, pollution etc.; market aspects include uses and users of product/service, analysis of domestic demand for last few years, analysis of external demand, analysis of product pricing, government control and subsidy, promotional strategy etc.;economic aspects include an economic rate of return, foreign exchange earnings, employment generation, value added, linkage effects etc.; financial aspects include cost of the project, debt-equity ratio, break-even analysis, financial evaluation, a financial rate of return etc. and management aspects include borrowers' experience and capability in terms of educational background, business experience, receptiveness to new ideas, organizational structure etc.

9   Only very few Western firms appear to have made any effort to adapt their designs to the different scarcities prevailing in developing countries ... Sometimes, indeed, the plant Western engineers design for developing country is more 'modern', i.e., capital intensive potentially labor saving than anything that exists in their own country.There are obstacles in overcoming the problem, possibly, the most important one is often the lack of an informed and critical client, determined to get a plant which will be very profitable ... (see for details Little and Mirrlees, 1968).

4 Securities markets and corporate financing

With the growth of private corporate sectors the role of securities markets as intermediary between the investor and the entrepreneur is considered pre-eminently important. According to textbook notions, stock markets usually perform the function of monitoring managerial activities through stock price mechanisms of firms and ensure efficient allocation of resources. Providing risk capital for investment, they also encourage risk taking by spreading risk. It can mobilize resources from different sources within and outside the country and direct smooth flow of funds from unproductive sectors to productive sectors ensuring return with reasonable liquidity and safety to the owners of capital. These markets could speed up the flow of long term savings from the comparatively capital rich countries to the capital hungry developing countries. The two functions of the capital markets - the domestic function of increasing and channeling the flow of long term funds on the basis of market criteria and the international function of expediting the flow of private long term capital abroad - are very much related as the development of the international capital market is dependent on the efficiency of the capital market in the domestic economy (Williams, 1966). Although effectiveness of these functions entails some puzzles[1], economic roles of security markets are being increasingly recognized. A stock exchange can provide 'marketability' for long term securities and this is crucial, since if they could not readily be sold they would not be attractive to buy. Thus, it can perform its functions as a catalyst by which the long term savings of the economy can be converted into physical assets either for the private sectors or for public sectors. This process is generally referred to as investment. As stock investment relates to ownership, it is always riskier than the investment in bonds or bank deposits. At some point, however, the tradeoff between risk and return begins to favor stock markets. The investor who is knowledgeable about a wider and more diversified universe can be expected to improve his average performance.

Having started anew from a war-ravaged base numerous political and economic problems surrounded Bangladesh that held economic growth below average. However, in 1976 with the change of government policy favoring private sectors, DSE resumed its activities to assume a dominant role in the economic growth of the country. The economic rationales like mobilization of resources through non-bank intermediaries, broadening of the ownership structure of corporate capital, deepening and diversification of the financial sectors were broadly considered for reactivation of DSE. The recent development toward privatization and that of an equity market in Bangladesh for mobilizing domestic resources appears to be encouraging. This may lead someone to believe that the equity market can be relied upon for providing sufficient long term fund necessary for industrialization of the country. Although equity markets record an increasing trend both in terms of number of the companies listed in the stock exchange and their market capitalization, a cautious investigation of its performance will result in skepticism. In the following sections an attempt has been made to evaluate its role in providing corporate finance in Bangladesh.

Alternative ways of financing

In the financial markets, basically there are two types of financing, viz., equity and debt. Equity issues differ from debt or bond with regard to ownership and return. Although ownership stems from equity, return is conditional on the earnings. On the other hand, debt is borrowing and does not give ownership right. It is an unconditional promise to repay principal and interest according to a fixed schedule. As a result ownership risk is associated with equity and not with debt. In general, the main purposes of issuing securities (an equity or corporate bond) are procuring funds for plant and equipment, collecting operating funds, repaying debt, ensuring management control, and promoting public confidence. Issues of equity shares are largely divided into those which require the payment of money and those which do not. In case of the former, equities are issued for cash while in case of the latter, free distribution of equity is undertaken in the form of stock dividend or stock split. In Bangladesh both types of issues exist. Since stock dividend and stock split increase the number of outstanding shares and tend to lower their prices to a level more accessible to the investing public, the practice itself makes it easier for individual investors to buy stocks, and at the same time, enhances the liquidity of shares. Usual types of equity and debt financing in Bangladesh are as follows.

Equity issues

Shares are usually issued for a consideration according to the following methods:

Public offering: In a public offering an issuing company offers new shares through a prospectus issue directly to the public for subscription at a stated price. In case of new companies, usually, the offer is made at the face value of the securities and in case of existing companies often at a market price. Companies in Bangladesh, until recently, required to make public offering at face value. They are allowed to issue shares at market price with the permission of SEC since 1992. No subscription rights are granted to registered shareholders under public offering. Companies, therefore, prefer to issue new shares at a market price then prevailing. This is the usual practice for offering new shares to general investors in Bangladesh. The SEC issued guidelines on initial public offering (IPO) in February 1995 which was amended in March of the same year. In terms of these guidelines, 55 percent of the amount of net IPO is reserved for applicants for a minimum lot (i.e., Tk. 5,000); whereas 30 percent is reserved for applicants for securities exceeding Tk. 5,000 but not exceeding Tk.500,000 and the balance 15 percent is reserved for financial institutions, insurance companies and financial and market intermediary companies applying for above Tk. 500,000.

Granting share subscription rights: In this case, the shareholders listed in the shareholders' register on the day the books are closed are given rights to subscribe for the new shares at a specified price and time period, although they are under no obligation to do so. If the shareholder relinquishes his right to subscribe to the new shares, these unsubscribed shares are then put up for public offering. In Bangladesh, some companies practice this form of subscriptions almost every year. In order to protect investors' interest the SEC issued guidelines in this regard in February 1995. These guidelines require that number of right shares offered for each existing share should not normally exceed 10, and that such right shares be offered to the investors, existing or otherwise, by a Right Share Offer Document.

Granting subscription rights to selected persons (third party allocation): Under this method, subscription rights are granted to selected persons who have special relation with the company, viz., its executives, large shareholders or important customers. However, such practice is restricted to extremely exceptional cases where a company is in the process of reorganization or considering the issue of new shares to another company for the purpose of strengthening the corporate relationship. Such a method is not widely practiced in Bangladesh markets.

Bond issues

Bonds are generally classified into Government or Public Bonds and Corporate Bonds. Among them, common types are as follows:

Government or public bonds: These include bonds issued by the government, bonds issued by public local bodies and bonds issued by public corporation in pursuance of the laws enacted for them. Bangladesh government has issued several types of bonds, viz., 8-Year *Pratirakkha Sanchaya Patra* (Defense Saving Certificate), 6-Year Bonus *Sanchaya Patra* (Bonus Saving Certificate), 5-Year Bangladesh *Sanchaya Patra* (Bangladesh Saving Certificate), 3-Year *Sanchaya Patra* (Saving Certificate), 5-Year Wage Earners' Development Bond and some other bonds registered and bearer with 2-5 years maturity. Annual sales targets of these bonds are set each year by the Ministry of Finance (MOF), but these are sometimes exceeded (Chowdhury et al., 1986). Due to lack of secondary debt markets in Bangladesh the purchasers of these instruments have to depend on interest income only. The conservative investors are deprived of any capital gain on these investments resulting from fluctuation of the market determined interest rates prevailing on any day implied by the liberalized economy.

Corporate bonds: These bonds are issued by the business corporations. Nine companies are enlisted with DSE on June 1995 as the issuer of corporate bonds. First issue of corporate bonds in Bangladesh was made in 1987. Investors who purchase this type of bond are usually long term investors.

Convertible bonds: Corporate bonds issued with the right on the part of the holder to convert them into company's share are called convertible bonds. During a specified time period after its issue a convertible bond can be converted into a stock upon demand of its holder to the issuing company. Recently some companies are issuing convertible bonds in Bangladesh capital markets. Among nine corporate bonds listed on June 1995 four bonds have partial right of option for conversion.

Warrant bonds: The holder of a warrant bond entitled to demand a certain number of new shares at a predetermined price any time during a specified period. This is different from the convertible bond in that the warrant bond is not convertible into stocks but merely entitles its holder to buy new shares in cash, while the convertible bonds can be converted directly into stocks. Such bonds are not issued till now in Bangladesh markets.

In order to meet the investors' divergent tastes, other types of securities like Asset-backed securities (ABSs), Exchangeable Bonds, Dual-Currency Bonds etc. are very often used for raising funds in developed markets. In view of the underdeveloped market condition, such instruments are yet to be introduced in Bangladesh capital markets. However, issue of some other securities, in addition to the existing ones, appears desirable.

Corporate securities and fund mobilization

In recent years optimism about an expeditious upgrading of the equity segment of capital markets capable of meeting the long term needs of corporate finance of Bangladesh has been observed among some sections of market observers. This may, perhaps, originate mainly from the persistent accumulation of bank deposits and heavy oversubscription rate of corporate securities over the past few years. Within a general framework, the significance of a stock market stems from its perceived classical role of allocating funds to the most productive sectors of the economy. Thus it is imperative that a stock market has or should have important links to the overall economy in which it works (Ando and Modigliani, 1963). According to the life cycle theory of Ando and Modigliani households project their resources or wealth over their expected life time and decide consumption flows that best suit their preferences. Part of the household wealth is held in the form of stocks. An increase in stock prices produces corporate gains resulting in higher wealth, which in turn results in additional consumption expenditures (see Bhatia, 1972). In Bangladesh, households are the largest group of shareholders although stock as a percentage of overall household wealth has always been small in the portfolio composition of stock investors (Ahmed et al., 1993), not to speak of the general public. Naturally, the impact of stock price changes on the household consumption should be insignificant. Another factor that might lead to this outcome is the pattern of distribution of stockholders in Bangladesh across wealth classes. The distributions of stockholding in Bangladesh are skewed in the direction of the relatively wealthy (Ahmed et al., 1993), who, it is argued, are less sensitive to the increases in stock prices when undertaking consumption decision, because of lower marginal propensities to consume (Arena, 1965). Recognizing the highly skewed ownership structure of Bangladesh companies as a fundamental issue, of late, the authorities have adopted several policies intended to broaden the base of share ownership which are as follows:

1 The government has withdrawn all restrictions on foreign investment,

permitting them to invest directly in primary and secondary markets.
2   The restriction on sale of shares at a premium has been withdrawn.
3   No permission is needed to issue Right or Bonus shares now within some limit.
4   55 percent of IPOs has been reserved for the minimum lot of Tk. 5,000.00.
5   Some fiscal measures have been aimed at primarily curbing tax evasion and encouraging savings and investment. Briefly these are (a) all capital gains

Table-4.1
Growth pattern of listed companies   *(In million taka)*

Year	No. Of Listed Securities	Paid Up Capital		Market Capitalization	
		Total Taka	% Increase	Total Taka	% Increase
1976	9	137.5	-	146.7	-
1977	11	230.5	67.61	248.5	69.36
1978	14	281.3	22.05	305.4	22.90
1979	18	365.0	29.77	393.7	28.93
1980	23	405.8	11.17	436.9	10.95
1981	26	528.1	30.12	603.2	38.08
1982	29	726.5	37.38	811.6	34.54
1983	44	1,001.5	38.04	1,211.3	49.25
1984	58	1,546.6	54.42	2,256.5	86.29
1985	72	2,059.7	33.18	3,492.6	54.78
1986	82	2,653.0	28.81	5,730.6	64.08
1987	92	3,149.6	18.72	12,670.9	121.11
1988	111	3,663.7	16.32	13,556.9	6.99
1989	116	4,539.2	23.90	15,350.5	13.23
1990	134	5,361.1	18.11	11,485.9	-25.18
1991	138	5,586.6	4.21	10,397.3	-9.48
1992	149	6,020.3	7.76	12,299.1	18.29
1993	153	8,201.7	36.23	18,098.7	47.15
1994	170	11,673.8	42.33	41,770.7	130.80
1995	201	19,438.0	66.51	56,518.1	35.31
1996	203	22,114.7	13.77	81,406.2	44.04

Note: Figures for 1996 are as on 31 July.
Source: Prepared from DSE Fact book 1994 and DSE Monthly Review (various Issues).

on disposal of securities have been tax exempt, (b) dividend income has been tax free up to Tk. 30,000, withholding taxes of 15 percent will apply for dividends remitted overseas to countries without double tax treaties, and (c) corporate tax rates have been lowered from 45 to 35 percent for publicly listed industrial companies and 50 percent to 40 percent for unlisted companies.

Let us now see the growth pattern of listed stocks with DSE in Table-4.1. DSE was reactivated in 1976 with 9 companies. The number of securities listed on the DSE rose from 9 in 1976 to 203 in 1996 with accumulative value of Tk. 22,114.7 million at issue prices. The growth of paid up capital was somewhat slow in 1990-91 when the growth rate of market capitalizations was also negative. This indicates the bearish market condition at that time. The period from 1984-1987 represents an unexpected growth of market capitalization which peaked in 1987 with 121.11 percent increase from the previous year. The situation suggests a bullish market condition. In connection with stock price behavior we have more discussions in Chapter 5.

Table-4.2
Funds mobilized by banking system, government saving schemes and stock markets in Bangladesh
(In million taka)

Financial Year	Corporate Securities*	Bank Deposits (Time Deposits)	Postal Savings	National Saving Bonds	Total of Col. 3 to 5	Ratio(Col. 2 as % of Col. 6)
(1)	(2)	(3)	(4)	(5)	(6)	(7)
1975-76	137.5	5147.0	430.0	567.0	6144.0	2.24
1976-77	230.5	7670.0	447.0	713.0	8830.0	2.61
1977-78	181.3	9169.0	468.0	826.0	10463.0	2.69
1978-79	365.0	12352.0	493.0	1023.0	13878.0	2.63
1979-80	405.8	15131.0	533.0	1196.0	16860.0	2.41
1980-81	528.1	21497.0	583.0	1482.0	23562.0	2.24
1981-82	726.5	25366.0	591.0	1783.0	27740.0	2.62
1982-83	1001.5	32639.0	688.0	2187.0	35514.0	2.82
1983-84	1586.6	48359.0	810.0	2646.0	51815.0	2.98
1984-85	2059.7	63024.0	949.0	3040.0	67013.0	3.07
1985-86	2653.0	74102.0	1075.0	3694.0	74871.0	3.57
1986-87	3149.6	90903.0	1195.0	4458.0	96556.0	3.26
1987-88	3663.7	113603.0	1551.0	6045.0	121200.0	3.02
1988-89	4539.2	136174.0	2062.0	7662.0	145898.0	3.11
1989-90	5361.1	159289.0	2697.0	9803.0	171789.0	3.12
1990-91	5586.6	178807.0	2977.0	19033.0	200817.0	2.78
1991-92	6020.3	202686.0	2983.0	27186.0	232855.0	2.58
1992-93	8201.7	224730.0	1253.0	18574.0	244557.0	3.35
1993-94	11673.0	252359.0	3218.0	11289.0	266866.0	4.37

Note: *Figures are for calendar years.*
Source: *Calculated from various issues of DSE Monthly Reviews; Bangladesh Bank Bulletin, October-December 1995 and Economic Survey of Bangladesh, 1993-94, Ministry of Finance, Government of Bangladesh.*

For getting a better understanding of the equity market performance we will examine its relative contribution in resource mobilization in Bangladesh. The extent to which the equity markets have been successful in mobilizing additional resources can be directly analyzed with reference to the share of corporate security issues to funds mobilized by other investment opportunities available in Bangladesh like the banking system, postal savings and other government saving schemes[2]. Table-4.2 presents the share of corporate securities in Bangladesh. As can be seen, the proportion of funds raised via the stock markets are small relative to banking system as well as government saving schemes. The increasing popularity of the equity markets since 1982-83 ensued due to different tax incentives offered and denationalization policy adopted by government. The corporate bond market, as noted earlier, came into being as a new investment vehicle since 1987 and this market has not yet been broad based. The attractiveness of bank deposits was magnified due to high interest rates until 1991. Government saving schemes were specially attractive due to high interest rates and tax exemption of income from this source. However, after 1991 interest rates on government saving schemes and bank deposits have been reduced significantly. Besides, tax benefits on government saving schemes have lately been withdrawn totally.

The ratio of new equity issues to gross domestic investment with some activity ratios are contained in Table-4.3. Drake (1980) has suggested that the

Table-4.3
Ratio of new equity issues to gross investment and listed securities turnover to GDP *(In million taka)*

Year	GDP	Gross Investment	New Issues	Turnover of Listed securities	Turnover / GDP Ratio (%)	New Issues / Gross Investment Ratio (%)
1985-86	466,230	58,850	593.4	34.3	.007	1.0
1986-87	539,200	69,490	496.6	152.4	.028	0.7
1987-88	597,140	74,310	514.0	120.8	.020	0.7
1988-89	659,600	85,190	875.6	154.3	.023	1.0
1989-90	737,570	94,430	821.9	187.7	.025	0.9
1990-91	834,390	95,960	225.4	100.4	.012	0.2
1991-92	906,500	109,850	433.8	261.0	.028	0.4
1992-93	968,800	128,370	2,181.4	403.6	.042	1.7

Source: Estimated from Economic Survey of Bangladesh, 1993-94, Ministry of Finance, Government of Bangladesh and DSE Monthly Review (various issues).

ratio of new issues to gross capital formation can provide a measure of the financial development, while Kitchen (1993) has suggested the use of various activity ratios as an indicator of financial development. In Bangladesh, the share of new equity issues to gross domestic investment is generally less than 1 percent[3]. It increased substantially in 1992-93. The turnover/GDP ratio of listed securities is also very low representing only a fraction of 1 percent although it has shown an increasing trend. This may, perhaps, be due to various incentives for encouraging equity investment and financial market liberalization policy declared by government together with lowering down the interest rates and withdrawal of tax benefits from different debt securities. The new issues abruptly declined in 1990-91 because of the political instability and market hesitancy about the government policy due to expected change of government ensuing at that time. The ratio of stock transactions to GNP in developing countries is usually a fraction of 1 percent with the exceptions of Taiwan, Singapore, Korea and Brazil. The ratio on the larger stock markets in developed countries frequently exceeded 10 percent, although low values were also recorded on the smaller European markets (Wai and Patrick, 1973, Table II).

Similar results can be obtained if the ratio of new equity to national saving is considered as Table-4.4 presents. In general, then, it may be concluded that the equity market has not been able to provide a strong alternative to the banking and various government saving schemes for mobilization of funds for

Table-4.4
Ratio of saving to GDP and new equity to national saving

Year	Ratio of Saving to GDP (as percent)	Ratio of New Equity to National Saving (as percent)
1985-86	3.22	3.96
1986-87	3.52	2.62
1987-88	2.97	2.30
1988-89	2.70	5.30
1989-90	2.73	4.09
1990-91	4.13	0.65
1991-92	5.85	0.82
1992-93	6.90	3.20

Source: Derived from Economic Survey of Bangladesh, 1993-94, Ministry of finance, government of Bangladesh and DSE Fact Book, 1994.

the period under consideration in spite of adopting various measures including tax incen-tives favoring the development of equity markets. The contribution of the equity markets to financial development represented by the ratio of new issues to gross investment for a period of 8 years from 1985-86 to 1992-93 has been insignificant.

Much of the market constraint is associated with the overall development of the country and hence investment in equities is likely to continue to be some highly risky affairs for a great many potential investors with pronounced risk aversion attitudes. The impressive increase in various government bond and bank deposits has taken place while their respective yield was falling. In fact, the rate of interest was 14 to 18 percent in 1990, had already dropped to 6 to 12 percent in 1995. The attitude behind such a trend cannot be interpreted in terms of irrationality on the part of general investors, rather in terms of enunciated risk aversion. In the presence of forceful structural, legal and other limitations, measures aiming at increasing the relative contribution of equities will most likely be of insignificant use. On the other hand, mechanisms that design to force industrial corporations to resort to the new issue market are of questionable effectiveness, in view of the relative difficulties to institute and execute them. Under these situations equity markets are likely to be restrained in the way of rapid development. Accordingly, transformation of short term deposits into instruments of long term debt and ownership need to be entrusted to a set of different institutions pending the eventual development of the capital markets of Bangladesh. This deviation in focus has substantial policy oriented implications.

Corporate financing in Japan is distinguished from that in other developed countries by a high ratio of borrowing from the banking system. The average net worth ratios[4] of Japanese firms (excluding financial institutions and insurance companies) stood at 19.3 percent at the end of fiscal 1991 which was far less than those of the U.S. (40.1 percent), Great Britain (44.2 percent) and Germany (57.3 percent). Their ratio of capital to total assets was at a low level of about 4.9 percent. Even if bond financing[5] is added to this, the average net worth ratios of Japanese firms stood at 23.8 percent in fiscal 1991 (Japan Securities Research Institute, 1994). Economic theorists might have argued that such high leverage should result in rapid growth of production while financial theorists might have preferred to focus its impact on price earnings ratio (PER). Whatever is the outcome of economic and financial theory, some historical facts appear to be relevant for understanding the debt situation in Japan.

At the time of Meiji Restoration in 1868 Japan was well behind most industrialized Western nations in terms of economic development. More than 1,000 unofficial currencies were in use in trade. Taxes were collected in rice and peasants and craftsmen were mainly governed by feudal lords. The situation warrants major changes in order to achieve rapid transformation of Japan into a money-based economy. Industrial growth was necessary to compete with European imports. It was required by the Meiji Emperor that land taxes would be paid in government-issued currency and that feudal lords would relinquish all taxation powers in exchange for a system of pension bonds.

Japan established its central bank in 1880 which issued a gold-based currency. Gradually many of the feudal lords sold their bonds for immediate cash. The city banks used the government pension bonds as reserves. More than 40 percent of the government budget was allocated either to pay interest on the bonds or to subsidize new industries directly (Barrett et al., 1974). Government had no other alternative since a few entrepreneurs had sufficient resources for industrial investment from their own. It has already been pointed out in Chapter 2 that these enterprises were subsequently handed over to private sectors at a nominal price which created a class of capitalists known as *zaibatsu*. Stock Exchange Ordinance was enacted in 1878 and Tokyo Stock Exchange (TSE)[6] and Osaka Stock Exchange were established immediately. In order to accommodate the large number of companies in the over-the-counter (OTC) market, a second section of Tokyo, Osaka and Nagoya was opened in 1961. First section stocks can be compared with listed stocks on the New York Stock Exchange (NYSE). Investment in first section stocks representing large companies is considered stable and safe investment. The trading mechanism is also similar to that of NYSE except the '*saitori*' system where the specialist is not allowed to trade for his own account or to have any public customer. Rather, he acts as 'brokers' broker'. The second section corresponds, by and large, to American Stock Exchange in the U.S. The companies listed in this section are all small and considered more speculative in nature than those listed on the first section. Usually small but growing companies are listed on the second section and subsequently transferred to the first section when they are able to meet relevant requirements. Before World War II, Japanese stock markets were speculative in nature and thinly traded stocks played only a minor role in industrial fund raising. Moreover, the *zaibatsu* companies did not have to depend on the external funds raised in the securities markets as those firms generated sufficient accumulated funds internally. These facts along with others can provide some indication about the traditional relationship among industries, banking, government and high degree of leverage in Japanese industry till today. The experience of U.S. and U.K. shows that industrialization was financed by a capitalist class that gradually accumulated its own internal financing strength. Bypassing this step, Japanese government effectively took the responsibility for financing both the banking system and the major industry groups like *zaibatsu*.

After World War II, the government again faced the huge task of reconstructing a war-ravaged economy. The democratization of securities was carried out by the Occupation Army's policies. Approximately ¥20 billion worth of stocks, called 'the released stocks', was collected by the bank of Japan and the government through property tax and similar instruments when the total sum of paid and issued capital was approximately ¥46 billion (Oka, 1991). All of them were then released to the public at a time. There was some doubt about the ability of the reorganized stock exchanges to handle a flood of new stock and bond issues. However, the share of the individual holdings to the total number of stocks at the Tokyo Stock Exchange (TSE) had reached more than 60 percent immediately afterwards. In the 1950s, there was a dramatic change in this share ownership. Individual investors' stocks were being transferred to institutional investors such as banks. The commercial banks absorbed most of these 'forced' equity issues. The government supported heavy use of bank loans as efficient and effective means of postwar industrial financing. A few entrepreneurs who could successfully overcome the difficulties involved in finance could rapidly expand their businesses in various fields in Japan. In general, they formed *zaibatsu* where government played a crucial role. Thus, the historical background may provide some explanation of a high debt-equity ratio of Japanese enterprises along with economic or financial theory.

In order to transform Bangladesh into an industrial economy, industries need to be able to compete with foreign counterparts in the import and export markets. Japanese experiences indicate that finance was the primary limiting factor to business success. The entrepreneurs who had sufficient accumulated funds to start an enterprise from their own resources in Bangladesh are limited in number. Besides, relative shares of equity markets are small and corporate bonds still represent an insignificant source of funds. In the initial stages of Japanese industrialization, persistence of similar situations has been observed when government facilitated industrialization through various means including financial support. These facts demonstrate the importance of finance, particularly debt finance in Bangladesh.

New issue market

A well developed new issue market or primary market can facilitate financing the planned process of economic development. New issue markets open the way for business corporations to tap a stable source of long term funds, enhance their social standing, attract talents and boost the morale of the employees allowing them to influence recycling of funds with optimum efficiency. Thus, these markets help them to strengthen their financial and business bases. Underdeveloped nature of the new issue markets causes liquidity constraints for both special financial institutions and commercial banks. Despite these advantages, the new issue market could not make any appreciable headway in Bangladesh markets until 1984 in which year oversubscription of new issues is observed for the first time. In the later years spectacular growth and oversubscription of new issues have been observed (Table-4.5). Recently, a handful of Bangladeshi companies has been offering new shares to the public *vis-a-vis* general investors have been showing interests to invest in shares. This is supported by the growing number of public offerings and higher rates of oversubscription. The peak year for public offering was 1988, when 21 companies floated Tk. 303 million of the new issues with an oversubscription rate of 138 percent. It is expected that in the coming years more funds will come to stock markets due to decrease in interest rates and abolition of the requirement to issue at par value[7]. Oversubscription has now become an order of the day in this frenzy new issue market. And its prevalence in most of the years indicates higher demand relative to supply. There are many shortcomings of the new issue market in Bangladesh despite its growth in the recent past, some of which are as follows:

1. As soon as the initial public issue is over, companies forget their duties toward protecting small investors who form the core of the investing public, by not sending the allotment letters, share certificates or refunding the

Table-4.5
Public offering of listed shares   *(In million taka)*

Year	Number of Issues	Amount Issued	Amount Subscribed	% of over / under Subscription
1977	2	17	5	-71
1978	1	15	8	-47
1979	2	9	3	-67
1980	2	5	2	-60
1981	5	17	13	-24
1982	2	6	5	-17
1983	5	13	8	-38
1984	12	309	412	33
1985	19	194	332	71
1986	9	81	123	51
1987	9	265	458	73
1988	21	303	722	138
1989	12	239	466	95
1990	11	158	195	23
1991	9	167	146	-13
1992	11	115	132	15
1993	4	143	152	7
1994	12	992	-	484
1995	25	1252	6936	454

Source: Prepared from DSE Fact Book, 1994, DSE Monthly Review and SEC quarterly Review (various issues).

application money in time in one or other pretext. Delay in allotment and delay in refunds of application money cause concern among the investors and raise the question, 'Who compensates the investor who waits for his refund to make his next investment?'
2. Despite the sharp growth in the activities of the stock market, no serious attempt has so far been made to tap the savings of the semi-urban and rural areas of the country.
3. Continuous oversubscription of shares will have its dampening effects, because repeated unsuccessful attempts discourage the prospective investors to venture into the capital market.
4. Companies making new issues are inadequately known to the investors with limited information publicly available. Investors in general have skepticism about auditors' reports.

In order to overcome the problems listed above, encouragement should be given for the evolution of a market maker who could hold a block of shares and bonds in one or a few specific scrips and thus impart greater liquidity. Disseminating information through making available to them along with illustrated tables and charts as well as holding meetings to brief them on the business of the companies and their financial position will bring them closer to the investors. This will go a long way in winning their confidence. Moreover, SEC's role should be as a 'promoter' rather than a 'regulator' in removing the undue delay in refunding, sending allotment letters, share certificates and the like.

Secondary market

A secondary market is a market for purchase and sale of already issued securities. In its pure sense, it refers to the stock exchange. Since securities markets are regulated and the subsequent dealings in securities are supposed to take place on the floor of stock exchange in Bangladesh, this market is expected to concentrate within the stock exchange floor. The stock exchange plays a crucial role in financing corporate sectors. The traditional concept of the stock exchange was that it is a voluntary association of capitalists controlled by themselves, for the concentration of income and wealth in the hands of a few. But this concept of stock exchange is no more tenable and the objectives have undergone a tremendous change toward resource mobilization rather than wealth concentration. Throughout the world the stock exchanges are considered as the unparallel institution for mobilization of savings and capital of the society and also a very sensitive barometer of business activities. It seeks to remove the disadvantages and impediments of the partnership form of business providing a marketplace for the equity issues for public limited companies and other securities. In the absence of a ready market for outstanding shares, new capital will not be encouraged to flow to expedite the growth of industrial sectors.

Most of the secondary market transactions in Bangladesh are undertaken in the DSE which was established in 1954. Before independence of Pakistan in 1947 only two stock exchanges were functioning in the areas of the then Pakistan. Both of these exchanges stopped functioning soon after 1947 due to large scale migration of the non-Muslims members to India. Thus, Pakistan did not have any stock exchange in August 1947. The need for such an institution was acutely felt and therefore, the Karachi Stock Exchange was organized in September 1948. Subsequently another stock exchange was incorporated on 28 April 1954 in the then East Pakistan in the name of East Pakistan Stock Exchange Association. It was renamed as East Pakistan Stock Exchange Limited on 23 June 1962 and it became Dhaka Stock Exchange on 14 May 1964. Although it was incorporated in 1954, the formal trading started in 1956 at Narayangonj. It was shifted to Dhaka in 1958. However, Karachi was considered as the principal capital market and Dhaka Stock Exchange (DSE) had to follow the tone and temperament of Karachi markets in those days. As mentioned earlier, DSE resumed its operation in the middle of 1976 after liberation of Bangladesh in 1971. The history of Bangladesh stock markets is of only about 40 years. The historical development of DSE is presented in Table-4.6 in a summarized form. This institution can play a vital economic role for achieving economic emancipation of Bangladesh. It can supplement governmental efforts to mobilize private capital and help government policy to inspire

Table-4.6
Historical development of DSE
- in chronological order -

1954	First established in the name of East Pakistan Stock Exchange Association.
1956	Formal trading started at Narayangonj.
1958	Shifted to Dhaka at Narayangonj Chamber Building.
1959	Shifted to own building at 9F Motijheel Commercial Area.
1962	Renamed as East Pakistan Stock Exchange Ltd.
1964	Became Dhaka Stock Exchange Ltd. (DSE).
1971	Suspended operations.
1976	Resumed operations with 9 companies.

private enterprises to succeed. Activities on the secondary market are concentrated in corporate securities only since the government securities are not yet permitted to trade on the exchange. These securities are traded for investment purposes as well as speculation. A high degree of speculation is associated with secondary markets of Bangladesh. Therefore, the genuine investors hesitate to invest their funds in stock exchange securities.

DSE is a self regulated organization but not well regulated one. They fail to regulate the exchange in a desirable manner and accept new entry. Stock broking appears to be a closed shop. 'Anywhere in the world stock exchanges are self regulating agencies, so long as they regulate themselves effectively. But when they do not do so, the SEC has the right and power to do so and our view is that the DSE has not regulated itself properly'(Euromoney, 1995). From this comment of the Chairman of the SEC of Bangladesh the role of DSE can easily be understood. It has the organizational and operational limitations that have the bearing on the efficiency of stock markets. DSE has 195 members, almost all of whom are individual brokers. Moreover, most of them are not active brokers. Only about 20 percent of the members reportedly engage themselves actively in securities business. Members should devote their time and energies to the securities business which is an imperative for the creation of an efficient stock market. They should genuinely regard the securities field as his business, recognize the public responsibilities of conducting this business and should have professionalism. In general, the present membership of the DSE does not fit this image.

Except for a minimum capital requirement of Tk. 1.0 million there is no financial stipulation in the listing rules. Nor is anything concretely mentioned about methods of trading, protection of customers, conduct of members, and the regulatory role of the exchange. Rules and regulations so far developed prescribing either its own activities or those of its members are inadequate to run an effective exchange. It would be considered as the nerve-center of all economic activities of Bangladesh if the market could be fully developed and properly regulated.

Table-4.7 shows the activities of DSE both in terms of trading volume and value. The figures represent a phenomenal upsurge in the rate of increases in all years except 1988 and 1991. The year 1994 recorded an increase of more than 600 percent from the previous year in terms of value but the rate of the increase in 1995 is 11.76 percent. In terms of average monthly volume of share turnover, the rate of the increase is more than 47 percent indicating a decline in share price in 1995. The government's declared market-oriented policies including foreign exchange liberalization, and promoting foreign investments in industries and securities are likely to enhance optimism among domestic and foreign investors resulting in the increasing operational dimension of DSE. Besides, public awareness about securities markets might have increased through some promotional activities including the use of mass media to acquaint the general public with the stock investment in recent times.

Table-4.7
Average monthly turnover of shares on DSE

Year	Number of Shares (in thousand)	Amount in Taka (in thousand)	% Increase in Value
1984	18	841	-
1985	49	2,689	219.58
1986	71	3,988	48.29
1987	156	14,805	271.27
1988	85	10,836	-26.81
1989	184	14,477	33.60
1990	259	16,215	33.60
1991	156	9,638	-40.56
1992	473	36,483	278.53
1993	443	48,237	32.22
1994	1,613	357,329	643.75
1995	2,383	399,408	11.76

Note: Monthly average for six months ending on 30th June 1995
Source: Compiled from various issues of DSE Monthly Reviews and DSE Fact book 1994.

The members of the DSE do not operate margin accounts for general investors. Their activities need to be directed for promoting the cause of stock exchange or the securities business at the desired level. They only buy and sell on behalf of clients on receipt of specific commission. There is no provision in Bye-laws of the Exchange for undertaking market making roles. Existing brokers are in favor of maintaining their oligopolistic position in the exchange and opposing any reform.

Since investors are equal partners in stock business, they may have representation on the governing body (Board of Council) of DSE. Without such restructuring it is likely that the DSE will continue to oppose reforms and overlook the investors' interest. The brokers' monopolistic attitude needs to be removed by increasing the number of active brokers and allowing new brokers substantially. Opening of CSE recently is a step forward to this direction. This may create some competitive environment in the stock markets of Bangladesh.

Regulatory framework

The securities markets in Bangladesh as elsewhere are governed by certain rules and regulations. Regulatory authorities of the Bangladesh capital markets consist of SEC (formerly CCI), RJSE, DSE, and newly established CSE. SEC is under the Ministry of Finance and RJSC is under the Ministry of Commerce. On the other hand, DSE and CSE are corporate bodies under Companies Act 1994. The RJSC partially implements the Companies Act 1994. There are some legislative acts governing the securities markets that are presented in Table-4.8. The former CCI operated according to Capital Issues (Continuance of Control)

Table-4.8
Laws relating to securities markets in Bangladesh

Law	Year	Executing Authority	Relevant Ministry
Companies Act	1994	Registrar of Joint Stock Companies (RJSC)	Ministry of Commerce
Securities and Exchange Commission Act	1993	Securities and Exchange commission (SEC)	Ministry of Finance
Securities and Exchange (Amendment) Act	1993	Securities and Exchange commission (SEC)	Ministry of Finance
Securities and Exchange Rules (SER)	1987	Securities and Exchange commission (SEC)	Ministry of Finance
Securities and Exchange Rules	1971	Securities and Exchange Commission (SEC)	Ministry of Finance
Securities and Exchange Ordinance	1969	Securities and Exchange commission (SEC)	Ministry of Finance

Act 1947. Under this Act the government gives consent to the issue of any security. With the establishment of the SEC under the Securities and Exchange Commission Act 1993, the office of the CCI was abolished. Simultaneously this

Act has been repealed with the passing of the Securities and Exchange Commission Act 1993. The Securities and Exchange Ordinance of 1969 has been amended and substituted by Securities and Exchange (Amendment) Act 1993. The SEC is responsible for implementing Securities and Exchange (Amendment) Act 1993 and other rules and guidelines in order to regulate the securities markets and the dealings in the securities. These provide protection to investors and regulate the securities markets as a whole. The ordinance establishes listing procedures, regulates insider trading, prohibits fraudulent acts, false statements etc. Securities and Exchange Rules (SER) of 1971 establishes the qualifications of membership in the exchange and the method of transacting business. However, no definite mechanism as regards monitoring and implementation of the above provisions was spelt out. Even the provision in the SER of 1971 to constitute a Securities and Exchange Authority of Bangladesh was omitted in SER of 1987. In the absence of any definite authority for implementing the rules and regulations, securities markets practically became nobody's business causing, *inter-alia*, improper trading, insider trading, fictitious trading, sleeping brokers, creative reporting, delayed reporting and so on. However, with the establishment of SEC in 1993 responsibilities of supervising the securities markets has been entrusted with it. In order to ensure healthy development of security markets the SEC has so far issued the following guidelines and regulations:

1. Initial Public Offering (IPO) to local investors.
2. Foreign placement or allotment of securities.
3. Issuance of right shares.
4. Sanction of issue of capital by Greenfield public companies.
5. Merchant banker and portfolio manager regulations.
6. Stock-Dealer, Stock-Broker and Sub-Broker Regulations.
7. Appeal Regulations.
8. Insider Trading Regulations.
9. Mutual Fund Regulations.

Accordingly, SEC has initiated taking disciplinary action against some activities not consistent with the declared guidelines and regulations. After long time the Companies Act 1994 has been enacted. It is likely to have a positive impact on the market if this law is properly implemented. However, it is observed that neither the RJSC nor the SEC has sufficient staff with professional background and other resources needed to discharge their responsibilities at a satisfactory level.

As a self regulatory organization, DSE has its own listing rules but they are generally viewed as outdated, and lacks objectivity and detailed provisions for listing and administration of listed stocks. Corporate listing with DSE, in many cases, is influenced by the requirement of regulatory authorities or the financial institutions, which impose a listing requirement as a condition for getting credit but attaching lesser importance to the other benefits of stock listing. DSE could not ensure regular and timely disclosure of information on listed companies in order to protect the interest of investors. Recurrence of violation of rules is observed due to weak or no enforcement of disciplinary actions by the respective authorities.

According to the needs of an emerging market some changes in the rules and regulations have been undertaken with the establishment of SEC although more need to be done. All the more important is the effective execution of the existing rules and regulations. Allegations are found about non holding of general meetings in due time, delayed payment of dividends, irregular publication of financial statements, delays in repayment of excess application money etc. Although the SEC initiated disciplinary action against some irregularities, they are reportedly very slow in their efforts.

Demand side of the market

Underdeveloped countries like Bangladesh are dominated by agriculture with small land holdings. Despite low income levels and low savings rates in Bangladesh, a variety of options are available for investment. The savers (individual and institutional) are the suppliers of funds and constitute the demand side of the securities markets. The available financial assets for investment in Bangladesh are commercial bank savings and fixed deposits, postal savings bank deposits, deposit pension schemes, insurance policy, various government savings certificates, corporate debentures, mutual funds, and stocks. In a well functioning capital market, the investors are concerned with risk and associated return for their investment. Riskier investment in equity offers a higher return than do the less risky debt instruments. Return on equity is not easy to summarize like the return on a debt instrument since equity return has two components - dividends and capital gains - that are subject to change according to price changes.

A major criterion for judging the effectiveness of stock markets is to measure the new capital they raise for firms and government. For Bangladesh the ratio of funds mobilized through issue of corporate securities is low. In most of the years the new issue is less than 1 percent of gross investment as it appears from Table-4.3. In this regard, Samuels and Yacout (1981) concludes for Nigeria that 'Despite a reasonably active secondary market, the primary market has not made a major contribution as a provider of funds. The new funds raised on the market for the private sector, as proportion of GDP, are low, being in each year less than 1 percent.' The process of capital market development in any country essentially rests on the savers (individual and institutional) and the issuers. These groups are fundamental components of the capital markets but they are yet to attain the stage of takeoff in Bangladesh. The savers in Bangladesh are in a disarray and surrounded with a number of limitations. An investor desirous of entering into an equity market is concerned to find an assured home of his investment. He needs to be fully aware of the required formalities, trading system and procedure of execution of deals on the stock exchange floor. While safekeeping of money in banks does not require constant watch or any special effort to make higher return, active association of an investor in the trading of stocks can contribute substantially to that end. The savers here are not conscious about different vehicles of investment and the securities market as a whole. All classes of investors tend to relate the return on a stock to its dividend payment, thereby usually overlooking the possibility of capital gains (Robbins, 1980). The notion of modern portfolio management based on the risk-return relationship has gained a headway in developed securities markets which is not familiar to the investors of Bangladesh. Investors need to be made aware of the functioning of the stock exchange and of the possible risks as well as of the possible returns. This can be attained through active but responsible promotional activities by the SEC, ICB, stock exchanges and shareholders' representative bodies in Bangladesh. Socioeconomic and political instability in the country significantly contributes to the preference for hoarding money, precious stones, gold, real estate etc. instead of long term investment in risky financial assets. The confidence of the investors has been shaken in the securities market due to the loss of their investments as a result of nationalization of industries after independence. They also need to have confidence in the macroeconomic performance of the economy which is considered as market risk or systematic risk. Simultaneously, they need to have confidence in the firm's product, its market, management and disclosure of information which is specific risk or unsystematic risk. The number of wealthy persons who could acquire the ownership of well-diversified portfolios by investing in shares, debentures or other form of securities as required for sustaining a corporate securities market is limited and the small savers are likely to constitute bulk of the fund supply in the market who are not in a position to spread the risk of capital loss through formation of a well-diversified portfolio. Countries which have highly skewed income and wealth distributions are unlikely to have the right mix of investors to keep the market active and fluid (Kitchen, 1993). By and large, Bangladesh demonstrates similar condition as already indicated earlier. Individual savings accrue mainly to the unsophisticated people, who are financially inexperienced and have conservative attitudes toward money. Such people are apathetic toward advanced forms of wealth-holding, and this threshold of insensitivity will be overcome only gradually and most likely through a fairly protracted learning process (Drake, 1980). The important point is that securities demand can be influenced easily by official decision. The experiences of Brazil demonstrate evidence in support of this. According to Ness (1974) the major incentives offered in Brazil include: (1) provisions for stockholders to deduct purchase cost of securities substantially from taxable income; (2) provision for part personal income tax exemption of dividends and for concessional rates of withholding tax for shareholders in those 'open capital' companies that undertook to achieve wide dispersion of equity; and (3) provisions for individuals and companies to discharge a proportion of their tax liabilities by subscribing to special mutual funds, withdrawals from which could not begin for at least two years[8].

Information is vital in influencing the demand for securities. Disclosure of accurate information is limited and the costs of obtaining it are inordinately high and therefore, investment in securities becomes extremely risky. Investors expect interim and more accurate information on company performance. Both investors and officials of listed companies in Bangladesh were of the view that the disclosure of information by the listed companies was not adequate. In addition to that companies do not make timely disclosure of information. Even many companies violate the regulation to pay dividends within 60 days after holding AGM. Investors believe that there are widespread manipulations and malpractices in the accounts of listed companies, and so in the conduct of the stock brokers (Ahmed et al.,1993). Absence of concrete guidelines for prospectus preparation, IPO and premium pricing is also discouraging for the investors. Efficient and reliable brokerage houses have not yet developed for supporting and guiding investors in taking right decision and most investors are not capable enough for financial information analysis. Thus, the investors in Bangladesh are exposed to high degree of risk in the face of frequent reported market manipulation and other abuses that make the elusive concept of business confidence.

Investors' attitudes toward stock investment depends on knowledge about stock markets, information flow affecting the stock price, ability to analyze information and opportunities open to them. Ahmed et al. (1993) found that in Bangladesh a significant variation in the degree of knowledge, volume of information and analyzing ability is observed between existing and potential investors and city dwellers have more information than rural people who constitute more than 80 percent of the population. Remoteness from the center of the city is a factor that keeps investors away from information on the stock market. The potential investors (particularly people living in the suburban areas) are therefore at a disadvantage, because of the cost, time and effort involved in stock investment.

According to the responses received from individual investors, absence of knowledge about the stock market appears to be the most important deterrent to stock investment. Amount of stock investment has been found to be positively influenced by the economic capacity of investors, knowledge about the stock market and ability to analyze information. Relative investment in stock to total financial investment has been found to be positively influenced by investors' knowledge about the stock market, their information seeking on the stock market, their ability to analyze information, and negatively influenced by years of formal education and daily working hours (Ahmed et al., 1993).

Institutional investors include commercial banks, finance houses, investment companies, life insurance companies, general insurance companies, and pension and provident funds of different organizations. Unlike individual investors, most institutional investors have large sum of money to invest. In essence the potential demand for security from institutional investors is very high. Ahmed et al. (1993) have indicated that:

Although institutional investors constitute a very large segment of the potential demand for stock market securities, they are reluctant to invest in these securities due to unavailability of securities in terms of both quantity and quality, and organizational and legal restrictions on security investment, although it was revealed that the officials of institutional investors have reasonable ability to analyze information for making sound investment (Ahmed et al., 1993).

According to Section 2(3) of Insurance Act 1938 'approved securities' for investment means government securities and any other security charged on the revenue of the government or guaranteed fully as regards principal and interest by government. Thus, the Act limits insurance funds to enter into the stock market. Besides, a sizable investible fund from provident Fund and Trust funds, cannot participate in the stock market as forbidden in Section 20 of the Trust Act 1882. In addition, the supply of good quality stocks for the institutional investors is limited in the markets. The trivial role of the institutional investors in the stock markets in Bangladesh can be explained, to some extent, by these factors. However, in view of the high oversubscription rate, 15 percent of IPO is reserved for financial institutions, insurance companies and other financial intermediaries as per guidelines issued by the SEC in 1995. Now institutional investors in Bangladesh require to be persuaded of the desirability of equity investments and measures need to be taken to relinquish them from the requirements to invest in government securities only. Inflation has negative impact on the real value and the yield of bonds, debentures, etc. due to their fixed capital value and rate of interest. This has led the support for use of price index (Wai and Patrick, 1973; Ness, 1974). Equity securities are conceived as a 'hedge' against inflation. Hence, indexation may influence a change in the composition of a portfolio of assets. The stock price index used by the DSE had been suffering from some serious shortcomings. A new index basically consistent with the IFC formula for emerging markets has been introduced recently. Besides, an equally weighted sensitive index covering 30 to 50 actively traded stocks may be useful.

Supply side of the market

The companies issuing securities, represent the supply side of the market and the situation is no good either. As we have seen in Chapter 2 that the industrial sector is relatively small in Bangladesh permitting a significant share for public sectors. In the private sector large firms are very often owned and controlled by foreign investors who have little need or desire to raise capital locally. Besides, the locally owned private firms are not willing to go public for fear of loss of control and secrecy. The companies in Bangladesh are reluctant to raise equity capital which is non inflationary investment financing as it is otherwise available more conveniently and at a relatively lower cost through the financial institutions. This results in heavy reliance on bank finance that leads, in general, to a high debt-equity ratio in the capital structure of firms in Bangladesh. Although it is necessary to have a wide range and adequate number of securities in the market to meet the diversified choice of investors, the Bangladesh market does not fit this notion. We have seen the relative market capitalization and firm size of different emerging markets in Chapter 2, where Bangladesh markets were found as the smallest of all. By the end of 1994 the number of listed securities was 170, but about 72 percent of the market is retained by five major industrial houses and seven multinational companies (Khan et al., 1995). There are some Greenfield companies coming to the market at unrealistic premiums based on unrealistic profit projections. Trading is still mostly confined to blue chip stocks. For example, 76.8 percent of total trading was confined to the 10 most active stocks between July 1993 and June 1994 (Edward, 1995). These indicate the narrow base of securities markets in Bangladesh.

Most of the IPOs are being heavily oversubscribed (Table-4.5). Despite the general lack of awareness about stock investment this has been taking place almost every year (Ahmed et al., 1993). This shortage in supply of variable dividend securities also makes the institutional investors divert large volume of their investible funds toward fixed income securities. 'It can be argued that in less developed countries only the most creditworthy firms can sell their securities via a capital market, that these firms also have prime access to bank loans, and hence that such firms have greater freedom of choice between different sources of finance (in terms of availability of funds), for example, between bank loans and security issues. Development of capital markets provides no reallocation of resources to such firms, (Wai and Patrick, 1973). Besides, repressed interest rates in a country may mean that the more creditworthy firms have ready access to bank loans at low, tax-deductible interest, specially in countries where high debt-equity ratios are accepted (Kitchen, 1993). There are 1,000 public companies registered with the RJSC but only 148 of them are listed with DSE as on 30 June 1994 (SEC, Annual Report, 1993-94). Different individuals and family groups are inclined to concentrate ownership and control of holdings of their companies that appeared to be one of the fundamental problems to the growth of stock markets. In order to augment the supply of shares two suggestions are offered by Arowolo. First, statutory companies could be advised to offer their securities either directly or through subsidiaries to the public permitting them to 'have a more direct say in the management of such companies.' Secondly, in respect of joint ventures between government and private sectors, 'the base of equity ownership could be substantially broadened if the government would divert itself of part of the ownership of such ventures as they become successful' (Arowolo, 1971). Security markets in Bangladesh are lacking many good quality securities due to nationalization of these enterprises. The securities would otherwise be made available in the market. Besides, multinational companies constitute some of the largest and probably the best operated companies in Bangladesh. These are either owned by government or foreign investors resulting in unavailability of these shares although they are listed with the DSE. Foreign companies need to be pursued for issuance of some local equity. In order to attain that objective, overseas borrowing may be penalized. This measure is consistent with nationalistic approach. In this regard Arowolo has noted that:

> The rise of economic nationalism in many countries already raises uncertainties as to the continued foreign ownership of many of these companies. The pressure for increased local participation in such companies is not confined to securing the appointment of a few local people as senior personnel who are usually without much responsibility in policy decisions. The offer of shares and securities on a voluntary basis to local subscribers might provide a safety valve and reduce the risk of nationalization (Arowolo, 1971).

It has been reported that there are some 3,000 small and medium scale sick industries of which many are defined as companies (SEC, Annual Report, 1993-94). Sickness is considered as a major cause of inadequate supply of good quality securities in the market. When the company is listed on the stock exchange, few shares are available for trading as majority shares are held by the original sponsors, it is observed. The sponsors often buy additional shares in the stock market to raise their holdings to 70 percent or 80 percent even though shares are initially floated in the primary market on 50:50 basis (Alam, 1989). The important factors identified behind non floatation of shares by the public limited companies are non profitability, weak financial condition, unwillingness of the entrepreneurs, relatively smaller company size, lengthy official procedure needed for going public etc. Among these factors weak financial condition is labeled as the most dominant one. Unwillingness toward public floatation is attributable to several other factors like fear of losing control (24 percent), too stringent disclosure requirements[9] (18 percent), and timely holding of AGM (22 percent) (Khan et al., 1995).

Many of the newly emerging enterprises are faced with multifarious problems, e.g., lack of an internal market, unfair competition from black market products, shortage of working capital etc.causing these securities less attractive. The issuers of the companies are represented by entrepreneurs most of whom are still in the process of transition from trade and other profession to industries. Consequently, the entrepreneurial ability of the average sponsors has not yet been able to attain the standard of optimum efficiency. Information about the company's assets, future prospects and even yearly financial statements are not furnished by the companies regularly. The rates of underwriting commission may vary with anticipated risks from company to company but the underwriting commission is fixed to 2.5 percent. This causes the high risk companies difficult to get underwriters at this rate. Furthermore, there are many securities which are not listed with the DSE but competing with securities listed there. Among them Unit Certificates of ICB, and various government bonds are important ones to absorb a sizable fund. If these could be listed for trading on the stock exchange, it would make securities available in the secondary market for investment and contribute to the development of stock markets. These could have its positive impact on the depth and breadth of the markets.

Policy implications

Formulating a suitable financial policy and their execution in a particular country is predominantly significant for economic growth. In this regard opinions are largely united against government interference with the pattern of interest rates and allocation of investible funds. Rather, these are to be determined by the free interplay of market forces (McKinnon, 1973; Shaw, 1973; Wai and Patrick, 1973; Porter, 1966; Ness, 1974). The package[10] of policy prescriptions offered by World Bank, IMF and other international agencies for developing countries contains recommendations to raise interest rates partly to tighten credit and partly to raise savings. This will make available more investable funds for economic development. However, the issue is ambiguous in terms of theory and empirical evidence. Strong support for 'free' interest rates (i.e., removal of any legal or oligopolistic ceilings upon interest rates in general and interest rates on bank deposits in particular) has been shown by McKinnon (1973). Artificially cheap institutional credit has the effect of distorting the allocation of resources between the modern and traditional sectors of the economy as well as inhibiting the integration of the informal and formal financial markets (Myint, 1970). McKinnon argues 'free' interest rates[11] not merely as the key to integration of different segments of the credit market but also as the centerpiece of a general economic liberalization program. This would reduce segmentation and shape an economy in line with development. In his own words, 'high rates of interest for both lenders and borrowers induce dynamism that one wants in development, calling forth new net saving and diverting investment from inferior uses so as to encourage technical improvement.' That implies promoting the integration of formal and informal financial markets, favoring enterprises and activities other than those that flourish under 'financial repression' and thereby changing the factor proportions in production. Myrdal (1968) points out:

> There would be changes in the relative prices of goods and services, the absolute change depending, in each case, on the extent to which capital was used in the production process, and changes also in the demand for factors of production. As a higher level of interest rates is more in harmony with the great scarcity of capital in the South Asian economies, these adjustments would generally lead to a more rational allocation of resources. More specifically, a higher level of interest charges would tend to induce greater economy in the use of capital in construction and in production processes, a desideratum in all the countries of the region. If very capital-intensive public investment projects were reappraised in terms of a higher interest level, many of them would appear inadvisable (even taking into consideration external economies and other benefits not reflected in their cost/return accounts). In the case of projects that would still be carried out, the costs of the services or goods that constituted their end products would rise.

Artificially low interest rates prevail currently in formal financial sectors of Bangladesh like other less developed countries. By contrast, very high interest rates are charged in the informal financial sector reflecting the scarcity of capital. McKinnon (1973), having indicated to high disparities of rates of return on existing and potential investments in these countries, notes:

> The capital market in a 'developed' economy successfully monitors the efficiency with which the existing capital stock is deployed by pushing returns on physical and financial assets towards quality, thereby significantly increasing the average return . . . Thus it is hypothesized that unification of the capital market, which sharply increases rates of return to domestic savers by widening exploitable investment opportunities is essential for eliminating other forms of fragmentation.

However, Drake (1980) has cast doubt on McKinnon's Statement. In his own words, 'Certainly, freedom in the capital market is necessary for overcoming fragmentation, but one doubts that this freedom is a sufficient condition for obtaining that result or even for unifying/integrating the domestic capital market. My scepticism is based upon the very uneven spread of information and understanding, to say nothing of great differences in economic attitudes and abilities, that persists in developing countries.' De Gregorio and Guidotti (1993) have indicated that real interest rates are not good indicators of financial repression or distortion. According to them the relationship between real interest rates and economic growth might resemble an inverted U curve. In their own words:

> Very low (and negative) real interest rates tend to cause financial disintermediation and hence tend to reduce growth, as implied by the McKinnon-Shaw hypothesis . . . On the other hand, very high real interest rates that do not reflect improved efficiency of investment, but rather a lack of credibility of economic policy or various forms of country risk, are likely to result in a lower level of investment as well as a concentration in excessively risky projects (De Gregorio and Guidotti, 1993).

That implies large negative or large positive real interest rates have the similar adverse impact. In this regard Japanese experience provides the most discouraging evidence for the advocates of financial liberalization. The Japanese financial system was controlled particularly in three areas, viz., interest rates, division of business and overseas transactions. This system, while partially inherited from their tradition and partially set up by the government around 1950 with the objectives to achieve economic growth. Senda (1991) has pointed out:

The most fundamental reason was to provide financial support for the reconstruction and independence of the Japanese economy, which the war had left in ruins. In other words, an artificially low interest rate policy was enforced in order to accelerate the industrialization of the Japanese economy and to increase its international competitiveness by providing low cost funds. To ensure a steady supply of loans (which tended to be in short supply) to the fields that needed them most, fund distribution was controlled by a system of division among financial institutions. Finally, regulations on cross-border transactions enabled the enforcement of an artificially low interest rate policy and prevented outflows of foreign currency reserves.

Other purposes of these regulations were to maintain financial order, guaranteeing the earnings of the financial institutions and protect them from foreign competition. In Japan, interest rate controls began during the Meiji era with interbank agreement on interest rates. After World War II, bank deposit rates were regulated primarily by the Temporary Interest Rates Law of 1947. Although this law is still in force, the control system is in the process of abolition. The separation of banking and securities businesses was introduced by the Securities and Exchange Law in 1948 which was patterned after the U.S. Glass-Steagall Act of 1933. Japan's foreign transactions were restricted under the Foreign Exchange and Foreign Trade Control Law (or 'Foreign Exchange Law') of 1949. However, as Japan gained the status as an IMF Article 8[12] country and joined the Organization for Economic Cooperation and Development (OECD) in 1964, regulations on overseas capital transactions were lifted after the enactment of the New Foreign Exchange Law of 1980. In the financial structure of the fast growth period that favored indirect finance, the security markets remained relatively underdeveloped. After 1975, however, the markets grew quite rapidly under the influence of the large scale floatation of government bonds and the internationalization of finance. The ratio of total securities outstanding to nominal GNP rose from 45.5 percent at the end of 1970 to 115.8 percent at the end of 1988 while the relative share of equities among all securities declined from 29.4 to 11.8 percent in the same period. The size of government bonds including Treasury Bills (TB), local government bonds and bonds issued by public corporations became very large that rose from 39 to 51.6 percent and corporate bonds from 9.2 to 21 percent (Tatewaki, 1991, Table-6.1). This figure indicates the relative weakness of equity securities and the growing dominance of debt securities specially the government bonds in the Japanese financial markets. Japanese financial liberalization process can be well understood from the following statement of Royama (1992):

Financial restructuring in Japan became a continuing process during the second half of the 1970s. The need to fund the large government deficits that emerged after 1975 started the liberalization. Government bond issue in a large scale was the major force pressuring the regulatory authorities to initiate a series of reforms that started the restructuring process. The Japanese financial system was under intense regulation. Monetary authorities and industrial self constraints restricted the working of a free market mechanism. However since the middle of 1970s when MOF started to issue huge amount of government bonds under the new economic circumstance of lowered economic growth, financial liberalization has evolved and a market mechanism has taken to resume their roles in Japan's finance. First, the liberalization took the form of deregulation of interest rates particularly on bank deposits. Banks introduced new deposits with interest rates determined freely in the market or with formula flexibility. At the end of March 1986, 88.2 percent of total bank deposits were those of regulated interest rates. However, the proportion decreased to only 36.0 percent at the end of March 1991.

It cannot be denied that all these regulations have significant contribution to the economic growth of Japan. It has now become one of the economic superpowers judging in terms of current account surplus, foreign reserves and net overseas assets. Thus, regulations and supervision have been proved to be useful that ultimately led Japan toward becoming one of the world's leading freer market system with predominant private sectors.

The analysis of the success or otherwise of equity markets from a macro economic perspective is not necessarily a straightforward process. A variety of different indicators and variables for judging aggregate efficiency have been suggested by a number of different authors (Wai and Patrick, 1973, Drake, 1985). However, it appears that prerequisites of decisive importance may restrain the immediate growth of both demand for and supply of equities in Bangladesh. Indeed, in the framework of a less developed country dominated by agriculture like Bangladesh, it would be rather difficult to find an efficient equity market. Development of confidence in financial instruments and the requisite change in institutions, their framework and attitude are basically a matter of time and not only of incentives. Efforts to accelerate the development of the equity markets shortly by some policy measures do not appear to be very promising in a developing market condition. As expected, not very much can be done to influence the standing, profitability and dividend policy of a firm by legislative measures only. In spite of various legal measures and tax incentives the market is still very small and extremely volatile. The swings in the stock markets of Bangladesh in 1996 illustrate how much the extent of fluctuations in the market index can be for such a market. Besides, inadequate disclosure system and legal framework, persistent political instability, lack of sufficient institutional structure, small number of large companies, narrow base of the market and low level of saving rates of 7.7 percent in 1993-94 (low even South Asian standards) are some of the issues that are clear indication of market weakness. All these have substantial impact on the adequacy, efficiency and reliability of the market. Conceivably favorable effects that legal and tax reform, such as exemption of dividend income from taxes up to certain limit, exemption of capital gain taxes, promotion of greater company disclosure, protection of minority, imposition of penalties for misdeeds of company executives etc., will likely to result in stimulating the demand for equities. But these may well be counterbalanced by the existence of various problems inherent in the developing markets. Overall environment is very much a relevant factor to be considered while making an assessment about the operational efficiency of stock markets. In the industrialized countries investors will find a home that is well defined with a well structured legal system, a reasonably competitive situation, reasonable controls over prices and inputs to maintain them within tolerable limits, and relatively open access to the international economy. But the situation in the developing countries is not necessarily the same. One must note here that public policies in developing economies need to help promote the necessary conditions for economic growth. The necessary elements here are savings and capital, educated people, entrepreneurs and organizations, technology and well functioning state. These are the issues which, by their nature, can't be achieved at a desirable level within a short time. In the absence of these determinant factors encouraged and promoted, accomplishment of any economic program including capital market development is difficult to attain up to the expectation.

The slow evolution of the equity markets, however, should not hamper the industrial growth of the country. The development of the capital market and particularly that part of the equity segment, does not constitute a condition *sine qua non* for economic development. It is rather the outcome of the overall development process of the country and a feature of a more mature economy (Cameron, 1967). In view of the situation prevailing in a developing country like Bangladesh, the potentialities of the banking system deserve greater attention and the necessary steps should be taken to enable it to play a decisive role as an agent of development. Moreover, regardless of how efficiently organized an equity market may be, it is difficult to ensure the flow of available savings toward the most desirable projects from the point of view of priorities for economic development. For, private profitability is not always a sound criterion for judging the desirability of an investment from the social point of view. Public segments of the capital market can play an important role for the developing market. Public debt management could provide a suitable transformation mechanism whereby various debt instruments can satisfy various investors' tastes of ensuring safety, liquidity and yield, while the private entrepreneurs are permitted access to necessary funds which otherwise might not have been available for them. Besides, with the passage of time there is reason to believe that institutional and individual investors will have better response to the issues of private firms since they have familiarity with dealings in securities. Equities were traded in developed economies only after public confidence had been developed by prior experience with government securities (United Nations, 1950). For developing an efficient stock market in Bangladesh, a viable secondary debt market needs to be promoted. A vibrant secondary debt market (involving the debt instruments issued by the government, semi-government and corporate bodies) is an essential part of the program to permit the conservative investors to enjoy the fruits of a fixed interest income stream as well as capital gains like the stock investors.

It is difficult to imagine the rapid expansion and strengthening of the securities markets within a short span of time in a situation of political, economic, financial instability and structural impediments prevailing in an economy like Bangladesh. A suitable base for financial stability must exist before an active securities market can develop and this is essential in order to win the confidence of the investing public in the instruments traded on the exchanges. In the absence of these conditions it is difficult to mobilize savings and to have a properly functioning capital market (Basch and Kybal, 1975). However, stability should not be equated with simply maintaining the *status quo*. For long term stability the structure must be capable of anticipating and assimilating evolutionary change. The need for stability in the broadest sense cannot be overemphasized, but this does not mean resisting change; instead the priority must be to ensure that change is allowed to evolve in a reasonable and systematic way (Lloyd, 1977). Usually, once the public loses confidence in the process of growth of the market, liquidity declines and the process of collapse continues.

In the present context of Bangladesh establishment of efficient contractual institutions in private sectors like a mutual fund which presupposes a relatively developed capital market is not likely to come about shortly. Even if such institutions are set up in the private sectors, there is no certainty that they would be able to acquire sufficient return generating good quality securities in requisite quantities and satisfy the market demand. In fact, at the present stage of development of the country the banking system - commercial, investment and development banks - needs to play a dominant role for financing economic development. Historically, corporate sectors in Bangladesh are less dependent on equity markets and more on bank loans or internal finance. It would then appear that a reorientation of the functions of the banking system in Bangladesh is far more promising and practicable than a swift change in the pattern of asset choice of mass savers. It is even conceivable that the banking institutions, operating within a circumscribed framework to prevent financial vicissitudes, may display initiative and enterprise reminiscent of the Credit Mobilier (Cameron, 1953) and the German 'Universal' banks (Gerschenkron, 1962). However, heavy reliance on banks for long term funds may sometimes lead to an extensive increase in money supply or even dispose some of the securities on the face of tight monetary policy. This may cut off the flow of long term funds unexpectedly entailing demoralizing effect on the capital market (Williams, 1966). Of course, it is not difficult to contain such undesirable developments through suitable measures to be worked out in advance.

In spite of the importance of banking system for corporate financing in the initial stages of development, necessary measures must be directed to remove the discrepancies and odds in the capital markets so that demand for and supply of equities are matched. It is desirable that government should proceed with positive steps to have an integrated program where the different segments of the financial market will be given due consideration in an orderly fashion. For working of efficient operation of the capital markets, government policy can motivate the fundamentals of it, particularly with regard to:

1 Expansion of participation and ownership base in the industrial sector, its attitude toward monopolies and restrictive practices.
2 Overall credit control mechanism including the level of interest rates.
3 Taxation allowing special incentives and disincentives which can inspire the investment, reinvestment and industrialization of the country compatible with the national objectives.
4 Encouragement for the gradual development of an institutional structure that will influence industrialization and financing including securities companies, investment banking in the private sector and enhancing the efficiency of the existing specialized financial institutions and commercial banks working in the field.

Apart from the various aspects of the general economic framework, there is also the indisputable need to institute and implement appropriate regulations and standards covering such issues as the rules of conduct of stockbrokers, accounting and auditing standards and so on. Accounting and auditing standards are particularly important since poor financial reporting will necessarily entail substantial tax evasion and substandard investment decision in any country. Brokers, sub-brokers and dealers should be honest but the reality of Bangladesh does not conform with the notion in many cases. Brokers' activities are not satisfactory in many countries, not only in Bangladesh. The core of the problem revolves around the conflict of interest arises mainly from the role of a broker as an agent, and the personal economic freedom for the broker to trade on his own account, underwriting new issues, acting as company promoter or director etc. This creates distrust among the investing public about stock markets. It is difficult to make a clear-cut boundary of their activities and therefore, it is desirable that their activities and responsibilities are to be determined through exchange of expert opinions. Then those should be well publicized and supervised by the concerned authorities. In the past the stock exchange council in the U.K. has been the main focus of control over the activities of its members and it has been authorized to reprimand, suspend or expel any member who (Briston, 1976) violates any of the rules or regulations of the exchange, fails to comply with any of the decisions of the council, is guilty of dishonorable or disgraceful conduct, acts in a manner detrimental to the securities exchange and unbecoming the character of a member, and conducts himself in an improper or disorderly manner or wilfully obstructs the business of the exchange.

It is likely that the asymmetry in information among investors is caused by poor communications and uneven disclosure by companies. This may result in a lack of confidence in the market by investors. Insider trading, even when it is nothing more than a quick reaction to slowly spreading information which is possible in the absence of an efficient information network, may induce others to shun the market. Drake (1980) has pointed out the need for official regulation and supervision to ensure full disclosure and wide dissemination of information in order to prevent market rigging, and to protect shareholders.

The SEC of Bangladesh who is responsible for overseeing the market needs to give attention to these issues so that proper transparency is ensured and code of conduct of the exchange members is well defined and adhered to. However, SEC should take care in applying such rules. Wai and Patrick (1973) warn of the 'danger of regulatory overkill . . . which may inhibit capital market development.' Alternatively, it may drive it underground, as happened in Kuwait. There the well-regulated official market, with only about 40 quoted securities did not provide sufficient opportunities for the financial community. This led to the development of the unofficial market (Souqal Manakh), where shares of new companies and of other companies in the Gulf, were traded. Again, about 40 companies' shares were traded, but payments with postdated checks creating a forward market in shares and the bubble burst in September 1982. It is, therefore, advisable for the authorities responsible for stock market regulation to follow a path in between under supervision and over supervision. Investors should have confidence but not feel overprotected.

Concluding remarks

Divergent opinions about the contribution and development of equity markets prevail among the academics and practitioners. There are indeed obstacles, inherent in the nature of underdeveloped economies like Bangladesh, to the germination and rapid development of securities markets. However, the constraints are not as binding as they appear at first sight. It appears to be pertinent to note that the appropriate policy for a country will depend on the condition of socioeconomic structure prevails there. Appropriate supply and demand inducements may have proved to be effective. However, the experience of securities market development in Japan indicates that it would be better not to impose a securities market upon an economy in which complementary economic and financial developments are not occurring. In Japan the new issue market failed to keep pace with the tremendous strides made by the economy along the route of industrialization, particularly during the growth period. An encouraging trend in recent years is observed in the growing participation by domestic as well as foreign investors in Bangladesh stock markets. Such investment can increase the level of activities of the markets and the financial resources to domestic firms. But it is unlikely to serve as a source of adequate long term funds solving the problems of savings mobilization, investment and growth at the early stages of development. In view of the present stage of market development associated with various legal and structural constraints as well as corporate practices of the country, there is reason to believe that the development of close relations between banks and industry as a means of promoting economic development appears to be unavoidable. Increased savings by all classes of investing public, and the utilization of those savings for productive investment, requires the existence of an appropriate network of savings and credit institutions, in particular an efficient banking system. Development banks are an invaluable source of long term funds in developing countries like Bangladesh. Likewise, surplus funds of the commercial banks can also be made available for industrial financing through efficient maturity transformation. Pressures for developing the internal efficiency of these institutions may straighten the efficient use of funds. It should be remembered that efforts to speed up the development of the equity market, although laudable, may not lead to immediate tangible results in the face of various fundamental weaknesses inherent in the market condition of Bangladesh. Despite the desirability of direct financing, it seems more desirable to give emphasis on indirect financing through financial intermediaries until a later stage of development of the country. Indirect financing should not be considered as impediment to the development of capital markets, but as a necessary step prior to, and as facilitating long term enduring growth of the latter. For promoting economic growth direct and indirect financing should be considered as complementary but not mutually exclusive. It does not mean ignoring the equity segment of the financial system rather the emphasis needs to be given to other so-called secured vehicles for fund mobilization. Simultaneously, regulatory authorities continue supervision of the market development in general and the trading activities in particular to make shares and bonds as attractive investment vehicles. In the absence of such supervision investors are likely to be more exposed to various market abuses including market manipulation and investment in security markets may decline undesirably.

Notes

1. Recent literatures have pointed out some puzzles that surround the operation of stock markets, viz., puzzle relating to raising new equity finance, and retentions, 'equity premium puzzles' and control function of stock markets. It is thus made questionable whether stock markets are best at doing these functions (For details see Mayer,1994; Mayerand Alexander, 1990; Mehra and Prescott, 1985; Reitz, 1988 and Weil, 1989).

2. The interest rates on different government saving schemes including Wage Earners Development Bond have been reduced in different phases lately and some have been discontinued. The three-year national investment bond and Six-year Bonus Saving Certificate are no longer available. Tax benefit on these investments has also been withdrawn totally in recent years, which is expected to result in a significant fall in the quantum of investment in such instruments in the days to come.

3. The gearing effect of new equity needs to be taken into consideration in measuring its contribution. That is, if the ratio of debt to equity is 3 to 1, then every Tk. 1 raised in new equity means total investment of Tk. 4.

4. Net worth is defined as the ratio of equity capital to total capital and total capital is broadly divided into liabilities and equity capital (capital and surplus).

5. Although funds raised through bond offering, technically, are regarded as non-equity capital,in view of their dependability as long term funds,some consider them as semi equity.

6. At present there are eight stock exchanges in Japan, viz., Tokyo, Osaka, Nagoya, Kyoto, Hiroshima, Fukuoka, Nigata and Sapporo. Among these stock exchanges Tokyo carried out about 86 percent of total transactions,Osaka about 10 percent and the rest is for others (Tatewaki, 1991).

7   The abolition of the requirement in 1992 has paved the way for public offering by the good companies that had achieved a net worth above the face value of their outstanding stocks.

8   The generous tax-relief provisions favors the 157 funds to be exhausted and also encourage the growth of mutual funds in general. These incentives produced striking rise in the volume of share issues, number of issuing enterprises, stock exchange turnover as well as share prices in Brazil.

9   Public floatation of shares require approval of capital issue and prospectus. For getting approval of capital issue, a company has to apply to the SEC with a filled in application form, Memorandum of Association, Articles of Association, Certificate of Incorporation, Certificate of Commencement, loan sanction letter, formal consent of the directors, resolution of the Board of Directors, and feasibility report. Approval of the prospectus requires the company to submit a draft prospectus, an underwriting agreement, an agreement with the manager of the issue, auditors' certificate of its accounts upto 5 years, and a 'No Objection Certificate' from the financial institution if the company has taken any loan.

10 Large part of the package concerns mainly freeing interest rates instead of fixing at high level, reduction of reserve requirements of commercial banks, and the removal of intervention in investment direction and interest rate subsidies.

11 This implies that the interest rate is the main determinant of savings and investment rates. This is questionable since it does not consider other factors like expected rates of growth, inflation and other factors pertaining to business confidence.

12 Article 8 of the IMF agreement prohibits direct restrictions on payments based on current transactions. Current regulations of the Japanese security markets allows a single foreign investor to hold up to 10 percent of the Japanese firm without special permission from the Japanese government.

5 Behavior and structure of stock prices

The significance of a well functioning and robust stock market as a corollary to a sustainable growth of the economy in general and private corporate sectors in particular is being increasingly recognized in recent years. In a modern economy with sizable private corporate sectors, stable security price and general economic development are so interwoven that the state of the economy and specially the investment climate thereof can easily be guessed by a mere review of the behavior of the stock markets. The stock markets to an economy, what a clinical thermometer is to a human body. It reflects the health of the economy. It is recognized that the stock market and economic activity move in a similar pattern that indicates investors' attempt to forecast economic trends. Thus, the stock price index is considered as a major indicator of the economy.

Stock prices, in general, are determined by the interaction of demand and supply. Stock differs from other consumer goods to the extent that stock itself can't directly be consumed like other consumer goods rather the income generated by it can be used for consumption purposes. Accordingly, determination of a stock price may be governed by the volume of net assets it holds. However, in spite of its considerable bearing on the price of a stock, net assets are, in a sense, the liquidation value of the enterprise and thereby not considered most suitable measure for a going concern. Basically, the most important aspect in the stock price mechanism is the amount of earning the investor's money will realize in a certain period. This is usually related to the dividend rate which can play a crucial role behind demand and supply relationship and thereby price formation. An anticipated future dividend is subject to uncertainties and influenced by many economic and noneconomic factors. Fluctuations in security prices are the function of a variety of factors. Interest rates, industrial production, commodity prices, savings, investments, population, employment, political and economic developments, technological changes, corporate profits, earnings or dividends, investors' feelings etc. are the prominent ones that can influence stock prices. As a result, many indeterminate factors come into play to complicate the pricing mechanism. All these may conveniently be divided into 'internal' and 'external' factors. While the former is related to the internal achievement of a particular industry or a company, the latter is exclusively the outcome of the stock market conditions affecting the stock prices in general. Chen, Roll and Ross (1986) have hypothesized a broad range of influences that could affect security prices. According to them the value of a share is equal to the present value of future cash flows to the shareholder. Any factor impacts on either the size of future cash flows or the discount rates used to value the cash flows will have its bearing on the price. The primary function of a stock market is to allocate resources to the most profitable investment opportunities. If stock prices provide accurate signals for resource allocation, firms are able to make correct production-investment decisions, and investors are able to choose the most suitable stocks for investment. These choices are possible if the market is efficient, that is, if stock prices 'fully reflect' all available information.

This Chapter seeks to examine the trends in stock prices with a view to discovering their behavioral pattern and also locate the main factors, both economic and non-economic, behind the stock price behavior in Bangladesh.

DSE trading system

In Bangladesh a company willing to offer shares for a public subscription must apply to the SEC for approval. The company so approved is then eligible to apply for listing on the stock exchanges. The stock exchange may list the security for dealings on the exchange floor if it is satisfied after making such inquiry as it deems necessary to fulfill the conditions prescribed for this purpose. Trading on the stock exchange is undertaken for the listed stocks only. According to the regulation of Bangladesh, public companies having paid up capital of Tk. 10.0 million or more are required to be listed on the stock exchange. No company with an issued and paid up capital of less than Tk. 1.0 million is listed on the stock exchange while companies with paid up capital between Tk. 1.0 million and 10.0 million can exercise their option for listing. The advantages of listing are increasing security's prestige, more publicity through media, raising security's marketability and easy accessibility to bank loans, tax concession etc. In spite of these advantages many companies do not prefer to be listed due to required disclosure of information, cost and necessary procedural formalities attached to listing process, unwillingness to make wide ownership and so on.

Shares can be acquired from the primary market or secondary market. Application for allotment of shares can be submitted in prescribed form when a public offer is made by any company. The prescribed application form is obtainable from the bankers to the issue, stock exchanges and the company office. Only one application in one name is permissible. If the applicant is allotted a share, he receives an allotment letter. He can either retain the allotment letter until a share certificate is issued or dispose of the allotment within renunciation period through broker signing the 'form of renunciation' usually attached at the back of the allotment letter. However, the investor receives the share certificate in exchange of the allotment letter subsequently.

Stock exchange is the legal platform for trading in the secondary market. Trading is conducted by the broker-members of the stock exchanges in Bangladesh. An investor can associate himself with the stock exchange trading only through a broker whom he can approach to execute his buy or sell order. DSE brokers are allegedly taking unnecessary long time to execute the order which often goes against the interest of the investor. In order to execute an order to buy or sell securities on behalf of his client, a broker is supposed to provide services at the time of executing a sell order as well as provide services and funds for a buy order. He charges a commission for such services which is 1 percent of the total value of the transaction. Thus, the stock markets in Bangladesh predominantly operate through the agents without any responsible market makers. The members of the DSE do not operate margin accounts for general investors. There is no provision in Bye-laws of the Exchange for undertaking market making roles.

While the stock exchange brokers must carry out trading of the listed stocks on the floor of the exchange in principle, off floor transactions are carried out through a kerb market in Bangladesh, notably during recent times. Trading of shares during floor trading hours as well as beyond trading hours is conducted among large number of interested investors assembled outside the stock exchange. Transactions are usually conducted through physical delivery of share certificates in the kerb market. Very often transactions take place at a distorted price. Fraudulent practices entrap people through trading on the false certificates have become a regular phenomenon in the country's kerb market centering the DSE. The unregulated kerb market has exacerbated the stock market manipulation and inflicted extensive damage to the market. Such unrecognized markets, if not guided properly, might have negative impacts on sound development of stock markets.

Trading takes place six days a week on the exchanges of Bangladesh. The market operates through 'an open outcry' with broker-members seated around a table with no access to outsiders. Dealing prices are recorded with a chalk on a black board by a member of the stock exchange staff. By the standards of large stock exchanges in developed countries, the technology is simple and not subject to technological failure. For a market of this size, the trading arrangements can, by and large, serve the purpose. However, in view of the growing size of the market, frequent allegations about the market manipulation, and recent upsurges followed by sharp downswings, credibility of the system as a whole has been brought into question. Computerization of the trading system and introduction of a central depository system (CDS) can bring improvement of the situation. Under central depository system for securities, transactions in securities are cleared on books merely by entering such transactions in the accounts concerned, with the stock certificates held in custody by a certain agency, instead of physically delivering them after each transaction. Since this system offers the advantages of rationalizing depository and delivery of large number of securities as well as preventing possible loss or misplacement, it has been in use now-a-days in many countries. Physical delivery of share certificates is not permitted under CDS. Consequently, people will be discouraged to go to the kerb market and thereby it may reduce the dominance of this market. It is true that computerization has proved efficiency, accuracy and speed of trading in many markets. But liquidity of the market may suffer from entire computerization. Order flows are generated, although at least partially, by subtle interactions of human activities on the floor, including behavior of the rivals, floor atmosphere, floor gossips and so on, all of which can hardly be held by computer. That means prices might be 'overshooting' or 'undershooting' if traders are just reacting to price moves on the screen without well understanding the reasons behind such moves. This may result in rather market volatility due to lack of exchange of information among the traders. The system, therefore, needs to combine the advantages of the technology - efficiency, accuracy and speed - with those of human interaction, visibility and information exchangeability on the trading floor so that maximization of liquidity and better market coordination can take place.

Till now little research has been conducted on the ownership and trading patterns on DSE. However, the widespread view is that most of the equity is tightly held by the families, relatives and friends. The shares of MNCs are owned by foreign parents and government who usually tend to decline to sell their shares in the local markets. Different informal estimates suggest that between 50-70 percent of equity is tightly held by families, relatives and friends. Institutions appear to be less dominant in stock exchange trading, although no reliable figures are available. According to informal estimates this share accounts for about 20 percent (Bichitra, 1996). However, all these estimates should be treated with caution.

Stock price indexes

Market always works for discovering true values despite efforts to conceal or distort them. Bangladesh's capital market is not an exception. The efforts to force investment at high levels than could be supported has usually been reflected in the poor performance of stocks. The industrial performance is poor and as such capital markets could only reflect such performance. A useful tool for studying overall price behavior of a market is a price index. Both the DSE

Table - 5.1
Equity prices in Bangladesh

Year	General index	Converted to a single base (1978-79)	% Relative variation in index based on immediately preceding year
1978-79=100			
1978-79	100.00	100.00	-
1979-80	99.48	99.48	-0.52
1980-81	102.85	102.85	3.39
1981-82	108.24	108.24	5.24
1982-83	114.06	114.04	5.37
1982-83=100			
1983-84	109.98	125.44	9.98
1984-85	138.91	158.44	26.30
1985-86	157.40	177.20	11.84
1986-87	322.55	367.90	107.62
1986-87=100			
1987-88	128.52	472.82	28.52
1988-89	157.51	579.48	22.56
1989-90	151.15	556.08	-4.04
1990-91	124.50	458.03	-17.63
1991-92	120.64	443.83	-3.10
1992-93	135.91	500.01	12.66
1993-94	189.50	697.17	39.43
1994-95*	289.66	1065.66	52.86

Note: *Figures indicate value for January 1995.
Source: Compiled from various issues of Economic Trends and Index Numbers of Stock Exchange Share Prices, Statistics Department, Bangladesh Bank.

and BB maintain share price indexes of the shares listed with DSE. The BB's 'Index of Ordinary Shares of Companies Listed in the DSE Ltd.' provides share price index taking different financial years as a base for different periods.

Both indexes rely on DSE's published price quotations to track prices of the shares of listed companies. Although the two indexes do not always yield exactly the same figures, they tend to agree in general.

Table-5.1 presents the stock price index prepared by BB. Transforming the index into a graph takes the shape like Figure-5.1. It is already noted that DSE remained inactive during the FFYP period (1973-78) due to government socialist policy adopted at that time. Although it resumed its operation in the face of a very unfavorable condition in 1976, it did not get momentum for a considerable time. Its operational activities were expanding very slowly. During the TYP period (1978-80) equity prices were hesitant and did not gain much ground as it appears from Table-5.1. In terms of annual index it declined from 100 in 1978-79 to 99.48 in 1979-80. However, during the SFYP period (1980-85) the price index rose from 102.85 in 1980-81 to 158.45 in 1984-85. The rise was almost steady throughout this period. By and large, the period was free from violent fluctuations in equity prices though there were significant rises

Figure - 5.1
Stock price trend in DSE

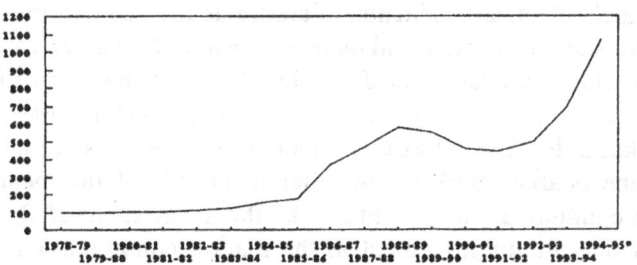

in prices in the face of a favorable situation in the industrial sector primarily due to government policy support for private sectors and denationalization. From the year 1980-81 the equity price index recorded a gradual rise compared to those of their respective preceding years. This rising trend continued and peaked in 1987-88 and thereafter it declined. During SFYP (1980-85) stock prices did not gain much ground, though a slight increase in prices recorded every year. The impact of Industrial Policy of the Government announced in 1982 along with some tax reliefs, concessions and the like allowed for investors in the government budgets during this period were believed to be the important factors behind this upward swing. Factors like expectations for the increase of stock prices, satisfactory earnings in many companies also contributed to this bullish tendency. The effect of all these was counterbalanced by the continued labor unrest, reduced production volume in some sectors, instability in political conditions, natural calamities etc. However, throughout this period the index went up in most of the months with greater magnitude. Although the index went down in some months, the decline proved to be a temporary phase as prices began to increase after a short time.

The TFYP (1985-90) started with an optimistic note. This was mainly as a result of the announcement of New Industrial Policy of 1986, relaxation of the rules of import of raw materials and machineries, larger size of TFYP and larger allocation to the private sectors and so on. The opening year of the plan period (1985-86) witnessed a moderate rise in equity prices and the trend was considerably accentuated in the following year (1986-87) when the General Price Index rose up to 367.90 from 177.20 in the previous year, i.e., the index became more than double within a year. The year 1987 has been marked as the boom period for the stock market of Bangladesh. Anticipations among investors for raising profits and dividends, emergence of a new class of investors, hedge against inflation, denationalization and holding company policy of the government, downward revision of interest rates, incentive schemes for export promotion, growth prospects of certain industries, exemption of income tax of individual shareholders, and reduction of corporate tax are the possible factors attributable for such rising price and thereby remarkable success of investment in share markets. However, since July 1987 the stock markets of Bangladesh were experiencing a bearish condition. Declining trends in most stock prices and the market index as well as the volume of transactions are the evidences supporting the bearish market. In order to get rid of this bearish market condition, a committee was constituted by the government of Bangladesh to suggest remedies for improvement in the market condition. The committee prepared an index covering only the active stocks and classified them into two categories: Multinational Companies (MNCs) and Local Companies (LCs). According to the report of the committee the MNCs stock price index increased five times by June 1987 over the base of 31 March 1986 against little more than two times in case of LCs stocks for the same period. The rates of overall price decline in December 1989 over 1987 was calculated 21 percent. It was also reported that though the overall price index had reflected fall by about 21 percent in 1989, in case of MNCs it was 20 percent and in case of LCs it was 25 percent. It was also reported that although the overall price index had jumped more than four times in 1987 in a period of 11 months, it had shown a fall of about 21 percent in 1989 over 1987 (Ministry of Industries, 1990). According to many knowledgeable stock market experts the damage was caused to the stock market due to political unrest, natural calamities and unprecedented floods in 1987 and 1988. However, it is believed by many that the market overreacted in this period without considering much of the economic fundamentals (Seok and Park, 1992).

It is evident that the period from 1978 to 1996 is characterized by a rising tendency in equity prices intervened sometimes with hesitant or falling price in Bangladesh. As regards to this increasing trend, it must be borne in mind that this occurred mostly in the years when the government policies have emphasized the private sector through divestment and allowed them to play their role in a wider range of industries. Throughout this period prices fluctuated violently though the direction and duration of the fluctuation were not similar in all the cases. The monthly rates of changes showed more cases of 'increases' than 'declines' as we approach to more recent years. Table-5.2 shows that prices were less stable in more recent times. The maximum variations are found in TFYP (1985-90) and the minimum in the TYP (1978-80). The degree of variations shows an ascending order. Again, during the TFYP both 'rises' and 'declines' were pronounced than earlier plans. The riskiness of the equity in

Table - 5.2
Average 'rises' and 'declines' of share price and their deviations

Measures	Rises			Declines		
	1978-80 (TYP)	1980-85 (SFYP)	1985-90 (TFYP)	1978-80 (TYP)	1980-85 (SEYP)	1985-90 (TFYP)
i. Averages	0.30	1.95	7.59	0.32	1.07	2.51
ii. Standard Deviation	0.22	2.63	11.36	0.30	1.28	3.59
iii. Coefficient of Variation	73.33	134.87	149.67	93.67	119.63	143.03

Source: Ahmed, 1992.

terms of standard deviation and coefficient of variation is pronounced in later years which is consistent with the increasing rate of 'rises' as the finance theory suggests.

In a study (Ahmed et al., 1993) we have considered the relationship between stock price and internal or micro factors. For this purpose nine independent variables have been taken to analyze the relative stock price. The independent variables are current ratio, debt-equity ratios, earning per share, book value of a share, dividend payout ratio, nationality of the company (i.e., national or multinational), size of the company in terms of paid up capital, current bonus dividend and growth of dividends while relative stock price has been taken as the proportion of stock price of individual company to the face value of that company. A correlation matrix has been prepared. It has been seen that the share price is significantly correlated with book value of a share, earnings per share, nationality of the company and debt equity ratio. According to regression analysis book value and nationality of the company have significant impact on stock price at more than 99 per cent level of confidence. Higher book value implies accumulation of past earnings. Thus, earning performance or dividend paying ability has been the leading influencing factor in share price determination. The implication of this factor is that the securities with high return potential command higher price. The significant relationship between the nationality of the company and the share price recognizes the fact that the investors have more confidence in the performance of multinational companies than local ones. This is consistent with the findings of the committee formed by Ministry of Industries (1990). As noted earlier in calculating the level of general price fall in 1989 it has been seen that the multinational companies accounted for 20 percent price fall while that of the local companies was 25 percent. Besides, the debt-equity ratio has displayed a negative relationship with share price.

Judged as a whole, TFYP period may be regarded as a period of rising stock prices although the rise was by no means steady. FFYP (1990-95) experienced fall in prices in its initial years which steepened in 1991 and continued during most parts of 1992. But the rate of decrease has slowed and gradually started to increase and culminated in November 1996. However, the market could not be sustained for long and since the second week of November 1996 the market experienced sharp decline. The stock price of Bangladesh underwent dramatic behavior. A sharp increase in general is observed for the periods of 1987-89 and 1993-96 associated with rapid fall following these periods. The aggregate behavior of stock prices reflects tone and temperament of the industrial sectors and related policies. The price rise that followed the bear market of early 1990s may be considered as an extension of ongoing reform policy of the government and firm commitment for liberalization and private sector development. Macroeconomic factors such as growth of the economy, increased flow of foreign exchange, deregulation of the market, lowering of interest rates; microeconomic factors such as changing corporate and financial strategies with introduction of fiscal and other incentives; institutional factors, specially establishment of SEC, are also relevant for price rises. However, it is apprehended that the market entered into an adjustment period and overreacted to some economic factors like a lowering interest rate, tax incentives and easy convertibility of Bangladesh currency associated with some market abuses including market manipulation.

While prices appear to be violent throughout the period, there have been periods of sufficiently long duration in which the direction of the changes has shown a remarkable consistency. Of course, during this period the equity prices unmistakably have shown an upward trend. Of the various factors affecting equity prices in Bangladesh, the impact of the annual national budget appears to be not deniable. In almost all the years prices either declined or behaved hesitantly on the eve of presentation of the budget as the investors' class, in general, had always expected a change in the dose of taxation on various sectors. However, the most potent factors governing the price behavior appears to have been, by and large, economic in nature although psychological and political factors have also sometimes resulted in wild and wide fluctuations in equity prices. Rumors and expectations about any factor had also their significant impact on the equity price behavior. Irrespective of the nature of a particular factor, equity prices were significantly affected when that factor directly or even indirectly affected the corporate sector in general and an industry in particular. On certain occasions, the equity prices have also moved under the impact of the corrective measures to curb the speculation-generated trends. This seems to be one of the major causes of price fall after the stock boom of 1987 and 1996 in Bangladesh.

In the history of Bangladesh stock markets the most significant event occurred in 1996 when the market behaved irrationally. In DSE all share price index rose from 770 in January 1996 to 3,700 points in the first week of November of the same year. But it dropped to 2,261.47 points on 29 December 1996 and again to 1,140.65 points on 8 April 1997. This abnormal price rise has taken place ignoring all micro and macro economic fundamentals. The price of shares of a company, having negative worth, increased three to four times. Even share price of a closed company also increased. The abnormal rise in share prices created an urge for mindless gambling among the various segments of people. Some people took the situation to become rich overnight. Suddenly the market started experiencing nightmares as the overpriced share market began sliding toward its rational level every day and subsequently crashed. The alarming fluctuation created a serious tension among investors and ultimately resulted in forced closure of floor trading for several days. Rise in stock price level appears to be too high that cannot be explained in terms of economic fundamentals of Bangladesh. It is difficult to segregate any single factor responsible for this price upheaval rather a combination of some factors including some policy issues might have contributed to such development. The likely candidates that might have some bearing on it are price manipulation on the exchange, lack of proper implementation of a circuit breaker, withdrawal of lock-in[1] system, absence of institutional traders on the exchange, lack of aggressive campaigning about economic fundamentals and its grave consequences etc.

Fluctuation in equity price is a usual phenomenon throughout the world. It is possible that a temporary supply of or demand for an extraordinary large amount of securities takes place sometimes. This may upset the balance between demand and supply. In order to stabilize the market, it is necessary to conduct some price supporting activities. Such activities are specially needed when the market is dominated by speculation and rumor. A circuit breaker implying a price limit and trading halt may work to stabilize the market especially when investors behave rather irrationally. The concept of a circuit breaker is not a new one. Yet it is one of the most controversial issues among all financial discussions. In the final analysis it is explained as a trade off between financial efficiency and stability. When one emphasizes financial efficiency, he must do it at the cost of more systematic instabilities. Similarly, when one emphasizes financial stability, he must do it at the cost of more competitive inefficiencies. The choice will depend upon the circumstances in which the market is situated and eventually upon the value judgement of a society. It is found in many countries in some form or the other and the rules are framed according to their respective needs. Advocates of efficiency objective contend that a circuit breaker would unduly delay price discovery, injure the investors forcing them to accept 'incorrect' prices anticipating trading halt. It is also argued that it causes deprivation of hedgers from market use when it is most needed. On the contrary, opponents argue for effectively limiting financial risks and hence systematic instability in critical times. They also contend that it may even facilitate price discovery by providing a 'time-out' during which counter orders can be generated. Bangladesh's market is relatively small even if it is compared with other emerging markets of South Asia. The presence of foreign portfolio managers with their huge fund can easily create an imbalance between demand and supply. This is needless to say that they will try to manipulate price with their profit motive. In view of the market condition of Bangladesh, financial stability needs to be supported by the authorities concerned and hence a circuit breaker should be executed effectively considering the cause of overall market development instead of the interest of any individual party. Simultaneously, wide campaigning through media against such irrational behavior and their consequences also need to be conducted. Legal measures should be instituted and executed effectively by the authorities concerned in order to contain manipulation of stock prices.

The implication of the withdrawal of lock-in system in the market is a subject of empirical investigation. However, it is unlikely to be positive in the market condition of Bangladesh. Experience of undertaking reform and stabilization programs shows that countries are prone to excessive foreign funds that ultimately prove unsustainable behavior leading to financial market failure. This is because excessive optimism is created among domestic and foreign investors and the policy-makers. Although better economic performance and large inflows of foreign capital justify such optimism initially, afterwards it does not sustain and in general results in a recession, crisis in the financial markets and capital flight. Investment in stock markets of Bangladesh by the domestic investors has got some momentum only recently that needs to be retained. Recent volatile stock market behavior is likely to have its negative impact on sound market development. The authorities should impose financial controls in an appropriate form to limit the potential damage. Regulations of cross-border transaction of financial capital are suitable tools. In the light of the experience of successful liberalization programs undertaken by East Asian countries in 1960s and 1970s, such moves appear to be appropriate in the context of liberalization and stabilization policies currently being pursued in Bangladesh.

Impact of dividend policy

The important aspect of the dividend policy is to determine the amount of earnings to be distributed to shareholders and the amount to be retained in the firm. Retained earnings are preferred to external sources of funds for financing growth. Conversely, dividends are desirable from shareholders' point of view following the 'bird-in-the-hand' principle. Proper balance between these two objectives needs to be evolved in formulating a dividend policy.

The shareholders of a concern, while investing their money, have one thing in mind, i.e., to earn profit on their investment which at least would not be lower than the rate of interest available for the same fund in the money market. The market rate of interest is the minimum which they expect to earn. This, however, does not mean that they will earn this every year on their investment. It all depends on the profits earned by the concern. If no profits are earned, the ordinary shareholders get nothing, notwithstanding the fact that if they invested it in the money market, they could have earned more. It is at this point that a dividend differs from interest. In case of ordinary shares, the dividend may or may not be paid as profits are earned or not, and even when profits are earned, the whole of it or a major portion may be transferred to the reserve fund by directors at their discretion but interest on debentures must be paid. Interest is, therefore, predetermined and fixed; the dividend is unknown and uncertain. Yet to a speculative brain or to one who is ready to undertake risk, investment in rationally selected shares offers greater return than the predetermined and fixed rates of interest. In fact, they expect to earn much more. If the concern earns profits, it will be too glad to share it in some form or other with the investors.

Dividend policy is the result of the action of various factors. One of the legal restrictions imposed is that dividend should not be declared from capital of the concern but only from the profit of the relevant year or any other undistributed profit (Companies Act 1994, Schedule 1). It is to be determined within the limit set by unappropriated surplus. It is true that the psychology of the investors demands high dividends, but that is not the only factor to be considered. Apart from legal restrictions there are many other factors which stand in the way of a high dividend being declared. If too high a dividend, quite disproportionate to that declared in other lines, is declared by a particular concern in a particular line, that would signify undercapitalization and attract funds from the public, thereby once more reducing dividends to normal. It is also known that in the field of finance, corporate savings have come to acquire great importance. Hence if the concern wants to be self-sufficient in financial matters, or at least depends on its own savings for a major part of its requirements, it is better not to declare a high dividend but to carry a major portion of the undistributed surplus to the reserve fund. There are certain industries, e.g., railroads, where profits are earned in the long run. Over a number of years no profits may be earned and no dividend declared. In speculative enterprises a high degree of uncertainty haunts profits. Accordingly, it is necessary to declare dividends at a low level which may be maintained all through the life of the corporation. The age of the concern also gets importance. It is true that a certain level of dividends becomes essential for new concern to declare in order to attract sympathy of the investors, but where it needs its own earnings for its growth, a cautious dividend policy is commendable.

All investors have one good reason to forgo dividends insofar as they originate at companies having growth prospects and continuing needs for new capital - which, after all, essentially describes the kinds of companies that most investors look for. New capital acquired from external sources is both expensive and hard to get. New capital acquired through retained earnings is both cheap and readily obtainable. It is cheap in the sense that its uses involve neither the payment of interest nor the allocation of earnings to new shares. They consequently produce higher earnings per share than other kinds of capital. Acknowledging this general principle, some economists have nevertheless argued that cost free capital may sometimes be undesirable. They contend that it may make managements sloppy in their investment decisions. They have argued that a management demanding a certain return from new projects to be financed with capital obtained externally will often settle for a more modest return on projects to be financed with retained earnings. Logically, retained earnings should not be committed to the business unless the return expected on them exceeds the shareholders' 'opportunity cost' (Loomis, 1968).

Considering all these viewpoints, the following general principles may be laid down regarding the distribution of profits among shareholders. In the first place, the company newly started should make it a point to pay no dividend or a very nominal dividend over a number of years after the commencement of business. Secondly, it should be the aim of the company to stabilize the dividend rate and in order to achieve that end, it must first reduce the fluctuation of profits to the minimum, so that a stable dividend policy may be ensured. Finally, it is for the company to pay out as dividend, in any year, only a portion of the surplus profits, not the whole of them, as a matter of financial prudence. How much of these surplus profits are to be paid as dividend is a matter to be considered by the management; no hard and fast rule can be laid down in this regard.

Economists, however, have long striven to make some broader points involving the relationship between dividends and stock prices. One important question remains there concerning the relative importance of retained earnings and dividends in determining a stock's price earning ratio (PER). Underlying this question is the proposition that both retained earnings and dividends convey a return to the stockholder. Dividends, of course, are some direct payoffs. Retained earnings, on the other hand, increase the value of the stockholders' investment and stimulate the power of the business to produce additional earnings. Since these are capitalized in the market, the value of stockholders' shares increases. The question then is which method of payment do most investors prefer?

Gordon (1962) says that for most companies generous dividend payout tends to lift price earnings ratios (PER), and niggardly payout to depress them. According to him, it is rational to prefer the certainty of a dividend payment now to the uncertainty of a possible future (realized through growth) flowing out of retained earnings. However, Miller and Modigliani (1961) have argued that dividends do not count. They have contended that investors are essentially indifferent to the level of dividends and that therefore they have virtually no effect on PERs at least if transaction costs and taxes are ignored. Still a third view has been pronounced by Friend and Puckett (1964) who have shown that in non growth industries - they included food and steel in this category - investors tended to value dividends somewhat higher than retained earnings but the opposite, they feel, is true for growth industries - identified as electronics, utilities and chemicals.

Thus, the issue is still unresolved and Black (1976) has rightly concluded 'What should the corporation do about dividend policy? We do not know.' We have already mentioned that stocks differ from ordinary commodities in that the purchaser of stocks does not expect to derive any benefit from the direct consumption of the stocks themselves. This necessitates the value of a stock to be considered in a way different from that we usually do with other commodities. The fundamental factor considered in purchasing a stock is how much profit the invested money will realize in a particular period and this depends upon a dividend rate anyway. Dividend, therefore, becomes an important factor behind stock price formation, as it is universally accepted that one can look upon a share as a profit sharing security. In the backdrop of the above discussion let us look to the dividend scenario of Bangladesh enterprises in Table-5.3. It is clear from this Table that with the increase of listed

Table - 5.3
Number of listed companies paying dividends

Year	No. of companies listed	No. of companies paying dividend	% of total listed companies	Number paying		
				5 to 15%	16 to 25%	26% and above
1980	23	15	65.22	-	-	-
1981	26	21	80.77	10	10	1
1982	29	22	75.86	12	9	1
1983	44	25	56.82	6	15	4
1984	58	35	60.34	8	18	9
1985	72	45	62.50	18	18	9
1986	82	43	52.44	14	21	8
1987	90	53	58.89	18	25	10
1988	111	46	41.44	17	16	13
1989	116	61	52.59	22	24	15
1990	130	77	59.23	40	25	12
1991	133	69	51.88	40	19	10
1992	142	62	43.66	31	21	10
1993	147	74	50.34	43	19	12
1994	157	65	41.40	29	21	15
1995	183	84	45.90	32	24	28

Source: Calculated from various issues of DSE Fact Book and Monthly Review

companies the number of dividend paying companies is also increasing in absolute terms but it is decreasing in relative terms. Among the dividend paying companies the median rate appears to be within the range of 16 to 25 percent while the number of companies within the highest range (26 percent and above) is small. Out of 15 years (from 1981 to 1995) the number of companies paying dividend 16 percent and above outweighed the number paying between 5 percent and 15 percent. It gives an impression that in general most of the dividend paying companies paid a good amount as dividend although the number of such companies is around 50 percent of the total listed companies.

Table-5.4 presents a comparative position of stock dividend yields, average dividend rates of the listed companies on the DSE and TSE and annual time deposit interest rates in Bangladesh and Japan. When seen from a long term viewpoint, the yield of dividend paying stocks has almost consistently been dropping till recently in both Bangladesh and Japan. The dividend yield of the

Table - 5.4
Changes in time deposit interest rate, dividend yield and average dividend rate *(Figures in %)*

Year	Time Deposit Interest Rate (One Year)		Stock Yield		Average Dividend	
	B'desh	Japan	B'desh	Japan	B'desh	Japan
1976	8.25	6.750	-	1.91	-	12.50
1977	8.25	5.250	-	1.82	-	12.68
1978	8.25	4.500	-	1.60	-	12.90
1979	8.25	6.000	-	1.57	-	12.98
1980	14.00	7.000	12.90	1.63	13.97	13.16
1981	14.00	6.250	12.20	1.55	13.88	13.38
1982	14.00	5.750	11.30	1.68	12.68	13.62
1983	14.00	5.750	9.90	1.39	11.98	13.76
1984	14.00	5.500	5.70	1.09	8.32	14.22
1985	14.00	5.500	10.70	0.99	18.20	14.50
1986	14.00	3.760	5.40	0.78	11.75	14.66
1987	13.25	3.390	3.50	0.63	13.41	14.72
1988	13.25	3.390	1.80	0.55	6.21	15.04
1989	13.25	4.320	2.90	0.47	10.17	15.56
1990	10.00	6.080	3.94	0.52	8.59	16.08
1991	9.00	5.250	5.42	0.64	10.24	16.42
1992	7.50@	3.820	4.60	0.90	9.50	16.42
1993	6.00@	3.089	4.13	0.82	8.39	-
1994	5.00@	2.174	2.08	0.76	7.91	-

Notes: 1. Time deposit interest rates are as of the end of each year. Since 1993 figures relate to one year time deposits of more than ¥ 10 million. 2. Stock yield and average dividend rates are based on dividend paying companies. @ Since 1992 individual banks are allowed to decide the interest rates on deposits within a range. This is the minimum rate set by the monetary authority, however, when taking the average of the actual rate offered by individual bank on one year time deposit these are 8.55%, 8.26% and 6.56% for 1992, 1993 and 1994 respectively.
Sources: Compiled from TSE (1995) and Japan Securities Research Institute (1994), Economic Trends, Bangladesh Bank-various issues and DSE Stock Exchange Review and DSE Fact Book-various issues.

listed companies in DSE was 12.9 percent in 1980 which declined rapidly afterwards. Undergoing some fluctuations during the period under consideration, it came down to about 2 percent in 1994. A similar trend is observed for the stocks of TSE. Average dividend rates of the Bangladeshi enterprises was 13.97 percent in 1980 which demonstrates a declining trend in subsequent years. However, the dividend rate of the Japanese companies appears to be steadily increasing. The important point is that the dividend rate and yield in Bangladesh are lower than the time deposit interest rate whereas in Japan although dividend yield is lower than a time deposit interest rate, a dividend rate is higher than that.

A low yield is attributable either to the low dividend or to the high market capitalization or to both as it appears from the following definition of the dividend yield:

$$Dividend\ Yield = \frac{Cash\ Dividend}{Market\ Price\ of\ Share} \quad \ldots\ldots\ldots\ldots (1)$$

An increasing market capitalization and a decreasing cash dividend are observed in Bangladesh. Moreover, the rate of yield decrease is more than the rate of decrease in dividends. This indicates that both lower dividend and higher capitalizations are relevant factors for explaining low yields. In case of Japan, businesses have mostly been taking a dividend policy that is enough to a certain fixed percentage of the face value as dividends steadily and continuously, while stock prices went up and remained high (TSE Fact Book, 1986). Accordingly, the dividend yield has gone down. Until recently the time deposit interest rate was much higher in Bangladesh, which was partly because of high rates of inflation. The dividend yield and dividend rate are relatively lower in Bangladesh when interest rates are compared. Recently, however, the interest rates have been revised downward along with low rates of inflation. A look at the investment indexes (PERs and dividend yields) in Bangladesh will also reveal a considerable fluctuation of these indexes. They undergo sharp fluctuations specially during a period of major policy changes. On the other hand, these indexes for Japan offer more or less stable condition over a relatively longer period of time.

There is a feeling among the laborers of Bangladesh that when high profits are earned, they should not be spent on fat dividends, but carried to reserve and depreciation funds and utilized for improving the standard of living of the workers. It is true that too fat dividends are not desirable, but dividends declared by companies in Bangladesh in most cases have not been excessive. However, in a period of prosperity, to the interest of the industry itself, it is necessary to build up as much corporate reserve as is feasible so that on the one hand it will lighten the problems of industrial finance in normal times and on the other, work as the main support in the dark days of depression.

Price earnings ratio (PER)

The price earnings ratio (PER) is an index obtained through dividing the stock price by the earnings per share to show the ratio between these two figures. As such, it is contemplated as a criterion for investment decisions. Having been used with stock yields in the developed economies since 1920s, investors particularly institutional investors have come to consider PER more important than yield in recent times. Formulation of PER has substantial relation with share valuation. Security analysts usually go through the process of discounting forecasted earnings or dividends to get a present value of a share. Conceptually the investment value of a share is equal to the present value of dividends expected from its ownership. In notational terms this can be expressed as:

$$P_o = \sum_{t=1}^{\infty} \frac{D_t}{(1+i)^t} \qquad \ldots\ldots\ldots\ldots (2)$$

Where P_o is the current price of the share, D_t is an expected dividend at the end of period t and i is equal to the investor's discount rate or opportunity cost applicable to the dividend stream. This is a general valuation model.

When the dividend per share is assumed constant year after year at a value of D then Equation (2) becomes:

$$P_o = \frac{D}{(1+i)} + \frac{D}{(1+i)^2} + \frac{D}{(1+i)^3} + \qquad \ldots\ldots\ldots\ldots (3)$$

If g is considered as a constant dividend growth rate, the valuation model takes the form of Equation (4).

$$P_o = \frac{D_1}{(1+i)} + \frac{D_1(1+g)}{(1+i)^2} + \frac{D_1(1+g)^2}{(1+i)^3} + \qquad \ldots\ldots\ldots\ldots (4)$$

Fortunately, there is a simple formula for the sum of this geometric series[2]. If i is greater than g then it simplifies to:

$$P_o = \frac{D_1}{i-g} \qquad \ldots\ldots\ldots\ldots (5)$$

Equation (5) is popularly known as constant growth model. Two assumptions underlying this equation deserve attention: a constant growth rate and infinite time horizon. Rather than forecast an explicit value of the dividend or earnings, many analysts start with ex post data of most recent years and project a growth rate g in subsequent years. There might have some variation between the actual and forecast. However, it should be recognized that the value for this growth rate g represents an average growth over the investor's time horizon, n years. Secondly, an infinite time horizon indicates mathematical convenience rather than investment reality. Instead of discounting over a finite time horizon of n years, where the value of n may vary between 5 and 50 years depending on the investors, it is assumed that discounting will take place over an infinite time horizon. It is, of course, recognized that the combination of these two assumptions implies the value of g must be an average growth rate over an infinite time horizon. The constant growth model is widely used and as such we will focus on this model. To arrive at the concept of PER, one merely has to divide both sides of the Equation (5) by earnings E. Then it becomes:

$$P_o/E = \frac{D/E}{i-g} \qquad \qquad (6)$$

Thus, as the model indicates, the key determinants of PER are the following:
1 D/E, the dividend payout ratio.
2 i, the discount rate used by the equity investors.
3 g, the growth rate of dividends.
Other things being equal, (a) the higher the payout ratio and the growth rate of dividends, the higher will be PER; (b) the higher the discount rate, the lower will be PER. It is needless to say that there is inverse relationship between payout ratios and the growth rate of dividends. This is because when the payout ratio is high, the retention ratio is low. A low retention ratio indicates a low rate of growth of dividends. It is obvious that the formula will yield meaningful results only if the value of the discount factor i is greater than the growth rate g. Otherwise, PER will be infinite or negative. This does not mean that PER is useless if the growth rate for certain companies is found higher in some years. It is only the long term growth rate which has relevance to the formulation.

The most common traditional index for investment decisions is the yield obtained by dividing the annual dividend by the purchase price of the stock. It enables the investor to determine the maximum price he can pay for a stock issue with a given dividend per share when he wants to secure a certain rate of return on the investment in comparison with the interest rate on savings and bond yield. In other words, the yield emphasizes the dividend rate. The implication of PER, on the other hand, goes one step further and underscores the relationship between the potential profit per share and stock price.

It is usually recognized that the yield on stocks should be higher than that on fixed-interest bearing securities like bonds and debentures because of the higher investment risk attached to stock investment than fixed interest-bearing securities. However, it is observed that with the rapid economic growth of the post war era and the development of economic policies, this relationship began to reverse itself around 1955 and stock purchase continued even when their yield fell below that of bonds and debentures. This phenomenon is known as

Table - 5.5
Comparative PER of the listed stocks at year end

Year	Price Earnings Ratio (Multiple)			
	Bangladesh	Japan	USA	UK
1986	10.30	47.3	14.91	11.84
1987	28.91	58.3	14.04	10.82
1988	8.07	58.4	10.38	9.49
1989	25.53	70.6	12.47	11.11
1990	12.09	39.8	11.66	10.10
1991	8.02	37.8	15.91	17.25
1992	8.87	36.7	15.24	21.74
1993	7.70	64.9	15.20	30.66
1994	23.12	79.5	12.70	17.81

Source: For Bangladesh estimated from various issues of DSE Stock Exchange Reviews, for others, TSE Monthly Statistics Report for First Section Stocks and Securities Research Institute, 1996.

'yield revolution'. As this 'yield revolution' emerged common in the United States, Europe and Japan, the emphasis upon the use of PER became stronger. Consequently, PER came to be recognized as one of the most important measures for investment decisions.

Table-5.5 provides a comparative picture of PER of Bangladesh, Japan, USA and UK. It is difficult to evaluate stock prices merely by looking at the figures of international comparison because of different accounting methods, discount rates used for pricing, and rate of profit growth. Nevertheless, it has some analytical relevance. This Table gives an impression that different standard for PER can be used for different countries. PERs for Japanese enterprises range from 36.7 to 79.5, for USA from 10.38 to 15.91, for UK from 9.49 to 30.66 and for Bangladesh from 8.02 to 28.91 for the period under consideration. The highest range is found for Japan and the lowest range is for USA. In Japan, PER suddenly dropped from 70.6 in 1989 to 39.8 in 1990 due to downward swing of Tokyo stock markets in early 1990. The common understanding is that Japanese share prices are relatively at high levels in terms of economic fundamentals. Table-5.5 shows that the highest PER is observed in 1987 and the lowest in 1993 in Bangladesh markets. This is consistent with the general price

Table - 5.6
Sector wise average PER of the listed stocks on DSE

Sector	1986	1987	1988	1989	1990	1991	1992	1993	1994	Average
Banks	25.4	85.5	9.2	-8.5	84.1	13.0	2.3	9.1	7.5	25.3
Investment	6.1	11.5	10.9	8.4	6.6	5.6	9.0	11.3	10.5	8.9
Engineering	4.9	8.5	8.9	35.0	8.4	5.7	9.9	4.7	16.0	11.3
Food & Allied Pro.	7.6	33.4	10.8	111.0	6.3	9.1	10.2	-0.2	6.8	21.7
Fuel and Power	9.1	11.2	11.1	12.2	6.7	5.3	12.7	11.0	11.3	10.1
Jute	-	0.1	-12.3	9.7	0.1	3.2	0.7	-0.5	14.5	1.9
Pharmac. & Chemicals	10.0	52.6	8.6	5.0	5.1	4.7	15.1	32.4	87.9	24.6
Paper & Printing	13.2	14.0	17.7	16.8	17.0	26.5	11.1	4.6	3.4	13.8
Service	6.1	6.1	6.1	6.1	6.1	6.1	3.0	3.0	2.0	5.0
Textile	4.1	6.4	9.4	4.7	9.7	9.3	8.7	7.0	4.6	7.1
Insurance	-	-	-	-	6.9	6.1	5.9	7.9	10.7	7.5
Misc.	10.1	12.9	9.1	7.8	-10.8	4.7	7.2	2.0	32.0	8.3

Note: PER calculated in December every year.

rise in 1987 and general price fall in 1993. Since PERs for Japanese and Bangladeshi firms display relatively high volatility, it would not be appropriate to consider this criterion as an absolutely proper standard for making investment decision. As PER has shown weak relevance to market reality, investors also need to pay attention to other measures such as a price-book value ratio (PBR). Based on the assets value of the enterprises and cash-flow multiple, PBR is stock price divided by cash flow (i.e., after-tax profit plus depreciation charges).

If we see the sector wise average PER of the listed stocks on DSE at Table-5.6, we find that the jute sector has the lowest PER as expected due to depressionary condition prevailing in this sector. Broadly speaking, 1987 shows higher PER in most of the sectors in comparison to other years. This corroborates the fact that higher market price of stocks was prevailing in 1987. In the period of rising stock prices, a strong tendency for the investing public to emphasize PER is observed at the time of stock purchase. But the rapid increase in stock prices caused by the excess demand pressures also results in a weakening of PER as a basis for investment decisions. In such a situation net worth of the company deserves greater attention implying investment decisions based on the ratio between price and net assets are more relevant. Strictly speaking, it is not easy to evaluate whether share prices are inflated by looking at indicators such as PERs and dividend yields. An international comparison of PERs, for instance, has to take into account different accounting methods, and also calculating a discount rate for share prices and long term rates of profit growth.

Dividend policy stabilization

Much has been written by authorities on corporation finance about stable dividend policy urging its necessity. Of course, the need for stabilization is not of the same degree of urgency in all cases, particularly so in 'closed corporations'[3]. But the urgency for stabilization is very great in case of corporations whose shares are widely distributed. Decisions regarding dividends and demand for external funds interact with each other as well as with investment. The determinants of dividends and hence retained earnings, and external finance need to be considered in order to attain planned level of investment. While analyzing dividend behavior, Lintner (1956) states that dividends represent primary and active decision variable and retained earning is a residual factor. Companies usually try to achieve a long run dividend payout ratio through a gradual process over a period of time. It is argued that the rationale for such a stable dividend policy is attributable to equity holders' preference for steady growth of income from their investment. Markets also pay for such stability. This indicates that lagged dividends and current earnings have their bearing on current dividends[4]. Among the shareholders, of course, two classes are to be distinguished - investors and speculators. So far as the speculators are concerned, they are in favor of constant fluctuations in the price of stocks. But the interest of genuine investors is altogether different. They desire stability in income from their investment. This in turn has its effect on the price of securities. For, only those securities will have greater demand from the investors which earn a stable dividend and consequently have a high and more stable value in the market. If the dividends declared by a security over a number of years are irregularly distributed, e.g., 8, 8, 6, 4, 4 averaging 6 percent, instead of 6 percent per annum, over a period of five years, then that security may command a lower price in the former case than the latter. In a study it has been revealed that about 70 percent of the investors in Bangladesh have preference for a moderate dividend payout ratio (Ahmed et al., 1993) suggesting a situation conducive for sustaining a stable dividend policy or maximization of the dividend in long run. Investment plans affect dividend policies in so far as there is a preference on the part of firms to grow through internal funds. In lean years when profits are low, firms may go for borrowing to keep the dividend rate stable. Alternatively, firms may resort to their own reserves for this purpose. A change in sales has its bearing upon working capital requirements and dividend payments. The effect of tax policies is also considered in the literature. Accordingly, empirical investigations on dividend behavior indicate that the impact of investment, external finance, change in sales and tax policies needs to be incorporated in explaining the dividend behavior. The demand for external finance is related to the firm's growth objectives. If the internal resources are not sufficient for the growth objectives provided by the market opportunities then the alternative open for the firm is external finance. The cost and risk associated with borrowing are relevant factors need to be considered in this case.

From the standpoint of the concern itself, a stable dividend policy is desirable for more than one reason. A corporation with stable dividend records finds good reception for any subsequent floatation and that at a premium too. It also improves the borrowing position of the corporation. A company on the road to progress will need money at every step for improvements and extensions. Such companies are, therefore, under frequent necessity of selling securities. The importance of this factor is all the more great in a country like Bangladesh where the propensity to invest in industrial securities is low. If stable dividend policy is pursued by the enterprises, it can help in augmenting the popularity of industrial securities.

One of the frequently raised issues about dividend policy is that dividend paid by the Bangladeshi enterprises is small and not paid in due time (Kashem, 1985). At times, however, this allegation may appear to be quite true, but a patient inquiry reveals that the policy is circumstantial. Our jute industry is a glaring example, where no dividend or a very low rate of dividends is paid for a long time. Otherwise, in general, the dividend declared seems to be reasonable. Of course, inordinate delay between declaration of a dividend and its payment is a real phenomenon in corporate behavior of Bangladesh enterprises. According to an instruction by the Ministry of Finance, government of Bangladesh companies should pay a dividend ratified by the shareholders in the AGM within 60 days after the meeting. But more than 54 percent of the investors reported it took more than 60 days after the AGM (Ahmed et al., 1993). The situation is expected to be improving with the establishment of SEC and some measures initiated by them in recent years. In this connection the relationship between the PERs of the DSE listed stocks and their dividend payment has been examined. For this purpose all the listed stocks have been classified into three groups, e.g., (i) those companies who never paid a dividend, (ii) those who paid a dividend every year and (iii) those who paid a dividend in some years continually. The averages of PER calculated for these three groups for two periods of time -1986 to 1989 and 1990 to 1994 - are shown in Table-5.7. First, let us see the average PER for the period from 1986 to 1989. Companies paying a dividend every year have the highest average PER representing 20.22 and the average PER of those companies who paid no dividend is the lowest representing 1.95. The average PER of the companies who paid dividends continually is 3.67 which is in between the two extreme groups. Again, PERs have displayed a similar trend for the five years period from 1990 to 1994. For this period PER of the first category appears to be marginally higher than the second category, and the third category companies are demonstrating lower level of PER for both the periods. These figures suggest that the market regards a dividend and a regular dividend is likely to be evaluated positively by the market which can stimulate the share price. Accordingly, stable dividend policy might have significant influence on PER of the enterprises in Bangladesh.

Table-5.7
Average PER of companies and associated cash dividend

Types of Company	Average PER	
	1986-1989	1990-1994
i. Paid Dividend Every Year	20.22	11.21
ii. Paid Dividend in Some Years	3.67	10.99
iii. Paid no Dividend	1.95	0.55

Notes: i. Two cases of abnormally high PER have been excluded. ii. Average PER of individual enterprise has been used for this purpose.

The question of stabilization of dividend policy has not altogether been neglected in Bangladesh, although it has not received the same sort of treatment as in other countries. Japan has demonstrated a policy of a stable dividend. If we look to the average dividend rate of Japanese firms at Table-5.4, it is evident that a stable dividend policy is followed by them. Most Japanese enterprises stabilized their dividend at 10 percent of face value and hence investing in stocks became more advantageous than keeping funds under the short term rate (Oka, 1991). As a result, 'the dividend per share remained unchanged under the fixed-dividend policy, which resulted in higher dividend yield' (Akimoto, 1991).

This stable dividend policy of Japanese enterprises, among others, might have its influence on the higher PER when compared with those of other countries. As a matter of practical policy, adoption of two sorts of measures is advisable in view of the preference for stable dividend policy in a country like Bangladesh. In the first place, efforts should be made by the management of each enterprise to declare dividends at such a level which can be maintained in the foreseeable future. Secondly, Dividend Equalization Fund may be instituted by the enterprises with the objective to equalize the rate of dividends over the years.

Individual shareholders generally prefer dividends. Corporations, on the other hand, prefer to minimize dividends in order to meet their investment needs. 'In a period when corporate capital is scarce, when corporate investment opportunities are expanding, and when capital gains are taxed at low rates, it is clearer than ever that dividends are a 'bad buy' for most stockholders'(Loomis, 1968). However, dividend and capital gain are assessed differently by individual and corporate investors in practice in view of the tax structure and other relevant factors prevailing in an economy. In Bangladesh, dividend incomes of individuals are not taxed up to a certain limit and the capital gains on sales of listed securities have been exempted from tax but dividend incomes of companies have not been exempted. In Japan, the dividend incomes of companies have not been exempted from tax rather tax is payable on such incomes at a usual rate while interlocking stockholding can avail the tax benefit when this is done by the borrowed fund (Nakatani, 1984). Corporations, in Japan, have typically relied more on debt financing than has been usual in other industrialized countries. Interest charges for Japanese nonfinancial corporations were approximately 53 percent of operating income in 1971 while the similar figure for U.S. nonfinancial corporations was approximately 35 percent (Flath, 1984)[5]. This might have induced the Japanese enterprises for interlocking stockholding and seeking high leverage very often referred to as 'overborrowing'. High share of Japanese business corporations in total share holding probably reflect these conditions[6]. It is evident that investors are mainly interested in buying the shares of the big companies who have higher degrees of goodwill and higher rate of a dividend. On the other hand, when a company is closely held, as occurs in Bangladesh, its management may prefer for a tax or expansion reasons to keep dividend payment low, thereby tending to reduce potential investors' interest (Robbins, 1980). Futatsugi (1986) shows that the reciprocal share holding of the Japanese firms has permitted them to ignore the obvious market demand for a higher dividend implied by the imperfections and uncertainties of the market. In this connection Baumol (1965) is quoted as:

...A very substantial proportion of American business firms manage to avoid the direct disciplining influence of the securities market, or at least to evade the type of discipline which can be imposed by the provision of funds to inefficient firms only on extremely unfavorable terms. A company which makes no direct use of the stock market as a source of capital can apparently, proceed to make its decision confident in its immunity from this type of punishment by its impersonal mechanism of the stock market.

Finance theory suggests that the tax deductibility of interest is a marginal advantage of debt financing since dividend payment is not allowed such advantage in case of equity financing. Corporations tend to balance it against the higher expectation of failure costs that undertakes higher level of debt financing. It has been argued that the tax deductibility of interest can't explain the higher leverage in Japan, because tax rates on corporate income are not significantly different from that of the U.S. (Wallich and Wallich, 1976). The higher leverage may be conceived as insulation from business failure costs, perhaps, because the Japanese government act as the tacit guarantor of private loans, at least to large firms (Caves and Uekusa, 1976 and Wallich and Wallich, 1976). Although corporate tax rates are comparable in the U.S. and Japan, personal tax rates are much lower in Japan. Both corporate and personal taxes have important bearing upon the overall marginal tax advantage of corporate debt financing. When capital gains are largely untaxed, a reduction in all other personal taxes increases the pass-through of interest income by a larger percentage than it increases the pass-through of equity income which comprises dividend and capital gains. Thus, the relatively low personal tax rates might imply that the marginal tax advantage is larger in Japan (Flath, 1984).

In order to restrain management from withholding dividend payments despite available earnings, Bangladesh had a penalty tax rate that was imposed if a company earned a certain level of profits and did not declare dividends. This was eliminated in 1978 so that management may retain more of the earnings and facilitate expansion. In Japan low dividend payments are sometimes appraised as disadvantageous for the capital market to play its due role as a pool of long term funds for business enterprises and in providing better investment opportunity for investors (Ahmed, 1988). Reintroduction of the former tax policy supports the securities market and capital formation in the long run on the one hand and exemption of tax favors in the short run on the other. It is rather desirable to follow a path that maintains balance between long run and short run objectives.

Concluding remarks

It is recognized that the influence of dividend decision in the stock price mechanism has some valid reasons. Dividends convey valuable information to the investors and it has been documented that managers' behavior also appears to be consistent with this view (Lintner, 1956). Although other alternatives exist through which managers can disseminate information (Pettit, 1972) but dividends are highly visible compared with other announcements in addition to its credibility of cash signals. Business enterprises in Bangladesh should, in their own interest, follow a stable dividend policy and this implies a conservative pay-out ratio. The shareholders should also realize that a conservative dividend policy may apparently be prejudicial to their interest in so far as they are not allowed to share in high profits. But really they are not losers. For, even in bad years it will be the policy of the concern to maintain the rate of dividends from the Dividend Equalization Fund even though no or very low profit is earned. Besides, by raising the confidence of the shareholders in a particular scrip, a stable rate facilitates capital appreciation which is beneficial to all concerned including the shareholders. Hence greater emphasis should be put on this aspect of the issue. Anyway, security markets provide investors a means to trade freely and timely, issuers to raise funds cheaply and smoothly and the economy to allocate resources efficiently. But the securities markets in Bangladesh have not yet developed to accomplish these functions at a desired level. Institutional structure has also been suffering from various limitations. Lack of professionalism, alleged oligarchy among the exchange brokers, weak legal framework and execution thereof have significant impact on securities market development. Price manipulation and other market abuses like insider trading, underhand dealing and the like are likely to stem from such situations. The efforts need to be directed toward eliminating these weaknesses of the market. The concerned authorities should continue their endeavor to such areas like broadening the active membership of the exchange, ensuring fairness and transparency, enhancing professionalism, increasing the number of securities listed, integrity, stability and liquidity of the market and so on.

Notes

1. Under lock-in system a foreign investor in shares cannot sell his shares within a year. In view of the large impact of foreign funds on the relatively small market of Bangladesh lock-in system was introduced. This was abolished in the budget of 1996-97.

2. We need to calculate the sum of an infinite geometric series:
   (A) $P_o = a(1 + X + X^2 + X^3 + ...)$ where $a = D_1/(1+i)$ and $X = (1+g)/(1+i)$.
   Multiplying both sides by X we have:
   (B) $P_o X = a(X + X^2 + X^3 + ...)$
   Subtracting (B) from (A) gives us $P_o = a/(1-X)$. Substituting for a and X in this formula, we find that $P_o = D_1/(i-g)$.

3. 'Closed corporations' are those whose shares are mostly held by family members, relatives and friends and these shares are not sold outside for retaining control.

4. Lintner's model can be shown as follows: $d_t - d_{t-1} = z(D_t - d_{t-1}) + x$, where D_t is desired dividend and z is coefficient bounded between zero and one, reflecting the rapidity of adjustment. The desired dividend is a fraction of current profits represented by $D_t = rP_t$, where r is target payout ratio and P is profits. Substituting for the unobserved d, the first equation can be re-written as $d_t = zrP_t + (1-z)d_{t-1} + x$.

5. However, according to Kuroda and Oritani (1980) the difference in interest as a fraction of earnings will diminish to some extent if financial subsidiaries are consolidated and financial lease payments are considered as interest.

6. In case of Japan this share is represented by financial institutions (43.8 percent) and business corporations (23.9 percent) while the share of business corporations in Bangladesh is almost zero (TSE, 1995).

6 Capital market theory and Bangladesh market

Under conditions of complete certainty, perfect capital markets and rational wealth maximizing behavior, the dominant normative proposition in the micro-theory of investment can be stated as ' . . . the firm should adjust its capital stock until the marginal rate of return on further investment (or reinvestment) is equal to the cost of capital' (Miller and Modigliani, 1966). Since by these assumptions, there can exist one and only one rate of interest for any holding period, and since it is assumed that all future cash flows are fixed, the solution is both well known and simple. However, many of the theoretical assumptions do not apply in practice. It is by analyzing the difference between the assumptions of the theory and the constraints of the reality that many of the ways of bringing them closer and thereby increasing efficiency will naturally emerge. Under certainty the saving can be invested in one kind of asset for certain earnings but in case of uncertainty, which appears to be unavoidable in the real world, anyone must have to undertake the liability of risk due to uncertain future earnings on assets or securities. The potential investors, individual or corporation, are faced with a capital market of considerable sophistication offering a wide range of investment opportunities. The prerequisites for 'a perfectly competitive market' are generally identified in finance literature as:

1. A large number of buyers and sellers exist so that no single buyer or seller can affect the price by his activities.
2. The products being exchanged in the market must be identical.
3. Both buyers and sellers must have complete information about all aspects of transaction without transaction cost.

Substantial empirical work has been done to test the efficiency of capital markets. The earlier works have been summarized by Fama (1970) and then by

Samuels (1981). Samuels concludes that only New York, London and Tokyo markets are reasonably efficient. However, no market will ever be perfectly efficient, and one can only rank stock markets by their degree of efficiency. Efficiency of the market operation of shares within a stock market suffers from some limitations. Samuels (1981) and Lloyd (1977) have identified some types of inefficiency in organized capital markets. These are: i) limited supply of securities with an inadequate number of traders in all cases and in many cases seriously so, ii) different risk preferences and perceptions of investors, iii) the number of buyers and sellers is limited and in many markets they have tended to become increasingly dominated by a section of investors, iv) inadequate market regulations and standards of disclosure of companies and lack of competent analysts and professional advisors, v) in most markets there are certainly no free entry or exit and transaction costs for various activities can be relatively expensive, and vi) the extent of knowledge regarding market conditions is far from perfect. In fact, in many occasions the markets have tended to flourish on insider information. These difficulties have considerable bearing on the efficient operation of a market and they need to be recognized and dealt with effectively. This Chapter will review the capital market theory and provide some empirical results.

Expected utility and investment decision

Since investment decision is related to consumption decision, both these issues need to be considered simultaneously. It is assumed that if the investor has wealth w_1 at period 1 in a two period horizon, he is to allocate it to current consumption c_1 and to an investment $(w_1 - c_1) = I_1$ in some portfolio of securities. This will provide terminal wealth $\tilde{w}_2$ which will be completely consumed at period 2, i.e., $\tilde{c}_2 = \tilde{w}_2$. It is also assumed that the consumer is faced with a perfect capital market. That is, selection of an investment portfolio can be approached by commencing with a set of fully liquid perfectly reversible and completely divisible assets (Tobin, 1965).

At period 1 investor faces the problem of allocating his resources, w_1, to consumption c_1 and I_1 so that maximization of satisfaction from consumption of period 1 and 2 can be attained. Thus, the consumption, expected consumption and standard deviation of consumption at period 2 will be:

$$\tilde{c}_2 = \tilde{w}_2 = (w_1 - c_1)(1 + \tilde{R}_p) \qquad (1)$$

$$E(\tilde{c}_2) = (w_1 - c_1)(1 + E(\tilde{R}_p)) \qquad (2)$$

$$\sigma(\tilde{c}_2)=(w_1-c_1)\sigma(\tilde{R}_p) \qquad (3)$$

Where ~ indicates random variable, R_p is the return on the portfolio p from period 1 to period 2 and σ indicates standard deviation.

While we may know the probability associated with any given outcome, we never can predict exactly what the result of an investment will be. With risk, a given expected return on one asset may be more desirable than the same expected return on another asset. For example, probability function $f(R)$ and $g(R)$ is defined as follows:

$$f(R) = \begin{bmatrix} .5 \text{ for } R = 5 \\ .5 \text{ for } R = 15 \end{bmatrix}$$

$$g(R) = \begin{bmatrix} .5 \text{ for } R = 0 \\ .5 \text{ for } R = 20 \end{bmatrix}$$

Although the expected return is 10 with either probability function, the probability of experiencing an outcome from these two probability functions is quite different. Rational investors may well be justified in disagreeing on the relative desirability of these two functions. Since the dispersion of probabilities differ, the risk also differs. In most work in the area of portfolio analysis under conditions of risk, the key to the solution of this problem of differing degrees of risk has been the expected utility axiom. That is, in order to characterize the investor as risk-averse, he is assumed to behave in such way so as to maximize expected utility. This is computed from the function $U(c_1, c_2)$, which is assumed to be monotone increasing. Thus,

$$\frac{\delta U(c_1,c_2)}{\delta c_1} > 0 \qquad \text{and} \qquad \frac{\delta U(c_1,c_2)}{\delta c_2} > 0$$

If R_p is the one-period rate of return[1] on portfolio p, then consumption in period 2 is $\tilde{c}_2 = (w_1 - {}_1c)(1+\tilde{R}_p)$ assuming, $w_1 - c$ is invested in p at period 1. Accordingly, $E(\tilde{c}_2)$ and standard deviation $\delta(\tilde{c}_2)$ of $\tilde{c}_2$ are related to $E(\tilde{R}_p)$ and $\delta(\tilde{R}_p)$ (For further details see Fama and Miller, 1972). It is customary to impose the following specific restrictions on the utility surface.

$$\frac{\delta UE(\tilde{c}_2)}{\delta E(\tilde{R}_p)} > 0 \quad \text{and} \quad \frac{\delta UE(\tilde{c}_2)}{\delta \sigma(\tilde{R}_p)} < 0$$

It implies that utility is increased by a higher expected return and decreased by greater risk. Since consumers are characterized as risk averse additional risk must be compensated by larger expected return to keep utility constant.

Stock market behavior in Bangladesh

In finance literature stock markets in the United States have been extensively examined. American capital markets are considered well organized and efficient. Presumably, market participants are well informed and sophisticated with interaction (competition) among participants eliminating any price dependencies. Only competitive rates of return are earned and prices adjust 'instantaneously' to new information. In England, the results are less decisive. According to a study 'considerably more dependence might exist in U.K. shares than in those of the United States' (Dryden, 1970). Using these capital market theories there has been little research that deals with developing securities markets like Bangladesh. With the resumption of DSE activities since 1976, the structure of the Bangladesh financial markets has changed and the number of listed securities has been increasing rapidly. Naturally, the functions of stock markets are getting increasing importance. It is, therefore, worthwhile to study the Bangladesh stock markets with the objective to clarify whether or not the asset pricing model works there. This insinuates that the risk-return relationship for the stocks listed on the DSE is to be examined. The answer to this question implies, among others, a test of Capital Asset Pricing Model (CAPM). An attempt has been made toward that end in this Chapter.

Among various investment options equity investment is considered as the riskiest of all owing to the fact that both the dividend income and capital appreciation components of equity returns are uncertain. Of course, the degree of risk difference is difficult to calculate. On the risk spectrum of various financial assets, government debt usually is at the lowest end of the risk scale, followed by bank deposits rising the risk up toward corporate bond and common stock in the following order:

High Risk	Common Stock (new issue)	High Return
	Common Stock (listed)	
	Mutual Fund	
	Corporate Bond	
	Bank Deposit	
Low Risk	Government Debt	Low Return

The hypotheses that the risk premium increases with the increase in the riskiness of security holding are equivalent to saying that there exist positive excess returns on higher risk securities when we move in succession along the risk spectrum of security investments. A risk spectrum may be distorted with the change of socioeconomic conditions[2]. The American evidence confirms the notion that common stocks are appropriately priced relative to other less risky securities in the sense of their rates of return being higher than on other securities. Ibbotson and Sinquefield (1976) have found that U.S. common stocks returned 8.5 percent per year compounded annually over the period, 1926-74, *vis-a-vis* 3.6 percent for corporate bonds, 3.2 percent for long term government bonds, and 2.2 percent for U.S. treasury bills, a rate which is approximately equal to the rate of inflation. Excluding dividends, common stocks returned 3.5 percent per year and the inflation adjusted stock returns were 6.1 percent per year, subscribing the notion that common stocks were good hedges against inflation.

Investors receive return on common stock investment in three forms: cash dividend, capital gain (loss), and distribution of capital in the form of rights offering and bonus shares. If the holding period is long, say 5 years or longer, then an investor would be expected to receive in all these forms. The overall returns one gets in the long run is called 'investment return'. If instead the holding period is short, say a month or greater, most of the investor's return will be in the form of price appreciation (capital gain) or depreciation (capital loss). As the stock prices are highly unpredictable, the short term common stock returns are 'speculative' in nature. Speculative return is thus distinguishable from investment return in that the former is highly unpredictable whereas, the latter is reasonablely predictable (Malkiel, 1981). However, common stocks are generally viewed as long term investment vehicles. In revealing some of the fundamental features of the Bangladesh stock market two questions are pertinent: i) What rates of return do investors earn on the average from their investments in the stocks? ii) How much risk do they bear? The rate of return on equity during an investment period is defined as the growth rate of the total market value of the stock from the beginning to the end of the period. It can be calculated as a ratio dividing the sum of the capital gain $(P_t - P_{t-1})$ and the dividend (D_t) by the amount of the initial investment (P_{t-1}) as follows:

$$R_t = \frac{(P_t - P_{t-1}) + D_t}{P_{t-1}} \quad \ldots\ldots\ldots\ldots \quad (4)$$

There are no ready-made return figures of stocks traded in DSE. Using the above formula we have calculated the average monthly market rate of return from the market index prepared by BB and average monthly interest rate on time deposit for a period of 16 years from 1980 to 1995 at Table-6.1. The Table brings out that the average monthly market rate of return for the period is 2.46 percent while the corresponding monthly interest rate on time deposit is 0.943

Table-6.1
Year wise average monthly return from shares and monthly rate of interest on time deposit *(Figures in %)*

Year	Average monthly market rate of return	Monthly rate of interest
1980 - 95	2.46	0.943
1980	1.21	1.167
1981	1.27	1.167
1982	1.39	1.167
1983	2.07	1.167
1984	3.64	1.167
1985	1.97	1.167
1986	3.68	1.167
1987	11.48	1.104
1988	2.24	1.104
1989	1.06	1.104
1990	-1.02	0.830
1991	-1.86	0.750
1992	-1.17	0.630@
1993	3.39	0.500@
1994	9.82	0.420@
1995	0.18	0.480@
Standard deviation	3.49	0.281

Notes: Time Deposit interest rate is as of the end of December each year and monthly rate is calculated through dividing one year interest rate on one year time deposit by 12. @This is the minimum rate set by the monetary authority as individual bank is allowed to decide the interest rates on deposits within a range since 1992.

percent. The average monthly rate of return is found considerably higher in most of these years than the monthly rate of interest on time deposit (considered as riskfree). In some years negative returns on stocks are also observed. The rate of interest varies from 0.420 percent to 1.167 percent while the rate of stock returns varies from - 1.86 percent to 11.48 percent during the period under consideration. Thus, the variation for stock returns is also higher than that of interest rates. In terms of standard deviation it is 0.281 for interest rates and 3.49 for stock returns. This subscribes the finance theory that higher risk is associated with higher return and low risk with low return. This is also true, in general, in case of the average return and risk combination of individual stocks as is evident from the analysis of the following sections. That is, the stock yielding higher rate of return is associated with higher risk and vice versa. It appears that stock investment in Bangladesh is attractive although fluctuations in returns are observed. This is what we mean by risk. However, after tax returns on various government bonds with a maximum investment limit sometimes may be higher than equity investment in Bangladesh[3]. When we see the average monthly rate of return for each year, we find that a rising tendency is followed by a falling one resulting in periodical fluctuation. Consequently, changes in rates of return do not move in one direction as is expected.

Capital Asset Pricing Model (CAPM)

The relationship between expected return and risk is the central theme of the capital market theory. It is with the problems surrounding choice under uncertainty that Markowitz (1952) and Tobin (1958) first concerned them. The origine of the theory lies with Markowitz, who was a pioneer in demonstrating formally that diversification of security holdings reduces the risk, unless the returns to the securities are perfectly correlated[4]. He has theorized that investors could diversify away all sorts of risks except the risk that comes with holding stocks in general. Later among others, Sharpe (1964), Lintner (1965) and Mossin (1966) have investigated the implications of this model for the equilibrium structure of asset prices and divided the total risk into two components. The first component is known as systematic risk or market risk and the second as unsystematic risk or non market risk. While systematic risk results from a common market factor, the unsystematic risk results from factors unique to a particular security or company or portfolio. In other words, systematic risk depends on the extent to which the asset price is sensitive to market swings and can't be eliminated by diversification. Unsystematic risk is independent of the market and can be eliminated by diversification. Consequently, it follows that the expected return on a diversifying portfolio becomes dependent upon the level of systematic risk. In more familiar terms, the expected rate of return on any asset can be written as the riskfree rate of interest plus the asset's normalized covariance with the market times the difference between market's expected rate of return and the riskfree rate. This model and the pricing result came to be variously known as the 'Capital Asset Pricing Model (CAPM)', 'capital market theory' or the 'market line theory'

Efficiency in resource allocation may be judged with reference to the pricing mechanism of the stock markets. CAPM is a method employed for knowing the stock prices that are set every day. It can serve as a real signal of the allocative efficiency of capital resources. The model relates the expected return on a security or portfolio of securities or other assets to the risk of investment. CAPM is aimed at providing analytical framework for finding possible solution to some of the problems inherent in classical economic approaches to investment decisions. One of such problems is the failure to explicitly recognize risk in relation to investment return. An investor using this model may deliberately choose a higher than average portfolio risk on which he would expect to receive a correspondingly higher return. The cautious investors may choose a lower degree of risk and receive a correspondingly lower return. The major assumptions underlying the CAPM are as follows:

1. Investors are risk averse who maximize the expected utility of their end-of-period wealth.
2. Investors are price takers and have homogeneous expectations about asset returns.
3. There exists a riskfree asset such that investors may borrow or lend unlimited amounts at the riskfree rate.
4. There are no market imperfections, investments are infinitely divisible, information is costless.
5. There is no transaction costs or taxes or interest rate change.
6. Capital markets are in equilibrium and all assets, including human capital, are marketable.

Some of these assumptions are obviously unrealistic, but they greatly simplify the model building process. Furthermore, even if these assumptions are relaxed, it is likely that the CAPM still holds approximately. Under these assumptions the model for security i would take the form as follows:

$$E(\widetilde{R}_i) = R_f + E(\widetilde{R}_m - R_f) \frac{cov\ (\widetilde{R}_i, \widetilde{R}_m)}{var\ (\widetilde{R}_m)} \quad \ldots\ldots\ldots\ldots (5)$$

Substituting β_i for $\dfrac{cov\ (\tilde{R}_i,\ \tilde{R}_m)}{var\ (\tilde{R}_m)}$, Equation (5) can be restated as

$$E(\tilde{R}_i) = R_f + \beta_i\ (E(\tilde{R}_m) - R_f)) \quad \ldots\ldots\ldots\ldots (6)$$

where $E(\tilde{R}_i)$ = expected return on security i,
R_f = riskfree rate of return,
$E(\tilde{R}_m)$ = expected return on the market portfolio, and
β_i = beta coefficient which measures the systematic risk of security i.

According to Equation (6), in equilibrium, the expected rate of return from a security is made up of the riskfree rate plus the risk premium multiplied by the beta coefficient of the relevant security or portfolio. For riskfree investment, therefore, β_i would be equal to zero and the investor's return is R_f. When $\beta_i > 0$, investors' expected earnings from that investment would be higher than R_f, i.e., $(E(\tilde{R}_m) - R_f) > 0$. If the riskfree rate on treasury bills is 6 percent and an expected rate of return on the market is 18 percent then the expected risk premium is 12 percent for risky assets. Using Equation (6), Table-6.2 presents the expected rate of return on risky assets for varying risk levels assumed. In this Table only systematic risk measured in terms of β_i has been considered. The unsystematic risk element $\alpha_i + \tilde{\varepsilon}_i$ which will be seen at Equation (7) in the market model, is not included since it is independent of market conditions and diversifiable. The market rewards investors with an appropriate higher rate of return for assuming systematic risk only because it is not diversifiable like unsystematic risk. A higher systematic risk is directly associated with a higher expected rate of return. This may have induced the risk averse investors to assume an additional degree of risk.

Table-6.2
Expected return for varying levels of systematic risk

β_i	$E(\tilde{R}_i)$
0.0	6%
0.5	12
1.0	18
1.5	24
2.0	30

A major breakthrough in the practical utilization of portfolio theory has come with Sharpe's (1964) development of the market model. He has suggested the use of a broad average like Dow-Jones Average as a surrogate for a market index. For security i the market model is:

$$\tilde{R}_i = \alpha_i + \beta_i \tilde{R}_m + \tilde{\varepsilon}_i \qquad (7)$$

Here α_i and β_i are parameters of respective securities, $\tilde{\varepsilon}_i$ is a random disturbance whose distribution is assumed to have expected value equal zero and $\tilde{R}_m$ is the aggregate rate of return on all securities in the market.

Apparently, this model identifies two elements of asset i - systematic risk and unsystematic risk. The former is represented by β_i and the latter is represented by $\alpha_i + \tilde{\varepsilon}_i$. β_i can be interpreted as a measure of risk contributed by security i in total risk as well as market sensitivity of the return on security i. A value of β_i greater than 1.0 implies a security with both above average market sensitivity and above average risk in the market portfolio, while value of β_i less than 1.0 indicates below average market sensitivity and risk in the market portfolio.

According to CAPM, systematic risk, commonly referred to as the beta of a security or portfolio is identified as the proper measure of risk of that security or portfolio. The average return on the portfolio is predicted to be directly related to the beta of the portfolio. While the concept of a beta has been contemplated with such considerable emphasis for practical purposes, this is still unfamiliar to the majority of investors and other market participants in Bangladesh. The correlation of the portfolio to the market index, measured by R^2, indicates how much of the variability in the returns on the portfolio or security is associated with variability in the market. The higher R^2 indicates the portfolio is more perfectly diversified. An R^2 equal to one would indicate perfect correlation.

CAPM suggests that high-risk, high return strategy will return more on the average than low-risk, low-return strategies and that high-risk, high-return strategy will bring greater losses in bear markets than will low-risk, low-return strategies. The average return of a portfolio is simply the weighted average of the average returns of its component securities where the proportion of value is used as weights. Moreover, the beta of a portfolio is a weighted average of the betas of its component securities, with the proportion of value used as weights. Finally, the beta of a well-diversified portfolio provides a good surrogate for its total risk, since almost all fluctuations in the portfolio's value will follow market swings.

Stocks with high beta values should have high returns on the average. They may be said to be in a high risk-return class. On the other hand, stocks with low beta values should have low returns on the average. They may be said to be in a low risk-return class. This relationship may be used as a basis for selecting an investment strategy. If one desires high return he should select stocks that will, in fact, have high beta values in the future. It may be noted that the accuracy of the association between the betas of two periods has been extensively tested by Blume (1975). Blume estimated betas on single stock portfolios, 2 stock portfolios and so on up to 50 stock portfolios and examined the correlation of betas between two periods. It has been observed while betas on larger portfolios of two periods are highly correlated, those of the individual securities are less correlated. This might be due to change in riskiness (beta) in a different point of time. In addition, a beta is estimated with a random error and if the random error is large, then the beta is less consistent in different time periods. The value of a beta in some cases increases while others decrease with the change of risk in different time periods and thereby cancel out when a large number of securities are combined in a portfolio. This leads to the high correlation of beta values of larger portfolios in two time periods than smaller ones. Blume (1975) and Vasicek (1973) have suggested methods for adjustment of beta values so that forecast can be made with better accuracy. However, in some cases it has been assumed that the beta is reasonably stable over time which procedure was used by Black et al. (1972).

Efficacy of CAPM and the developing market

There are two important problems in testing CAPM. First, it is concerned with expected returns, whereas we can observe only actual returns. Second, the market portfolio should include all risky investments, whereas most market indexes contain only a sample of common stocks (Roll, 1977). The important points of Roll's criticism in his own language are as follows:

> Deviations from the return/beta linearity relation are frequently linked with some other phenomenon. The validity of such linkages is criticized using the Jensen measure of portfolio performance as an example. If the 'market proxy used in the calculations is exactly (not significantly different from) ex-post efficient, all of the individual Jensen performance measures gross of expenses will be identically (not significantly different from) zero. They can be (significantly) non-zero only if the proxy market portfolio is (significantly) not efficient. But if the proxy market portfolio is not efficient, what is the justification for using it as a benchmark in performance evaluation?

This statement explicitly questions the use of security market line. In a more specific term, his objection about the use of a market portfolio is as follows:

> The theory is not testable unless the exact composition of the true market portfolio is known and used in the tests. This implies that the theory is not testable unless all individual assets are included in the sample.

The importance of Roll's objection is clear. But operational efficiency of CAPM is better than many of the economic models. Myers and Rice (1978) have refuted this critique to the extent they have shown that under fairly general conditions, performance tests using the CAPM can give meaningful results. There is a general agreement that β is a useful measure of the risk of a security or portfolio and high beta securities are priced to yield a correspondingly high rate of return. Fama (1976) has focussed on the term 'market' in the following words:

> Thus, in deriving testable implications of the hypothesis that the capital market is efficient, we structure the world in terms of 'market' that assesses probability distributions on future prices then sets current prices on the basis of these assessed distributions. Strictly speaking, this implies that investors have monolithic opinions about available information and act single-mindedly to ensure that their assessments are properly reflected in current prices. What we really have in mind, however, is a market where there is indeed disagreement among investors but where the force of common judgements is sufficient to produce an orderly adjustment of prices to new information.

Capital market theory is likely to contribute substantially to explaining the behavior of relatively efficient markets, and can be a powerful tool of analysis. CAPM has been tested in several statistical studies using different methods[5]. The results showed substantial support for the model. Many of the results are summarized by Modigliani and Pogue (1974) in the following words: '1) The evidence shows a significant positive relationship between realized returns and systematic risk. However, the slope of the relationship (γ_1) is usually less than predicted by the CAPM. 2) The relationship between risk and return appears to be linear. The studies give no evidence of significant curvature in the risk-return relationship. 3) Tests that attempt to discriminate between the effects of systematic and unsystematic risks do not yield definitive results. Both kinds of risk appear to be positively related to security returns. However, there is substantial support for the proposition that the relationship between return and unsystematic risk is at least partly spurious - that is, it partly reflects statistical problems rather than the true nature of capital markets.' Nichols (1993) has pointed out that 'Indeed, these theories have become such an essential part of doing business that one finance textbook urged students to tattoo their prescriptions on their foreheads'.

Of late, the capital market theory is under attack from various sides. A group of critics believes that a new financial paradigm will emerge from the study of nonlinear dynamics and chaos theory. Some argue that investors are not always rational. Moreover, the validity of a beta has been questioned by another group including Fama (see Fama et al., 1992). Some efforts have been applied in determining whether the Japanese stock market prices securities in accordance with efficient market hypotheses (EMH) and CAPM. The empirical findings are not consistent with these theories[6]. Again, certain phenomena appear in the stock markets throughout the world which defy rational expectation. It is empirical regularity that the returns of small firms, on average, exceed those of the large firms in January[7]. To the extent the risk-return tradeoff shows up only certain months of the year much of the modern finance theory is brought into question. Fama et al. (1992) have questioned the CAPM and concluded that the model has failed to describe the last 50 years of average stock returns. In other words, they have described a beta as a wrong measure of risk. Such growing skepticism has led people to question modern finance theory in general and EMH and CAPM in particular. It is argued that CAPM 'fixes too high a cost of capital for some companies that should be encouraged to reinvest more freely, it fixes far too low a cost of capital for others, and it gets the right number for still others only by coincidence'(Lowenstein, 1991). Ross (1976) introduced a multi factor model known as Arbitrage Pricing Theory (APT) which he claimed as more flexible and robust than CAPM and possibly immune to the testing problems associated with CAPM. According to Shiller markets are more complex than theories would indicate. In his behavioral model he has attempted to explain market behavior as it did in the Black Monday Crash of October 19, 1987. 'There is no good economic reason why the nation's corporate equity should have lost nearly a sixth of its value in less than three hours . . . it appears that what happened on that day is old-fashioned speculative panic. People began to fear that because of the fears of other investors, stock prices would crash, and in effect they created the crash in an effort to get out of the market'(Shiller, 1992). So complete rationality does not hold and the investors' 'variable tendencies' can contribute toward developing such situations. Shiller continues, 'Investors may enter buy orders so that they can profit from future price increases, thereby causing further price increases. These further price increases may encourage yet more investors into the market and so on: a feedback loop - that is, a vicious circle - creates an upward trend in prices; the bubble grows.' Similar behavioral patterns might have caused bubbles burst. It follows that the investors' attention should be more on company fundamentals. In that effort managers should find 'relational investors,' long term investors like those in the Germany and Japanese systems who consider the company's real value for the long term.

However, in view of the complexity prevailing in the financial markets, it is reasonable to think that no one number nor single answer would provide an adequate explanation of the problems. Simultaneously, it is also true that multidimensional models are associated with problems that only a privileged can fully conceive. Moreover, the results of the study of MacKinlay (1995) 'suggest that multifactor pricing models alone do not entirely resolve CAPM deviations.' 'Whatever the shortcomings of using the CAPM to estimate the risk-adjusted discount rate, it may be no worse than the alternatives, and may even be better in countries which do have organized capital markets' (Kitchen, 1993). In fact some weaknesses of the CAPM have been identified but a better alternative asset pricing theory has not yet been developed in order to invalidate it. Stigler (1966) has put it as follows: 'The answer is that it takes a theory to beat a theory. If there is a theory that is right 51 percent of the time, it will be used until a better one comes along.' Thus, it is likely that CAPM and EMH will continue to dominate in spite of their limitations until some better workable alternatives are available.

The use of CAPM to allocate resources to projects of developing countries may lead to a misallocation of resources because of the market imperfections and distortions are likely to be greater in these countries. Its applicability in less efficient capital market seems to be much less certain. Market imperfections may be dominant in developing markets, particularly during their formative stages. However, capital market theory may tend to be increasingly relevant with the development of markets and environment. In case of a developing market like Bangladesh the efficient market hypotheses may be, a priori, suspect for a variety of reasons. Errunza (1977) in his paper has commented: '...However, at present, it is doubtful whether substantial insight could be gained from application of CAPM to the developing markets. This is because many of the LDC markets are not very active and available LDC stock market indexes are of doubtful quality, consistency or reliability.' The presumed 'inefficiency' implied by such markets might stem from structural as well as institutional issues such as the following: i) in developing economies, capital markets have difficulty in detecting and discriminating among investment opportunities; ii) composition of outputs may respond sluggishly to changes in relative prices; iii) a dichotomy exists in financial activities between organized and centrally controlled banks, acting loan windows at subsidized interest rates, and private and unorganized money markets catering largely to demands outside government control; iv) the capital markets are 'fragmented' in terms of information and communication; v) temporal horizons are short; vi) investment preference is given to physical assets rather than financial assets (Shaw, 1973). This may result in lack of financial development, particularly in capital markets, consequent upon certain market imperfections such as transaction costs, lack of timely information, costs of acquiring new information, and possibly greater uncertainty about the future (Goldsmith, 1971; Mason, 1972; Shaw, 1973). If some or all of these factors are operative, it is likely to suspect that they may be reflected in market mechanisms. In general, the principle seems to survive, although not entirely unscathed. The inefficiencies, even in organized markets, mean that the risk is not proportional to the variance of return. Risk estimates may be extremely hazy because of lack of information (Kitchen, 1993). Errunza (1977) has pointed out 'portfolio suppression' (political and economic instability, monetary and fiscal policies which result in high and unstable rates of inflation, interest rate controls, lack of capital market institutions, high transaction costs, etc.) as obstacles to foreign portfolio investment in the securities of developing countries. However, the study of Gandhi et al (1980) on Kuwait stock markets has observed substantial scope for gains through diversification. Agmon and Lessard (1977) have reported in a study of four stock markets in Latin America over the period 1958-68 that risk could be diversified away to the level of about 16 percent to 30 percent in these countries, whereas 70 percent of the risk can be diversified away in the U.S.A. by holding a diversified portfolio. Obviously, diversification in these countries does reduce risk, but not to the same extent as in developed countries.

Testing methods and empirical results

In this study data used are end of the month price, data relating to dividend and stock split, if any, of the 25 selected stocks listed on the DSE. The end of the month price data is considered as the beginning price of the next month. These data were taken from the Investment Scoreboard data published in the Stock Exchange Review, a monthly publication of the DSE. We have calculated the monthly return of each stock from these data using Equation (4). In case of unavailability of stock Exchange Review, the respective data are collected from the daily Bangladesh Observer where the daily stock price data are published.

The selected 25 stocks representing most of the industries were considered for the period of five years from 1985 to 1989. The investigation was done for this period considering easy and reliable data availability. Market return is calculated from the General Price Index data constructed by Bangladesh Bank and dividend data preserved in the computer of DSE to use as surrogate for market. During this period the number of companies listed on the DSE was as follows:

1985 - 72
1986 - 82
1987 - 90
1988 - 101
1989 - 112

Accordingly these samples cover 34.72 percent in 1985, 30.49 percent in 1986, 27.78 percent in 1987, 24.75 percent in 1988 and 22.32 percent in 1989 of the population.

Risk can be measured in many ways. A measure is focused here that emphasizes the impact of swings in the market on the return from a security or portfolio. If there were no prospect of a bear market, there would be little risk in the common meaning of the term. Stocks are considered risky because their price can go down. Typically, the more sensitive a security or portfolio is to the swings in the market, the more it goes down in a bear market. In order to measure it, the slope of a regression line relating return on the portfolio to the return on a broadly-based portfolio usually used to represent 'the market' is considered. The slope of such line is termed as 'beta'. More formally, it is the covariance between R_i and R_m divided by variance of R_m. The covariance is:

$$\frac{\sum_{i=1}^{N}(R_{it}-\bar{R}_i)(R_{mt}-\bar{R}_m)}{N} \quad \text{and the variance is:} \quad \frac{\sum_{i=1}^{N}(R_{mt}-\bar{R}_m)^2}{N}.$$

For the purpose of this study, return calculated from the General Price Index of Bangladesh Bank has been used to measure R_m. It is important to recognize that beta may not provide an adequate measure of the total risk of a stock. However, for well-diversified portfolios, the majority of the variation in return is attributable to changes in the return on the market. Thus, a beta provides a good measure of risk. It seems worthwhile to examine the results of a test of CAPM to see if higher return has been associated with higher risk as measured by beta. Sharpe and Cooper (1972) examined the listed stocks of New York Stock Exchange whether following alternative strategies, with respect to risk would produce returns consistent with CAPM. The general approach of Sharpe and Cooper with some modification has been adapted for the stocks of DSE[8]. A beta at a point of time is measured using 12 months of previous data. This procedure is repeated every year. Table-6.3 presents the realized rates of return and the betas of different assets during the period from 1985 to 1989. This risk-return relationship in most cases appears to be consistent with general principle of a higher beta is related with higher return.

Table - 6.3
Rates of return, standard deviations and betas for selected stocks

Name of the Stocks	Average Monthly Return	Standard Deviation	Beta
Glaxo Bangladesh	0.1397	0.4570	2.2660
National Tea Co.	0.0187	0.0863	1.1570
Singer Bangladesh	0.4630	0.1443	0.9016
Burma Eastern	0.0808	0.2363	0.7123
Paper Converting	0.0212	0.0851	0.6004
Bangla Process	0.0019	0.0795	0.5762
Bangladesh Lamp	0.0375	0.1182	0.5661
Second ICB Mutual Fund	0.0944	0.1301	0.5245
Pubali Bank	0.0103	0.0798	0.5223
Bangladesh Shipping Co.	-0.0057	0.0479	0.4962
Ashraf Textile	0.0262	0.1042	0.4024
First ICB Mutual Fund	0.0637	0.1602	0.3915
Oxygen Bangladesh	0.0919	0.2535	0.3541
Uttara Bank	0.0244	0.0730	0.3461
Monno Stafflers	0.0203	0.0513	0.3309
Islami Bank	0.0056	0.0557	0.2865
Monno Ceramic	0.0236	0.0845	0.2818
Apex Foods	0.0294	0.0775	0.2267
National Bank	0.0105	0.0640	0.2220
A.B. Bank	0.0226	0.1579	0.1960
Delta Jute	0.0018	0.0057	0.1368
Bengal Carbide	0.0491	0.1044	0.1223
GMG Industrial Copn.	-0.0035	0.0239	0.0678
Bangas	0.0422	0.1183	0.0234
ICI	0.0042	0.0624	0.0155

Note: 8 months from January to August have been considered for 1989.

In order to get portfolios with different beta values we have divided stocks into five risk-classes based on the beta value of each security. In other words, selected stocks are divided into five classes ranking them by their respective betas. Classes or strategies are numbered from 1 to 5 where number 1 is the lowest risk class or strategy and number 5 is the highest risk class or strategy. An equally weighted portfolio is formed of the stocks that comprised each class. That is, stocks are bought and sold until the portfolio contains an equal investment amount in all stocks of a particular risk-return class at a point of time. Rebalancing is, therefore, required both to accommodate changes in the set of stocks in a class and to account for price changes.

Table-6.4 shows what would happen, on average, if an investor had done

Table - 6.4
Average return and portfolio beta

Strategy/Class	Average Return	Portfolio Beta
5	0.06	1.13
4	0.03	0.54
3	0.05	0.37
2	0.02	0.24
1	0.02	0.07

this for the period from 1985 to 1989. It appears that the strategy/class on the basis of beta value can be followed by an investor of the DSE. If any investor wants to pursue the high beta strategy, he simply divides his funds equally among the stocks in the highest beta class. In terms of average monthly return for each strategy, strategy 5 provides a return of 0.06 per month while strategy 1 provides 0.02. It is observed that although the values do not maintain perfect uniformity in respect of each class, the general relationship is of the expected type, i.e., portfolios composed of securities in lower risk-return strategies or classes tend to provide lower average return. The coefficient of determination between strategies and return is about 0.71.

The estimated values of a portfolio beta for the five strategies are also seen in the Table. Returns obtained with strategy 5 moved 13 percent more than the market as a whole. On the contrary, returns obtained with strategy 1 moved only 7 percent of the market as a whole. In this case also the values do not decrease with perfect uniformity. However, the general relationship appears to be of the expected type, i.e., portfolios composed of securities in lower risk-return classes tend to move less with swings in the market. The findings of this study are consistent with that of Yalawar (1988) who concluded that 'The return risk relationship as envisaged by the CAPM is operative over a greater part of active equities market in India.'

The next logical step is to examine the relationship between the return that would have been earned and the risk (beta) from following alternative strategies. The relationship appears to be positive and linear. The equation of this relationship is:

$$\bar{R}_i = 0.017 + 0.04\beta_i \quad \dots\dots\dots\dots\dots \quad (8)$$

By and large, stocks with higher betas have produced higher return. In fact, R^2 between return and risk (beta) is 0.71. That is, about 71 percent of the variation in expected return is explained by differences in beta. It follows that beta has explained a very significant portion of the difference in return between these portfolios. Accordingly, this study suggests with clear and easily interpreted evidence that, as the general equilibrium theory indicates, there is positive relationship between return and beta. Of course, only one strategy is found to be riskier than the market. It is pertinent to note that due to many factors including shorter time period, smaller number of companies, market inefficiency and so forth, the results are likely to conform less than what should be. However, the main results of this study show that roughly 30 percent of total risk of a portfolio of stocks listed on the DSE can be eliminated by diversification and the remaining systematic risk, measured by beta, can't be diversified away.

These results broadly suggest that the investment in risky assets is rewarded in Bangladesh for the risk taking. It tends to show that the expected realized rate of return is related to the systematic risk as opposed to total risk of securities. Since the unsystematic risk is relatively easily eliminated, markets should not be expected to offer a risk premium for bearing it. Besides, the beta gives the systematic risk of a security or a portfolio relative to the risk of the market index. Thus, it is often convenient to speak of security or portfolio risk in terms of systematic risk or beta. Since the beta is assumed to be reasonably stable over time (Black et al., 1972) buying of stocks/portfolios with a higher forecast beta would lead to holding portfolios with higher realized return.

DSE has introduced a new price index since 1986. We have considered this new index to test the CAPM using a different method. Table-6.5 provides the annual return of equities in nominal terms for a period ten years from 1987 to 1996. This return is measured by the changes in the index, and the dividend yields. The sum of the two shows the return for each year receivable for an investment in the index at the beginning of the year. This may be considered as a proxy for the return attainable by the 'average' stock market investor. We have assumed a risk-averse investor, who holds a diversified holding which approximates to the market index. Following the CAPM we may have the relationship below:

$$E(R_m) = R_f + \text{risk premium} \quad \ldots\ldots\ldots\ldots\ldots\ldots(9)$$

Where $E(R_m)$ is expected return on the market, and R_f is the riskfree rate of return. For R_f we have taken the return on treasury bills (TBs). These returns are lower than that of long term government securities, but the latter are more subject to inflation risk and also lower return when the investor is forced to sell

Table - 6.5
Nominal returns on ordinary shares, TBs and risk premium

(Figures in % per annum)

Year	Return on equity	Return on TBs.**	Risk premium
1987	34.64	8.00	26.64
1988	74.04	8.00	66.04
1989	10.66	8.00	2.66
1990	-12.28	7.50	-19.78
1991	-22.32	7.00	-29.32
1992	-13.98	7.00	-20.98
1993	40.71	4.00	36.71
1994	117.90	3.50	114.40
1995	2.16	3.50	-1.34
1996*	41.44	3.50	37.90
Arithmatic mean	27.30	6.00	21.31
Standard deviation	41.80	1.97	42.55
Geometric mean	23.19	5.63	20.34

Notes: *This year's figure is estimated based on the information of 31 July. **The rates are for end of December each year and accordingly, the figures represent the return for buying TBs on 1 January and holding them for one year.

before maturity. If we compare nominal return of risky securities with corresponding return on riskfree treasury bills, we find higher return for the risky securities. The difference between these two constitutes a risk premium - reward for risk taking in equity investment. In 6 out of 10 years of investment results in DSE stocks, the risk premium was positive. Table-6.5 provides arithmetic mean giving the average return, standard deviation measuring the riskiness of equity investment and also the geometric mean. It is evident from these that higher risk in equity investment is associated with higher rate of return and lower risk in treasury bills associated with lower rate return.

Thus, the implications of these results are substantial. That is to say, the price changes of stocks listed on the DSE - reflecting a less developed country - are likely to conform to the general stock price behavior predicted in the finance theory. The findings of this study are expected to deepen the insights of the academics, investors, investment analysts, policy makers and other interested parties.

Accounting information and security market

Information plays a very important role in security markets. It influences security price formation and thereby influences the optimal portfolio selection. Economic theory of choice postulates that the decision maker seeks the best option out of available alternatives in order to attain optimum results. Accounting information can aptly play a vital role by indicating, in concrete terms, the result of economic actions. In enterprises where individuals invest and manage the business simultaneously, then ownership and management are inseparable. But in a typical joint stock company, most investors provide money and do not participate in the management which is accomplished by somebody else. Thus, the concept of 'absentee investors' emerged. The investors purchase shares of the company with the expectation to get return from it in the form of dividend and capital gain. They will retain the shares if these are considered relatively profitable and will sell if these are considered unattractive. Thus, the investors mainly depend on the management's report usually in the form of financial statements reflecting enterprise's economic and financial performance. Accounting principles indicate more than merely to provide information to the shareholders. While users may differ like shareholders, creditors, and managers, their economic decisions are similar. All of them consider the actual or potential net gain. Chambers (1979) has pointed out:

> At no point has it been necessary to consider the idiosyncratic features of decision-makers, the users of the information. It should be apparent that any party interested in the financial affairs of an enterprise is interested in its solvency, its debt-dependence, its asset composition and its rate of return. All four are expressive of aspects of its performance, and anyone or more of them may be suggestive of trading and financing prospects. Accountants cannot know how the assessments of users will take account of the specific features of a given enterprise. They can have no idea of 'degrees of relevance' of information to particular users, or of the rate of exchange at which some relevance may be 'traded off' for some reliability (or any other characteristic) by any user . . . In the light of that ineluctable ignorance, the only course to adopt is to ensure the 'representational faithfulness' of the indicators of solvency, debt-dependence, asset composition and rate of return - for between them, those indicators embrace every element of periodical

financial statements.

Capital market theory assumes efficient markets. Resource allocation activities take place through pricing of securities available in the market. Efficient security pricing is, therefore, tantamount to efficient fund allocation by the market. The securities are said to be efficiently priced if investors can expect appropriate rewards for bearing risk. The relationship between security prices and information made available to the market has been explained by the EMH. It was Fama (1965) who told that there was no way to beat the markets and only unforeseen events can affect prices. Random events are as likely to affect stock prices positively as negatively. Thus, investors are rational and rational investors trade only on new information, not on intuition, that can be derived from Fama's hypothesis. That means price of securities observed at any time are based on 'correct' evaluation of all information available at that time (Fama, 1976). However, capital market efficiency is defined in a number of ways (Rubinstein, 1975). Financial economists use the term 'efficient' in a sense different from other economists. In a 'financially efficient' market, prices fully reflect all available information. On the other hand, an 'economically efficient' market allocates resources in a way which is 'Pareto efficient', i.e., no one can be better off without someone else made worse off. Much of the finance literature on capital market efficiency focuses on the informational efficiency. An interesting point is that capital markets in some countries are hopelessly 'inefficient' in economic sense, yet the market may be 'financially efficient' in that new information arrives randomly and stock prices adjust instantaneously reflecting the new information. Accordingly, the random character of stock price behavior is attributed partly to the informational efficiency of the markets (Fama, 1970). However, the capital markets in developing countries are informationally efficient, yet inefficient in other senses (Sharma, 1983). It has been recognized for a long time that one important role of accounting information is to facilitate the decision making of interested groups. Staubus (1961) has stated that accounting is an information activity for decision making[9].

In developing countries, particularly, lack of confidence in an unknown management or in the economy itself has often resulted in hesitancy on the part of prospective domestic investors to entrust their funds to an enterprise. The auditor, through his independence, competence, and integrity supplies the needed credibility for financial reports. As has been proven in many developed countries like the United States and the United Kingdom, the existence of a well-recognized and well-established accounting profession has influenced significantly the development of domestic capital markets

(Washington SyCip, 1967).

Earnings reports, inflation accounting, segment reporting etc. are all considered to be required from the recognition that accounting should function by providing relevant information for decision making of interested groups. When annual announcements are considered as accounting information announcements, price activity in the announcement week is greater than that of the nonreport period. It is also confirmed that investors consider annual announcements as having more information value than interim announcements (Otsuka, 1983). According to Beaver (1970) if an announcement contained new information about the expectations of a company, then that new information would be immediately impounded in the price of that company's stock. This may take place either through the changes in the equilibrium price of a security or reflect in terms of value. Beaver has hypothesized that either one or both of these reactions can take place depending upon risk preferences of investors and the extent of changes in the expectations of the market vs. the expectations of individual investors. Abnormal price changes would result from changes in the expectations of the market as a whole and abnormal volume activity would reflect changes in the expectations of individual investors (Beaver, 1970).

However, Lev and Yahalomi (1972) have shown that while Beaver found reaction to earnings announcements on the New York Stock Exchange, such reaction was not found on the Israeli Stock Exchange. They attributed the differences in results of the two studies to one of the following factors: a) the Israeli stock exchange does not react to earnings information, b) changes in the structure of the Israeli stock markets and the earnings announcement processes are sufficiently different from the New York markets to preclude such a reaction, and c) the results of the tests are incomparable on the basis of statistical probabilities. Deakin et al. (1974) have pointed out that if there is no abnormal reaction in price or in volume, this might be due to the fact that the market has either: a) anticipated the announcement, thus the formal announcement itself has no information value; or b) the announcement is of little or no use to the investor and the process which generated it is of no use to the investor; or c) the market does not efficiently absorb new information as hypothesized in the efficient market literatures; or d) sample design and the methodology chosen are insufficient to test these hypotheses. About 50 percent or more of all information about an individual firm that becomes available in the market during the year is captured in that year's earnings figure (Ball and Brown,1986). Beaver (1970) has indicated that investors do shift portfolio positions at the time of the earnings announcements, and this shift is consistent with the contention that earnings reports have information content.

Systematic risk arises from the relationship between the return on a stock and that on the market and it is also clear from the foregoing discussion that the risk of a firm should be determined by some combination of the fundamentals of individual firm and the market characteristics of that firm's security. Beaver et al. (1970) have studied the relationship between systematic risk (beta) of a stock and accounting measures of risk (fundamental firm variables). They considered seven variables of the firm and the beta on a firm's stock. These were:

1. Dividend payout ratio, i.e., dividend divided by earnings.
2. Growth in a firm's assets in terms of change in total assets.
3. Leverage, i.e., senior securities divided by total assets.
4. Liquidity, i.e., ratio of current assets to current liabilities.
5. Firm's asset size.
6. Variability of earnings in terms of standard deviation of the earnings-price ratio.
7. Earnings covariability using an analogous value for accounting income. They termed this as 'accounting beta'.

They have used these seven accounting variables to compute cross-sectional correlation coefficients between each variable and the systematic risk for 307 firms and concluded that accounting risk variables can be used to select and to rank portfolios such that the ranking has a high degree of correlation with ranking the same portfolios according to systematic risk. The evidence is consistent with the contention that the accounting risk measures are impounded in the market risk measures. Apparently, it appears that information contained in financial statements is useful in estimating risk and deserves importance from the viewpoint of portfolio investment.

Let us now see the contents of financial statements published by the companies of Bangladesh. A typical annual report and account that usually presented to the equity holders of Bangladeshi companies contain the accounting information in the form of a comparative Balance Sheet and a comparative Manufacturing, Profit and Loss Account of two years - current year and previous year - supplemented with a yearly Schedule of fixed assets. Announcements are made by the companies through press for declaration of dividend, right offer or other affairs. However, press reports providing various information is not adequate. Companies Act and Securities and Exchange Rules (SER) of Bangladesh have provided some rules for disclosure of company information. Although it is not precise in some occasions, the contents, timing and quality of these statements does not fit the essence of these rules in most cases. Although it has been stipulated in the SER to provide interim information to the stock exchange and shareholders within one month after the end of first six months of accounting year, shareholders in most cases, do not get any interim information from the company on its financial performance (Ahmed et al., 1993). In the same study it has been revealed that more than 50 per cent of the companies fail to hold annual general meeting (AGM) within nine months after the end of their accounting year. It implies that shareholders and other users of information do not formally get information on corporate performance in due time. The qualitative aspect of information depends mainly on the intention of the company rather than on rules. The method of preparation is determined by both accounting assumptions and conventions which permit the exercise of discretion by the accountant within generally accepted principle. However, these conventions and practices have been subject to various criticisms. For instance, Carrington has noted that:

> ...concern has concentrated on the failure of published accounting reports to give adequate warning of the imminent financial collapse of apparently substantial businesses and on the inadequacy with which asset values are stated, often leading to sacrifice of shareholders' interest predatory takeovers. Difficulties in making valid inter-company comparisons, and distortion of trends, through inadequately disclosed items or transactions have also received adverse comments from financial analysts . . . Others have been frustrated by accounting data rendered irrelevant by arbitrarily determined expense apportionments, depreciation provisions and inventory valuations. Economists also have long criticized accounting for use of unrealistic measures lacking any reasonable relationship to economic values (Carrington, 1977).

However, it would not be right to conclude that information provided in these statements are totally irrelevant. Rather, nature and quality of information need to be considered according to the objectivity and practicability. According to various accounting conventions, statutory requirements, accounting standards, and modern practices, the published accounts might normally be expected to contain six components. These are the balance sheet, the profit and loss (revenue) account, auditors' report, notes to the accounts, fund flow statement and comparative figures. These components can provide a good measure of the extent to which accounts are prepared with the objective of communicating information. The investigation of the accounts of Bangladeshi companies has revealed that:

> In general, public enterprise accounts are out-of-date, incomplete, poorly designed, not properly consolidated, and invariably produced in English. The accounts of quoted and other companies are only better in comparison. Banks tend rigidity to follow the prescribed formats, with both its merits and its inadequacies. The accounts which our initial overview indicates as best are

those of the multinationals. Even here, there are deficiencies, and we suspect the accounts would not compare well with the accounts prepared by the parent company in the country of origin. Nevertheless, according to our tests the multinationals stand out in comparison to other categories. Since the multinational use Bangladeshi accounting expertise, we wonder why there is no apparent 'transfer of technology' to improve the standard of other categories of entities (Parry and Khan, 1984).

It is more serious when the inadequacy occurs within the dominant public enterprises and when the actual content of the accounting reports reveals so many deficiencies and anomalies. The type of information provided in the annual reports is purely historical and does not deal explicitly with risk considerations nor future cash flows associated with equity holders' investment. Future earnings probability has long been of great deal of interest to the investors, security analysts and accountants. Accordingly management should include, in the reports and accounts of Bangladeshi companies, information relating to future cash flows of the firms. Investors should be provided with the firm's future profitability, management's plans and capability, social responsibility as well as market and industry forces and other related items of information in addition to these financial statements. Some public enterprises have made some commendable efforts to use their reports to convey information about their activities.

The results of this study may raise some questions about adequacy, nature and content of information set postulated by the capital market theory. Obviously, the information set is not complete and it is much smaller than the information set available in advanced economies. In this connection it can be seen what kind of information usually the investors get about companies listed on TSE, one of the leading stock exchanges in the world. According to Deakin et al. (1974) 465 information releases were classified as either quantitative information releases or qualitative information releases. Quantitative information releases were defined as those releases related to earnings and provided numerical analysis of either sales, production, earnings or dividends. Specific figures or ratios may be quoted for a company, or the company's position may have been revealed on the basis of comparison to other companies or to a market average. Qualitative information releases are more subjective in nature and are defined as those which require the reader to exercise judgement to determine the possible effect on earnings of this announcement of prospective events. It includes such information as technology discoveries, purchases or exchanges of discoveries, new product information, new investments or disinvestments, new operating or marketing policies, corporate adjustments necessitated by competitive environment, new financing arrangements and new or prospective sales of individual projects or sales to individual customers where no immediate effect on total earnings could be determined. Equipped with such information investors, particularly individual investors, could be considered in a better position to predict their investment cash flows and assess the risk associated with these cash flows.

In the light of the above major deficiencies about company information which can greatly influence on the efficient operation of the markets in Bangladesh may be summed up as follows:

1. Information contained in published company accounts is inadequate.
2. The extent to which information published in accounts is out of date by the time it is publicly available.
3. The existence of a number of unscrupulous companies which use their accounts in order to conceal fundamental facts about the financial position of the company.
4. The non existence of a structure of extensive public analysis and criticism of such information as is published.
5. The non existence of both high standards and effective machinery to enforce those standards and a strong, independent financial press for ensuring the accountability necessary to keep and improve these standards.

Capital markets in Bangladesh are still in its infancy and investors are not so skill in evaluating business and economic performance like those of the developed countries. No empirical research, perhaps, has yet been conducted focussing on the type of market parameters relating to Bangladesh markets discussed in this Chapter. ICB could offer some guidance in this regard but ICB and its schemes were in 'serious lapses' as we have seen in Chapter 3. With the establishment of SEC, it is expected that it will come forward to accomplish this responsibility for the investors. This may accelerate the development process of the stock markets. Further research into the characteristics of stock markets of Bangladesh using various methodologies would be of value. However, in order to attain sound business enterprises as well as sustained economic growth of the economy of Bangladesh, the current problems of accounting system need to be addressed immediately and rationally so that induction of foreign capital, justification of taxation, proper industrial financing and development of capital markets in the right direction can take place.

One possible implication arises with the CAPM application is the issue of calculating the cost of capital. A popularly accepted method of calculating cost of capital depends on the CAPM theory to defend the use of a beta. Our empirical analysis shows this method may bring forth good results in practice. Of course, introduction of a well designed accounting system and availability of accurate and adequate information in time can make it better. It appears to be a good example of a theoretically elegant model that gives a good answer for asset pricing. However, theories and methods that are dependent on the CAPM require careful attention and scrutiny when they are applied to the analysis of actual problems.

Concluding remarks

The results of empirical testing of CAPM in Bangladesh have presented an appealing approach for investment decisions. As such, it can possibly contribute substantially in explaining the behavior of relatively less efficient developing market like Bangladesh. In view of the deficiency in information set available in developing countries like Bangladesh the results are likely to be questioned on its adequacy, nature and information content. Of course, it seems difficult to provide sufficient information about future because of the existence of real world uncertainty. Probable future events can be foreseen to some extent through many sophisticated statistical tools. Moreover, in view of the heterogeneous nature of investors' expectations, any attempt to aggregate individual investors' expectation will face difficulties. Despite these facts, efforts should be made to make accounting information more relevant qualitatively and quantitatively to investors' needs. It is true that accounting information is not the only source of information to the security markets. Government pronouncements, press releases are also there. They are ultimately reflected in the reported financial statements which the existing and potential investors are supposed to use in making their investment decisions. In fact, the investors are implicitly interested in the prospective market values of the shares and possible fluctuations in these values which imply the associated return and risk. Existing and potential shareholders are interested in information that is likely to make predictions about the future behavior of different elements related to the future values of investments. However, based on different tests Sharma et al. (1977) have also concluded that stocks on the Bombay Stock Exchange obey a random walk and are equivalent in this sense to the behavior of stock prices in the markets of industrialized countries like U.S.A. and U.K. However, its applicability is likely to be less certain in view of the market imperfections. It should be remembered that the capital market theory does not incorporate such an intangible factor as human psychology, instead investors are considered rational to make the model rather simple. This makes the capital market theory less credible in approach and questionable in its applicability.

Appendix-6.1

Mean-Variance Approach of Markowitz

Markowitz two-parameter mean variance approach may be summarized as below.

In the portfolio selection model, an investor is to choose fractions $x_1, x_2, \ldots, x_N$ of total fund that will be invested in N assets subject to constraints.

$$\sum_{i=1}^{N} x_i = 1 \quad \text{and} \quad x_i \geq 0 \quad i = 1, 2, \ldots, N$$

If the returns for a period on individual assets, $R_1, R_2, \ldots, R_N$ are jointly distributed random variables then the return and expected return on the portfolio are:

$$R_p = \sum_{i=1}^{N} x_i R_i$$

$$E(R_p) = \sum_{i=1}^{N} x_i \bar{R}_i \quad \text{where,} \quad \bar{R}_i = E(R_i)$$

Here E is used as expected value operator. The variance of return, $\sigma^2(R_p)$, on the portfolio is (where σ_i is the standard deviation of the ith security):

$$\sigma^2(R_p) = \sum_{i=1}^{N} x_i^2 \sigma_i^2 + \sum_{i=1}^{N} \sum_{\substack{j=1 \\ j \neq i}}^{N} x_i x_j \sigma_{ij}$$

Where σ_{ij} is the covariance of returns between two securities i and j. Besides, σ_{ij} is the correlation of the two returns multiplied by their standard deviation, i.e., $\sigma_{ij} = \rho_{ij}\sigma_i\sigma_j$, where ρ_{ij} is the correlation coefficient of the returns to i and j, and σ_i, σ_j are the standard deviations of returns to i and j. Substituting σ_{ij} in the above equation, we get:

$$\sigma^2(R_p) = \sum_{i=1}^{N} x_i^2 \sigma_i^2 + \sum_{i=1}^{N} \sum_{\substack{j=1 \\ j \neq i}}^{N} x_i x_j \rho_{ij} \sigma_i \sigma_j$$

In order to explain the impact of diversification on risk (measured in terms of variance or standard deviation) a case of two securities 1 and 2 is presented for simplicity. 100 percent of funds can be invested either in 1 or in 2, or diversified between 1 and 2. It may be assumed that $\sigma_1 = \sigma_2 = \sigma$.

(a) If 100 percent is invested in 1 (i.e., $x_2 = 0$; $N = 1$) then $\sigma^2(R_p) = \sigma_1^2 = \sigma^2$.
(b) If 100 percent is invested in 2 (i.e., $x_1 = 0$; $N = 1$) then $\sigma^2(R_p) = \sigma_2^2 = \sigma^2$.
(c) If x_1 invested in security 1 and x_2 in security 2 ($N = 2$; $x_2 = 1 - x_1$), then

$$\sigma^2(R_p) = x_1^2 \sigma^2 + (1 - x_1)^2 \sigma^2 + 2 x_1 (1 - x_1) \rho_{12} \sigma^2$$
$$= \sigma^2 [x_1^2 + (1 - x_1)^2 + 2 x_1 (1 - x_1) \rho_{12}]$$

Now $x_1^2 + (1 - x_1)^2 + 2 x_1 (1 - x_1) = [x_1 + (1 - x_1)]^2 = 1$
or $x_1^2 + (1 - x_1)^2 = 1 - 2 x_1 (1 - x_1)$

If correlation coefficient, $\rho_{12} = 1$, then $\sigma^2(R_p) = \sigma_1^2 = \sigma_2^2$ as in (a) and (b) above indicating no diversification. Diversification takes place only when $\rho_{12} < 1$. Then,

$$\sigma^2(R_p) = \sigma^2 [1 - 2 x_1 (1 - x_1) + 2 x_1 (1 - x_1) \rho_{12}]$$
$$= \sigma^2 [1 - 2 x_1 (1 - x_1)(1 - \rho_{12})]$$

If $\rho_{12} < 1$, then $(1 - \rho_{12})$ is positive and $(1 - x_1)$ is positive. Then $2 x_1 (1 - x_1)(1 - \rho_{12})$ is a positive number, z, and $\sigma^2(R_p) = (1 - z) < \sigma^2$. Accordingly the variance of return can always be reduced by diversification as long as correlation coefficient is not perfectly positive, i.e., $\rho_{12} < 1$.

Notes

1 One period rate of return on any investment is the capital gain (the market value of the investment at period 2 less the market value at period 1) plus dividend, divided by the market value at period 1.

2 For instance, risk spectrums may be distorted with the change of an inflation rate and fixed return investment may become less attractive than some equities.

3 With some exceptions these options are open to individuals only, even with certain maximum limit. This interest policy, possibly, is aimed at encouraging the small savers who are justifiably feeling too exposed to the risk of market manipulation and other abuses associated with some market constraints. In recent years interest rates on bank deposits and various government bonds have been reduced significantly.

4 See Appendix-6.1 for further details.

5   Some representative empirical studies on CAPM are: Fama and MacBeth (1973), Black et al. (1972), Miller and Scholes (1972), and Sharpe and Cooper (1972).

6   Some of the studies concerning Japanese markets that rejected the applicability of theoretical conjectures are: Maru and Royama (1974), Konya (1978), Hoshi (1986), Yonezawa and Maru (1984), Sakakibara (1986). However, the study of Lau et al. (1974) showed that investors in the TSE were compensated for bearing systematic risk.

7   In Japanese markets this phenomenon, known as seasonal and size anomaly, is found not only in January but also in other months of the year. See Kato and Schallheim (1985) and Ahmed (1992) for details.

8   The differentiating features of this study are mainly: First, they require 60 months of data to estimate a security's risk-return class, for the purpose of this study it requires only 12 months. Second, they use annual returns, monthly returns are used in this study. Finally, they apply the model in a developed market, it is applied in a developing market in this case.

9   It is possible to identify four specific ways in which published accounts can contribute to the process of economic development, viz., resource mobilization, resource allocation, resource control and national planning. In order to make these contributions published accounts should possess the characteristics of relevance, understandability, reliability, completeness, objectivity, timeliness, comparability and appropriateness.

7 Corporate finance and governance structure

The nature and structure of capital markets and corporate finance differ in different countries. In case of capital market development in advanced countries there was no initial perception of the eventual structure. Rather, they emerged in response to the changing conditions. The experience acquired by the developed capital markets may be employed in less developed countries to expedite the development of an efficient capital market. In Bangladesh, the problems of capital markets have been more serious and complicated due to inadequate savings and unorganized capital markets. The problems have come to the forefront in recent years with various policy measures emphasizing private sectors, deregulation and freer market economy have been envisaged by the government. Extensive discussion on corporate governance in recent years has increasingly drawn the attention of business community as well as academics for dealing with many of the problems associated with financial markets. The way managers are made liable to board of directors and thereby to stockholders is an important aspect of the functioning of a free enterprise economy. It is assumed that a corporate governance system should be designed primarily to ensure that the actions of a company's managers and directors accurately reflect the wishes of its shareholders (see for example, Easterbrook and Fischel, 1981; Lowenstein, 1988). However, there are major differences in the operation of management accountability in different countries. For example, the U.S. and British systems are classified as predominantly market-based in contrast to the bank-based system in Japan and Germany. In bank-based system, shareholders and lenders have close contacts with management through a variety of channels. Hence the ownership and control in this system appear to involve less problem than that of the U.K. and the U.S. market-based system. Stockholders' supremacy has hardly been a conspicuous feature of the corporate scene of Japan. This is not consistent with the theory underlying the system. Where market forces predominate in the capital market, shareholders can conveniently trade titles to ownership of a fraction of a company, while hardly being aware of their role as its owners. This contrasts with the bank-based systems associated with long term commitment and greater knowledge about borrowing firms developed by banks in the Japanese and German systems. These systems do not necessarily suffer from the same problems of recognizing and enforcing accountability to shareholders and lenders. Moreover, the economic performance of both Japan and Germany has far exceeded that of the U.S. and the U.K. in the post war period. This achievement can be partly attributed to the bank-based system of corporate governance in Japan and Germany. Capital markets in Japan experienced a radical structural change after World War II as a consequence of legislations introduced by the Occupation Authorities and the need to rebuild the war-ravaged economy. Besides, the Japanese capital market has been evolving continuously since the war. Thus, the 'traditional' practices have been adapted to a much more complex reality. The conventional standard economic theories developed in Anglo-American countries cannot give adequately convincing explanation of Japanese financial system. Japanese corporations with large number of enterprises organized to some extent in heterogeneous industrial groupings, have made a major contribution to growth. They are linked through reciprocal shareholding, and lender-borrower or buyer-seller relations demonstrating a financing and management system different from the West. Major commercial banks (city banks) have been the central organs of the present grouping. This type of affiliation among firms and financial institutions is not found so extensively in any other industrialized country[1]. U.S. government reports attribute Japan's competitive success in part to features of the Japanese system (Task Force (U.S.), 1990). Harvard Business School's major, multi-disciplinary study of American Management's time horizons recommends, as a way to combat 'short termism' among U.S. managers, restructuring American corporate governance so that it resembles Japan's more closely (Porter, 1992).

In neoclassical economic theory, the firm maximizes its profits or its market value. Under this paradigm, the objective of financial corporate groups must be to increase the profitability, individually or collectively, of the member firms. According to Caves and Uekusa (1976) while the joint profit maximization applies to the pre World War II *zaibatsu*, this is not true of the present day corporate groups. On the other hand, according to Kobayashi (1980) grouping increases the monopoly power of individual firms so that they can maintain stable sales networks at a lower cost, and at the same time, stabilize the price of the product they sell which, in turn, raise the profits of member firms. This Chapter examines the Japanese corporate finance and governance structure in the light of the existing theory. This will also shed light on their implications for a developing market like Bangladesh.

Individual shareholders

Since the Securities Democratization Movement, initiated under the leadership of the Securities Democratization Committee in November 1947, had released to the general public the large number of shares gathered in the hands of Holding Company Liquidation Committee upon the dissolution of the *zaibatsu*, share ownership by individuals exceeded 60 percent[2]. Apparently, a new phenomenon of large scale individual shareholding appeared for the first time. This was accompanied by a large degree of managerial independence as the prewar *zaibatsu* control mechanisms were abolished (Suzuki, 1992; Okazaki, 1993). However, with the reopening of the TSE in April 1949 a gradual process of transferring shares of individuals started through selling their recently acquired shares to large companies and financial institutions, often indirectly through securities houses. As a result, this proportion started declining year after year while the share of ownership by business corporations and financial institutions have gradually increased.

The share of individual stockholding has been more than 69 percent in 1949 and coming down to about 33 percent in 1975, to only about 26 percent in 1985 and less than 24 percent in 1994. On the contrary, the share of business corporations and financial institutions has risen from less than 16 percent in 1949 to about 61 percent in 1975 and more than 64 percent in 1994. When considered the share of financial institutions separately it also has shown a rising trend recording 9.9 percent in 1949 to about 34 percent in 1975 and to about 41 percent in 1994 (TSE Fact Book, 1995). Of course, the share of business corporations was little higher during 1971-73 than 1975 which is believed to be due to liberalization of capital markets in the early 1970s. This, however, does not indicate that the individuals' investment ratio (savings) has dropped. Rather, their investment preference has shifted from risky assets to riskfree assets. Among the riskfree assets the time deposits, which yields relatively higher earnings, has increased sharply from 26.6 percent of total household investment in financial assets during 1960-64 to 46.5 percent during 1975-79 (Yonezawa and Maru, 1984). One of the reasons often cited for individuals' relative preference for bank deposits and the like is the preferential treatment of interest income. By the Small Saving Tax Exempt System introduced in 1963, interest income from bank deposits not exceeding ¥ 3 million per individual and from postal savings deposits not exceeding ¥3 million per individual has been tax exempt. Interest income from deposits exceeding this upper limit can be taxed at 35 percent separately from other types of income if the depositor opts to do so. Substantial preferential tax measures for individual income from stockholding have been provided as well. First of all, in principle capital gains have not been taxable. Dividend income not exceeding ¥0.5 million can be taxed separately from other types of income at lower rates (20 percent for dividend income of less than ¥0.1 million per stock, and 35 percent for dividend income between ¥0.1 and ¥0.5 million per stock) (Aoki, 1984). From individual investors' viewpoint the following important reasons can be identified for the decline in the relative share in stock investment.

Attractiveness of stock investment

Average returns on stock investment have declined significantly from 4 to 5 percent around 1955 to a meager 1 percent after 1976 (Japan Securities Research Institute, 1986). Although new shares are issued at market price, returning of premiums to shareholders, thus gained, has not been carried out satisfactorily.

Diversification of investment

Since the investment in stock involves risk, the rational investors will diversify investment in order to avoid risk. But as far as individual is concerned, he is far away from optimum diversification in a real world due to financial and other limitations. In the stock market analysis the assumption of a perfect capital market in the sense that investor can buy as much as he wants of any investment asset without transaction cost is not applicable in real world condition. These are likely to have their bearing on the decreasing rate of investment in risky assets and the increasing rate of riskfree assets. The share of stock investment, which is considered as the most risky among all financial assets, has been getting down sharply from 20.6 percent of household assets in 1960-64 to 13.1 percent in 1965-69, 11.4 percent in 1970-74 and 7.9 percent in 1975-79 but the transition of investment ratios in securities other than stocks has shown an almost stable condition (Yonezawa et al., 1984).

Asset selection also depends on the level of investment, rules relating to investment, class of investors which in turn, perhaps, has influence on risk diversification. Yonezawa and Konya (1982) have shown that the entry into different segments of the market for different types of investors is regulated in Japan. For example, only stock markets are open to individuals whereas stock, *gensaki* (repos) and call markets are all, without regulation or with regulation, open to corporate investors. However, call markets are not open to industrial corporations. Besides, corporate institutions have larger amount of investable funds than individual and better diversification is possible by them. Obviously, corporate investors have a better possibility of eliminating unsystematic risk.

Cost volume

Transaction costs, information costs etc. are independent of the volume of investment and these costs are relatively high for the individual investors. Of course, individual can diversify investment through investment trusts. But in Japan they do not appear to be so attractive due to sharp decrease in the level of earnings from them since the second half of 1960s.

Whatever the reasons, if this trend continues, the importance of individual investors in the stock market will come down to a point where trading in stocks would loss momentum and formation of fair prices would be hampered. The effectiveness of stock markets may be weakened to such a level where it would be difficult for corporations to raise funds by selling their equity shares at market price. It implies that the stock market may be prevented from playing its due role as a pool of long term funds for business enterprises and in providing investment opportunity for the investors. Moreover, strengthening of control by corporate investors over other corporations through increasing stockholding may weaken the institutional device of joint stock company as an economic agent.

Corporate shareholders

The change in the ownership structure cannot necessarily be explained from the side of individual investors' behavior only. Corporate behavior has also its bearing on it. For understanding Japanese corporate capitalism, it is imperative to analyze the corporate practices like interenterprise relationship and cross shareholding that fostered business groups. Not only in Japan, the phenomenon of business groups can also be seen in many other countries where the market mechanism is the fundamental instrument of resource allocation. In these economies, the group is considered as an integral part of the resource allocation mechanism where internal organization can conceivably work as one of the institutional devices. Williamson (1975) has recognized this issue.

(1) Markets and firms are alternative instruments for completing a related set of transactions; (2) whether a set of transactions ought to be executed across markets or within a firm depends on the relative efficiency of each mode; (3) the costs of writing and executing complex contracts across a market vary with the characteristics of the human decision makers who are involved with

the transaction on the one hand, and the objective properties of the market on the other; and (4) although the human and environmental factors that impede exchanges between firms (across a market) manifest themselves somewhat differently within the firm, the same set of factors applies to both (Williamson, 1975).

Naturally, the resource allocation function is accomplished under the direction of the manager or through the market by market mechanism. Relative efficiency of the alternative ways for each transaction is a determinant factor for applying them in practice.

The cartel, the trust and the Konzern have long been familiar forms of enterprise combinations, but such a traditional approach is not adequate to explain the Japanese situation. The words like *zaibatsu, kigyoshudan* or *keiretsu* are used to give a meaningful explanation in Japanese context. These are the expressions referring to the combines, the estate of wealth, and by extension to the source of this wealth. In the vocabulary of some Japanese, these terms are used to indicate only the family dominated combines. And now-a-days these words not only carry the connotation of a family dominated combines but also has a time dimension. Many Japanese hold that the *zaibatsu* developed following World War I and *kigyoshudan* following World War II even though some *zaibatsu* like Mitsui and Sumitomo were the key Tokugawa merchant houses while Mitsubishi and Yasuda began and flourished early in the Meiji period.

In the West combines have grown on one industry or a group of closely related industries, with a view to achieving a monopolistic position. It was not so in Japan. The hierarchical value system of the nation, the special role of the government in the economy, the cumulative power of capital, the effective lobbying for privilege are the important factors which might have contributed to the unique development of combines in the form of *zaibatsu* and *kigyoshudan* or *keiretsu*. The similarities and dissimilarities between prewar *zaibatsu* and postwar *kigyoshudan* or *keiretsu* will make their meaning clear. Important similarities are as follows: Firstly, both of them have integrated a financial institution, such as, a bank, a general trading company (*sogo shosha*), and manufacturing companies into a group. Secondly, the large firm consists of many firms under an umbrella (*keiretsu*). Thirdly, both of them have dominated and led the Japanese economy since the Meiji Restoration of 1868.

Significant dissimilarities are also there. Firstly, the capital control structures are different from each other. In *zaibatsu* the capital control structure was vertical (pyramid structure) and centralized by the holding company. But in *kigyoshudan*, the interlocking directorate and cross shareholding have been developed into a horizontal and decentralized control system of management and capital. The control pattern over the subsidiaries and affiliates has been changed into a mutual control relationship. Secondly, The family monopoly domination over the capital in the prewar *zaibatsu* was thoroughly abolished by the Supreme Commander of the Allied Powers (SCAP) and in the postwar *kigyoshudan* the interlocking directorate, cross shareholding and the group presidents' meetings control and coordinate the business activities as a whole. Finally, the financial power of a bank within a *kigyoshudan* is much stronger than in the *zaibatsu*, because the bank has taken the place of the power of the *zaibatsu* family or that of the holding company. Thus, the important difference between *zaibatsu* and *kigyoshudan* in the managerial and capital control can be described as of pyramidal structure and circular structure respectively. The typical structures of these two types of groups are shown schematically in Figure-7.1 and Figure-7.2. These distinguishing features are very significant to understand the long term orientation of the Japanese firms' group behavior. The post war antitrust law not only prohibited the establishment of holding company but also restricted a financial institution from owning more than 10 percent

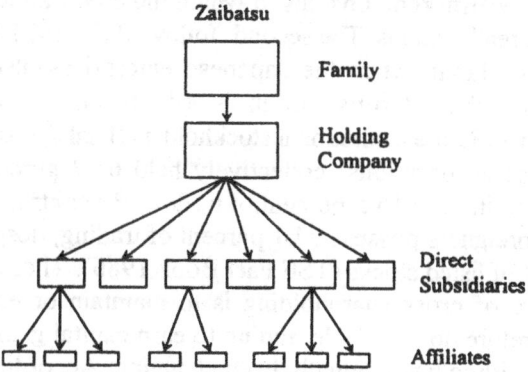

Figure-7.1
Structure of prewar business group

(the limit was 5 percent in 1948 but raised later according to the revision of Anti Trust Law, 1953) of outstanding equity of any single company in order to prevent financial institutions from functioning as *defacto* holding company. The result has been the formation of a new type of business groups through interlocking of stocks by a number of firms, including banks. This has raised corporate shareholding and lowered that of the individuals.

The two great waves of stock interchanges occurred in the early 1950s and early 1970s. In the first period, the *keiretsu* emerged from the remains of the prewar *zaibatsu*. In the 1950s and 1960s the BOJ used to limit total bank credit and directed the bank's sectoral allocations in general and sometimes in considerable detail through its direct and frequent contact with commercial banks in addition to interest rate policies. These policies had their likely effect

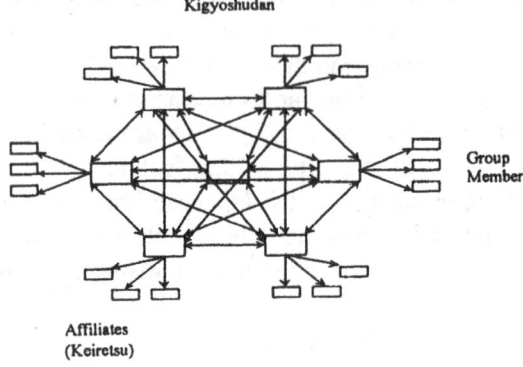

Figure-7.2
Structure of postwar business group

to increase the interfirm relationships in which the credit allocations could be modified through reallocations. The second followed the 1971 liberalization of capital flows into Japan when the Japanese enterprises also increased the holding rate within the enterprise group in order to face the offensive of the foreign capital. In 1985 the institutional stockholders (banks, insurance and non-financial business corporations) collectively held 61.7 percent of the listed shares but engaged in only 16.5 percent of trades. By contrast, security firms, individuals and foreigners possess 74.1 percent of trading, despite holding less than 34.3 percent of listed stocks (TSE Fact Book 1986). These figures suggest the major motive of cross shareholding is to maintain or enhance business relations and therefore do very little trading to earn capital gain. However, the motive of stockholding has gradually been changing. According to Yonezawa et al. (1984) the share of the non-financial business corporation was about 2-3 percent of the transactions before 1972 but it became as high as more than 10 percent after 1972. Since the plant and equipment investment of corporate institutions appeared to be stagnant after 1972, they were inclined to the investment in financial assets. Besides, there was hyper inflation due to excessive money supply at that time. In this inflationary process, price of stocks and other assets had been rising. Under the circumstances, enterprises were encouraged to search for profit from such investment without disturbing group ties. Corporations accounted for 30.5 percent of the total volume of trading in 1986, or double the 15.1 percent in 1975 on Japan's stock exchanges.

During the same period corporate ownership of publicly traded stocks rose to 66.3 percent from 61.5 percent, with a turnover ratio also doubling from 9.2 percent to 17.9 percent. The rise in the corporate share of the turnover is primarily attributable to the rise in the turnover ratio (Japan Economic Journal, 1987). However, in contrast to extensive intragroup stockholding there is little intergroup stockholding except for unilateral ownership by financial institutions (Okumura, 1982).

The intragroup stockholding may be viewed as 'exchange of papers' in the sense that the increase in assets of each corporation is canceled out by the increase in stockholdings of the other. But it does not create any problem for raising funds in Japan due to existence of 'overborrowing' situation. That is, the enterprises in postwar Japan, particularly the large enterprises, have heavily relied on money borrowed from the banks in order to raise external funds. This implies relatively less importance of share capital in the capital structure of Japanese enterprises. As a stopgap, sufficient money is readily available from the banks. Thus, the enterprises may ignore the qualities of raising share capital. However, when debt payments are not met, control rights are transferred to the creditors and managers lose their control benefits. This ensures that managers have a strong incentive to perform. This is consistent with some literatures on capital structure as a state-contingent allocation of control (Aghio and Bolton, 1992; Hart, 1989).

Dr. Scott (1986) emphasizes the importance of analysis of the six enterprise groups: Mitsui, Mitsubishi, Sumitomo, Fuyo, Sanwa and Dai-Ichi Kangyo in order to understand the modern economic structure of Japan. Three groups - Mitsubishi, Mitsui and Sumitomo - are based on prewar *zaibatsu* ties. These ex-*zaibatsu* groups consist of dozens of large corporations, along with a major city bank as the main bank and a giant general trading company, most of them using the same former name. The other three groups - Fuyo, Sanwa and Dai-Ichi Kangyo - comprise a somewhat smaller number of companies, but they also include a large city bank and a general trading company. The enterprises in these groups do not have prewar *zaibatsu* ties as those of the first type and they are less cohesive. These groups have much more economic power. For example, there are only 162 industrial companies in all six groups combined in 1985 which accounted for only 0.001 percent of the total number of corporations, but they controlled 15.37 percent of the total assets and 16.43 percent of total turnover (*Kigyo Keiretsu Soran*, 1986). Members of the groups are linked primarily by cross stockholding[3] and bank loans from the group's main bank. It has already been noted that the motive behind such cross stockholding is not the search for investment earnings directly rather strengthening their business relations or creating a stable spectrum of stockholders in order to provide a stable and supportive business environment.

It is a phenomenon of so-called 'stable shareholding arrangement' (*kabunushi anteika kosaku*). Nakatani (1984) explains it as a shock absorbing, 'mutual insurance' arrangement that benefits both the company and employees in the long run. McDonald (1989) views it as part of Japan's reciprocal corporate relationship that contributes to 'collective risk reduction'. In other words, it is an institutional device to combine the best of the two worlds - to have the benefits of the impersonal equity market without its impersonal nature, namely the instability and risks it entails. These are also known as *mochiai*[4] effect. Of course, this is likely to result in chronic shortage of shares on the market.

These merits of cross shareholding are subject to some social costs. The stable shareholding arrangement reduces the competitiveness of capital markets at the expense of outsiders, particularly the small individual shareholders. From the standpoint of the cross shareholders, it helps cement business ties at low cost as long as share prices are rising. In fact, their unrealized capital gains from such cross holdings can be used in Japan as collateral for loans treating them as 'latent capital'. On the contrary, cross shareholding becomes a burden when share prices decline. For example, in 1990 share prices declined to a considerably large extent. Corporate shareholders found the value of their shares decline by about 40 percent. Reportedly this has discouraged some banks to hold more shares at the request of their clients because of low returns *vis-a-vis* stressing the competitive efficiency implied by the financial liberalization.

Critics of Japanese business practices have alleged that cross shareholdings keep share price high and promote extensive business ties and consequently make takeovers of Japanese companies virtually impossible. In the U.S.-Japan Structural Impediments initiative talks in 1989-90, the U.S. side emphasized for changes in disclosure and other rules concerning cross shareholding. Japanese side has responded favorably and initiated some changes. In late 1990 the MOF enacted a rule requiring members of giant corporate groups, *keiretsu*, to disclose more about transactions within the group. Besides, a new rule requiring to report holdings of 5 percent or more in a company has been enacted. However, after an extensive literature survey it is concluded by Gerlach (1992a) that the criticism of *keiretsu* as a closed trading system underestimates its significance and viability in the Japanese economy. Imai (1990a,b) also has emphasized that the *keiretsu* is rational, evolving organizations that have engaged in market competition. There is no clear evidence that they impede entry into business or discriminate against foreign firms in their transactions. Nakatani (1990) argues that *keiretsu* system has been effective and resilient as the pillar of Japanese-style capitalism. Of course, he has agreed with their exclusionary position. In response to the foreign criticism, he suggests the government to offer incentives to the *keiretsu* groups so that they welcome foreign companies to join them without attempting to weaken them.

Ownership and control

According to the famous managerial theory of Berle and Means separation of ownership and control takes place through dispersion of company ownership to a large number of individuals and concentration of control in managers who pledge loyalty to the corporation. That is 'company ownership without control' and 'managerial control without ownership' has been recognized. The modern corporate governance literature has treated this separation as the efficient response to economic forces. It is argued that the increasing complexity of business is a more important cause of separation than the dispersion of stockholding. Existing owners lack the skill and information necessary either to run modern corporations themselves or to monitor the decisions of those who do (Chandler, 1990). Efficiency became the standard in the corporate governance debate. To increase the value of the corporation, control is delegated to managers with specialized skills. But this delegation also gives managers the discretion to advance their own agenda at the shareholders' expense. The structure of agency cost described in the modern reformulation as the sum of a) bonding costs, as managers tried to assure that they would do a good job; b) monitoring costs, as shareholders tried to oversee managers; and c) a residual loss that could not be eliminated (Jensen and Meckling, 1976). In equilibrium, there would be no other costs to eliminate. Any observed costs would be either the bonding or monitoring costs, whose elimination would cost more in increased residual loss, or the residual loss, whose elimination would cost more in offsetting bonding or monitoring costs (Roe, 1993). The purpose of corporate governance, thus, became minimizing the sum of the costs involved in aligning managers' and shareholders' incentives and in unavoidable self interested managerial behavior (Jensen and Meckling, 1976). The most enduring institution for minimizing agency cost has been the independent director. Other means to minimize the agency costs have included managerial labor markets, incentive compensation tied to stock price, capital markets that denied bad managers access to capital, and high debt that heightened fear of bankruptcy (Williamson, 1975). The concept - that shareholders would bridge their separation from managers by electing nonemployee directors to monitor management performance - has reached the status of conventional wisdom. However, substantial doubt remains as to independent directors' effectiveness (Gilson and Roe, 1993). Since the Japanese companies favor the company ownership by the companies through interfirm or cross stockholding, it has demonstrated a different situation[5]. Besides, Japanese firms depend more on debt than on issuing stocks. Thus, it is often observed that the bank has controlling power over the firm even though it is not a large stockholder. Equity financing does not demand a periodic return and it is, therefore, considered less effective as a control device, particularly when partial ownership of the bank remains within the group. This means that creditor needs to be taken into consideration in order to explain the control system in Japanese firms. While the bank may be owned by, and own shares in other group members, it is clear that it funds itself with deposits from outside investors in order to provide a reliable commitment for group firms. The group of firms solves their problems through mutual monitoring in normal times but the bank emerges as a 'monitor of last resort' in insolvent states acting on behalf of ultimate investors (Diamond, 1984). The bank is also monitored by the cross holding arrangement, by its depositors, and as a deposit taking institution, by the regulatory authorities as well.

The arrangement of maintaining allocation of voting rights in the event of an equity issue or the sale of group shareholding usually warrants the intervention by the main bank. It does so by allocating these holdings proportionately among group members (Sheard, 1986). While the arrangement suggests that the group's combined holdings in each member firm should provide the group with firm control, combined group holdings seldom exceed 50 percent. However, since residual shareholdings are widely dispersed, effective control is possible with less than a majority of shares. It is also well known that Berle and Means referred to both 'immediate control' and 'ultimate control' of firms. That is, if firm P is controlled by firm Q and Q is controlled by a particular person Z, then P is ultimately controlled by Z. Generally speaking, the ultimate dominator can be found by tracing large stockholders back to the beginning of the ramification. Prewar *zaibatsu* is a good example. From whichever corporation we start, if we trace the large stockholders, we eventually reach the holding company, and finally the family (Figure-7.1). On the contrary, postwar Japanese firms, which are characterized by interfirm stockholdings, the ultimate dominator is not found (Figure-7.2)[6]. Adapting it to the needs of the reality, the structure of Japanese corporate governance has substantial contribution to its development process. Thus, the Japanese industrial structure providing an alternative evolutionary path casts doubt on the standard classical model of corporate ownership mediated through securities markets as the best form of financial development, successfully providing ownership, diversification, and liquidity in just the right proportion.

Market segmentation

Business organizations - either public or private limited companies - may raise long term funds through private sources by ploughing back of profits and issue of shares or debentures to the affiliated enterprises. If this happens, it means a considerable share of long term finance is not marketable nor raised through the capital markets. Therefore, the capital market may be divided into two segments - internal and external. All those long term finances arranged privately without recourse to the investors in general are included within the scope of internal markets. Finances raised from the public fall under the scope of external markets.

It is the share price mechanism through which capital market evaluate, monitor and interfere for corporate control according to the text book notions. In the case of ailing firms, demand for the shares falls resulting in low share price as well as difficulty to raise funds from the capital market. Such condition suggests liquidation through a legal process. Alternatively, the assets of the firm may be rationalized through a takeover mechanism. Fama and Miller (1972) have indicated that even with the difference in preferences among shareholders the firm maximizes its profit and thereby market value of the firm following the 'market value rule' which assumes a perfect capital market. But these assumptions are somewhat artificial since imperfection and uncertainty are common in real world situations. Financial economists generally regarded the existence of a competitive market for corporate control for being in disciplining managers and ensuring that they operate their firms efficiently. A competitive capital market is necessary because its existence makes continually the managerial teams subject to the prospect of replacement. Jensen and Ruback (1983) concluded that:

> ...the evidence seems to indicate that takeovers generate positive gains, that target firm shareholders benefit, and that bidding firm shareholders do not loss. Moreover, the gains created by corporate takeovers do not appear to come from the creation of market power. Finally, it is difficult to find managerial actions related to corporate control that harm shareholders; the exceptions are those actions that eliminate an actual and potential bidder, for example, through the use of targeted large block of repurchases or standstill agreements.

This statement does not recognize any system like 'life-term employment' which appears to be possible in Japan mainly due to the existence of internal capital markets.

An internal capital market in Japan enables firms, as opposed to individuals, to diversify their risks and affords the management of firms insulation from external capital market forces, particularly from the market for corporate control (Nakatani, 1984). Following Nakatani (1984) and Williamson (1975) financial corporate grouping may be viewed as a kind of internal capital market. The large firms in a financial corporate group are able to avert sudden bankruptcy or takeover because of the back up received from the financial institutions and other business partners of the group. Fruin (1992) argues that the interfirm networks facilitate 'organizational learning', which is considered as the key concept in explaining the efficiency of the Japanese system. The relationship among companies goes beyond just production and sales activities and extends to exchanging technical information and even engaging in joint research and development activities. In this way, each company can share the various information that it has accumulated, giving rise to invisible assets that are available to all the companies participating in the network. The shareownership of the firm remains largely in tact as a result of the 'stable shareholding arrangement' which characterizes corporate organization in the internal capital market. Thus the operation of an active takeover market has been blocked largely as a result of associations and 'stable shareholding arrangement' among corporations (Okumura, 1981). *Keiretsu* is often viewed as an evil of the Japanese system due to its exclusivity. It can doubtlessly be an obstacle for a new comer who tries to penetrate the market, for *keiretsu* is founded on continuous, long term commitments among its members. The internal capital market can be seen, not only as a means of allowing the firm to diversify risks, but as a way to give managers the necessary autonomy from the external capital market which in turn, ensures life-term employment system. Under this condition, management is able to take a long term view of investment without being preoccupied with the firm's short term profit position, its share price movements or with the threat of a takeover as is the practice elsewhere. Of course, in order to attain better efficiency, the internal capital market has the mechanism through which intervention in the internal management by the 'main bank' usually takes place.

In this connection Aoki's (1980, 1982) model of cooperative game between stockholders and employees is noteworthy. Corporate members may wish to engage in a game among themselves where the aim of the game is to determine important policies, such as distribution of organizational rent, growth rate of the firm and corporate financial policy. This cooperative game is possible only when the firm is insulated at least partially from the imperatives of market forces. Business group in Japan is regarded as a means of insulating group firms from the external market pressure. Interfirm shareholding is used to undermine the general shareholders outside the group over policy-making process of group members. With little possibility of takeover bid managers' actions may go against the interest of general shareholders. It is argued that in a contractual governance system, factor providers' shared control, accomplished through cross holdings, does not diminish the returns to any other party. Gilson and Roe (1993) have offered an explanation other than exploitation for the implicit difference between the value of controlling factor provider shares and the value of noncontrolling public shares. All types of shareholders will unanimously favor maximizing the corporation's share value when separation applies. In case of relation-specific investment separation does not apply. In this regard they have pointed out '... noncontrolling shareholders may well approve of the nonmaximizing behavior. So long as the 'extra' return to factor providers is less than the increased productivity resulting from the relation-specific investment, noncontrolling shareholders are better off than if factor providers maximized share value but did not make the investment.'

Shareholding by business corporations or financial institutions is usually not found in Bangladesh. Internal capital markets favor diversification of risk which, in turn, may create confidence among investors. This may be more relevant for those markets where persistently high degrees of stock market fluctuations are observed.

Capital structure decision

Leverage decision is significant in influencing shareholders' return and risk. Market value of the share is affected by the capital structure decision. Japanese enterprises demonstrate a generally high rate of debt to equity ratio. The shareholders' equity for all nonfinancial companies listed on the TSE in 1985 was 23.4 percent (TSE Fact Book, 1986) which is quite low by the U.S. standards. According to Nakatani (1984) the ratio of equity to total assets is considerably lower for a group affiliated firms by 4 to 9 percentage points. This follows that the group behavior of Japanese enterprises appears to have contributed to the low equity level. This high level of debt may be seen in terms of 'Pecking Order Theory' of Myers (1984). Pecking order theory explains a situation when it seems to be not convincing to the potential investors about the investment opportunities of the firm due to asymmetric information that managers might have. They consider management's endeavor to exploit them in favor of the 'existing' shareholders. This may result in under valuation of new issues which are necessary for favorable investment opportunities. The decision rule then appears to be, 'Issue debt when investors undervalue the firm, and equity, or some other risky securities when they overvalue it.' Recent empirical evidence for the U.S.A. also shows that the announcement of a new equity issue reduces the value of previously outstanding shares by 30 percent of the value of the issue (Asquith and Mullins, 1986). Following Myers and Majluf (1984) pecking order suggests that for financing new projects, it is better to use financial slack (cash on hand and marketable securities) than any other sources. However, if the financial slack is not sufficient for the project then low risk debt[7] may be used as second choice. It is desirable to issue equity when debt becomes relatively risky. Besides, the literature on costs of financial distress supports less borrowing for risky firms (Myers, 1977).

Like Japan the industries of Bangladesh also demonstrate a higher debt to equity ratio. The loan giving agencies previously maintained a policy of 60:40 and 70:30 debt-equity ratio depending upon geographical location and nature of industry. This ratio has been raised to 70:30 and 80:20 respectively later. As we have seen in Chapter 3, this high ratio of debt could not yield an expected result, rather a huge volume of nonperforming loans is being piled up. The higher leverage of Japanese industries can be meaningfully interpreted with pecking order theory. This is because of the fact that the Japanese industries are less risky due to existence of strong business ties among group member firms through cross shareholding. In the absence of strong business ties in Bangladesh investment in business becomes a more risky affair. In order to attain the desired level of effectiveness of higher leverage, reduction of business risk is an imperative as argued by pecking order theory and demonstrated by Japanese experience.

Dividend decision

Under the assumptions of frictionless perfectly competitive market and absence of tax, it is a well-known proposition in the neoclassical world developed by Modigliani and Miller that financial resources may be raised by issuing new equity or long term debt or by retaining profits by the existing firms. Any of the alternative ways of financing are equally good to the firm. But the real world is different in terms of prevailing tax system and regulatory mechanism applicable to both financial intermediaries and non financial corporations. A distinct pattern of corporate finance will emerge depending on such real world phenomena. In Japan, individual shareholders are likely to prefer capital gain to dividend because of favorable tax treatment. Corporations, on the other hand, may prefer to minimize dividends in order to meet their investment needs. They also receive preferential tax treatment on intercorporate dividends while realization of capital gains is taxed at the regular rate of 42 percent (Nakatani, 1984)[8]. Futatsugi (1986)[9] shows that the total of dividends drawn by individual shareholders will always decrease if at least the payout ratio of any member of the reciprocally shareholding firms is less than 1. He has shown it by comparing two situations - before issuing cross shareholding and after issuing cross shareholding - between two corporations. Table-7.1 gives a hypothetical picture. None of the corporations has additional funds through the issue of cross shareholding and they cannot expand their productive capacities. It is assumed that *ceteris paribus*, annual profits will remain the same and not change the payout ratio. Row (5) of Table-7.1 shows higher dividends received by

Table-7.1
Comparative position of dividend before and after reciprocal share holding between two corporations

Particulars	Before issuing reciprocal/cross shareholding		After issuing reciprocal/cross shareholding	
	Corporation		Corporation	
	A	B	A	B
1. No. of shares issued	30	50	60	80
a) Individuals	30	50	30	50
b) Corporations	-	-	30	30
2. Proportion of shares held by individuals	All	All	1/2	5/8
3. Profits earned	620	930	620	930
4. Payout ratio	1/2	1/3	1/2	1/3
5. Dividend paid to individuals	310	310	620x1/2x1/2 =155	930x1/3x5/8 =775/4
6. Dividend paid to each corporation for mutual holding	-	-	930x1/3x3/8 =465/4	620x1/2x1/2 =155

Source: Developed on the basis of Futatsugi (1986).

individuals before issuing cross shareholding. But from shareholding ratio and payout ratio it follows that of the 465/4 in dividends, which A received from B, 465/4x1/4 will flow back to B and of the 155, which B received from A, 155x1/8 will return to A. This process will continue infinitely. Thus, the dividend paying ability of the corporations will increase. The total effect of this process is calculated by summing the following geometric progression.

$$\begin{bmatrix}620\\930\end{bmatrix} + \begin{bmatrix}0 & 1/8\\1/4 & 0\end{bmatrix}\begin{bmatrix}620\\930\end{bmatrix} + \begin{bmatrix}0 & 1/8\\1/4 & 0\end{bmatrix}^2\begin{bmatrix}620\\930\end{bmatrix} + \ldots = \begin{bmatrix}32/31 & 4/31\\8/31 & 32/31\end{bmatrix}\begin{bmatrix}620\\930\end{bmatrix} = \begin{bmatrix}760\\1120\end{bmatrix}$$

Now the individuals' dividends will be 760x1/2x1/2 = 190 and 1120x1/3x5/8 = 233.3 which is also smaller than before introducing cross shareholding. Corporations have the incentive to resort to cross shareholding for better financial position disregarding the external capital market. In this connection

Baumol (1965) is quoted as:

> ...A very substantial proportion of American business firms manage to avoid the direct disciplining influences of the securities market, or at least to evade the type of discipline which can be imposed by the provision of funds to inefficient firms only on extremely unfavorable terms. A company which makes no direct use of the stock market as a source of capital can apparently, proceed to make its decision confident in its immunity from this type of punishment by its impersonal mechanism of stock market.

It then appears that the cross shareholdings of the Japanese firms have permitted them to ignore the obvious market demand for a higher dividend implied by the imperfections and uncertainties of the market and the funds thereby made available at the disposal of the firms are likely to have been used more profitably.

Of course, the purchase of stocks with low dividend yields is creating problems for most Japanese institutional shareholders. Banks have cash flow requirements for payment of interest to depositors. Insurance companies face restriction on declaring dividends without adequate reported income and they are generally not allowed to treat capital gains (even where realized) as income. Most nonfinancial corporations are, at least partially, financing their shareholdings by loans with associated interest payments (Hodder and Tschoel, 1985). Thus there is a set of institutional shareholders who need substantial dividend yields, but traditionally follow policies of buying and holding shares to enhance business relations with the firm issuing those shares. Consequently, the purchase of low yielding market issues squeezes these institutions' ability to meet other commitments (Barnea, Haugen and Senbet, 1981). Besides, the importance of cross shareholding is likely to decline on the face of market liberalization policy of the government in recent years that needs for raising the firms' competitive efficiency.

The main bank system

It is a feature of corporate enterprises in Japan that most large firms have close financial, shareholding and managerial ties with a particular bank, known as the 'main bank'. Despite its popularity the Japanese 'main bank' remains vague. However, Economic Research Association (ERA) of Japan defines a main bank so as to fit the financial group (*kinyu keiretsu*) concept. It defines 'financial group' in principle by the amount of financing that a bank supplies to a particular borrowing company. When a given company has taken out the largest amount of loans from a particular bank for the past three years or more years consecutively, the company is viewed as belonging to that bank's financial group. According to ERA, nearly all the companies listed in the First Section of TSE have a main bank (i.e., belonging to a financial group). Of course, these companies borrow not just from their main bank, but from a number of other banks and financial institutions as well.

Main bank ties evolved gradually in the 1950s as banks became closely involved in restructuring and other operations of the client firms, supplied them with capital, acquired ownership stakes, and appointed some of the client firms' personnel (Suzuki, 1992; Okazaki, 1993). While firms had clear incentive to borrow, lending to highly levered firms would seem extremely risky from the bank's perspective. The main bank relationship allows the group member firms continued borrowing up to seemingly extraordinary debt to equity ratios. This relationship tends to be both a long term and very close, with the main bank being privy to extensive and confidential information on the firm's operations as well as its medium and long term plans. Accordingly, the main bank's loan evaluation was typically accepted with little question by other lenders (Hodder and Tschoel, 1985). Evidence supports that the reformed firms tended to perform worse than their industry peers due to diffuse postreform ownership structure and limited monitoring of managers. Thus, *keiretsu* and their main banks are proved to be economically rational institutions (Yafeh, 1995).

The main bank is usually a major shareholder of the firms in the group. The main bank for firms with bank borrowing which were listed in the First Section of the TSE in 1980 was the largest or second largest shareholder in 39 percent of the cases and among the top five shareholders in 72 percent of the cases (Sheard, 1986). The intensity of the main bank relationship appears not only in its nominal loan share and shareholding but also as a risk bearing agent. In a conventional capital market, the shareholders are the residual risk-bearers, but in the internalization of capital markets within the group in Japan, the main bank's corporate-insuring role gives it the character of, what could be termed, a quasi-residual risk bearer. There are striking examples that illustrate this relationship. When Ataka (a large trading company) went to bankruptcy in 1977, its two main banks took almost all losses. Foreign creditors of Ataka lost nothing, although their loans were basically unsecured (Prindle, 1981). Nitto Chemical (1966), Nihon Special Steel (1964), Fuji Heavy Industries (1963), Hitachi Zosen Corporation (1986-88), Sanko Steamship (1985), Itoman and Company (1993) and many others can be cited as examples of main bank intervention following the financial or managerial crisis occurred in the group member firms. A survey of 320 listed firms in 1977 with accumulated losses revealed a high level of representation by the main banks of the group (*Toyo Keizai Shimposha*, 1978). However, the most common form of bank assistance in Japan is the granting of interest reductions or exemptions on bank borrowing for a specified period and often sending some top ranking officials to the concerned enterprise. One way that group affiliated firm make surrogate insurance payments to banks during normal business times is by maintaining a high level of bank deposits, particularly with the main bank, thus serving to raise the effective interest rate (Washio, 1974). The banks in Japan, as a wide spread practice, hold a portion of their loan in the form of deposit which is known as *buzumiryodatekin* (compulsory deposit).

Under uncertainty, usually financial transactions are costly because of the cost incurred for collecting information about the borrowers. It is, therefore, desirable to establish stable long term business relationships with borrowers than to rely exclusively on short term spot transactions. Osano and Tsutsui (1985) have shown that implicit contract relationships are prevalent in the Japanese bank loan market. Kester (1990) characterizes the corporate governance of a *keiretsu* firm as relying on a complex interaction between the shareholding, credit holding, and long term business relationships that exist between the firm and its stakeholders. The largest creditor, which is almost always either the main bank or an insurance company in the same *keiretsu*, holds an average 21.9 percent of the firms' outstanding debt and 6 percent of its outstanding equity. The firm's largest five creditors (that are members of the same *keiretsu*) hold 49.8 percent of its debt and 18 percent of its equity. Moreover, many nonfinancial firms within the *keiretsu* extend large amounts of trade credit to those firms in which they have equity interests (Prowse, 1992). Corporate grouping in Japan seems to provide an ingenious device for such relationship which demonstrates a favorable condition for an implicit contract between a bank (as creditor) and group enterprises for 'side payments'[10] and thereby maximize the firm's value under uncertainty. Because large shareholders are also large debtholders in the same *keiretsu* firms, it also suggests that they may facilitate policies that attempt to transfer wealth from debtholders to shareholders and from shareholders to debtholders. Maximizing the combined wealth of bondholders and stockholders for the firm's operating decisions may fail to maximize the separate as well as the combined wealth of both groups at the time when the firm's debt is risky and side payments between them are ruled out.

In Bangladesh, policies have been devised to discourage investment in bank deposits and government saving schemes recently. One is revising downward the interest rates on these assets and the other is withdrawal of tax benefits so far enjoyed by the investors from such investment. These policies apparently aimed at channelizing the funds to direct investment instead of flowing to the banks. But the question arises whether people with excess money would find it profitable and feel secure to invest in company shares which are apparently highly risky. Even with the sense of security attached to fixed interest investments in government saving schemes, it is likely that people will prefer to save in the banks because of the lack of expertise, salesmanship on the part of the Directorate of Savings of the government and a maximum limit imposed on such savings on the one hand as well as convenience and nearness of the banks to the customers on the other. Moreover, investment in company shares is still of questionable attractiveness because Bangladeshi companies, excepting a very few, still suffer from credibility gaps. Investing public feels shy in investing in company shares because they are not sure whether they will get back their principal, not to speak of a dividend. Under the circumstances, there is a genuine apprehension that a sizable amount of money saved by the public might have gone for speculative trade, hoarding, purchase of real estates, gold and other unproductive assets. People may individually decide to invest directly in a productive sector in the external capital market. Alternatively, when funds come to the banking sector, this sector may take investment decision which is known as indirect financing. Japan has demonstrated a good example of the latter. This largely explains why in Japan the new issue market has failed to keep pace with the tremendous strides made by the economy along the route of industrialization. Until recently the open market in Japan was far smaller than what it could have been[11]. It suggests the desirability of emphasizing the indirect financing through banking system to promote industrial financing at the initial stages of a country's economic and financial development.

Japanese experience in the context of Bangladesh

It is obvious that the securities markets in an underdeveloped country should be viewed and assessed in relation to the country's limited economic and financial development. Thus any specific measure for fostering the growth of the securities markets should be introduced as part of a general program for economic and financial development (Wai and Patrick, 1973). Moreover, the condition and structure of a capital market depends upon varying factors. Before 1914 a major element in the growth of the London Stock Exchange was the issue and subsequent trading of the securities of railway, tramway, canal, dock, gas, electricity and water companies, operating in Britain and in the colonies (Morgan, 1965). In the less developed countries like Bangladesh, such activities invariably belong to the government sector where they are not financed by shareholders and rarely by the issue of debentures or bonds. If the average size of corporations is usually small like Bangladesh, the market would not be very important for the high cost of small issue and for several other reasons as well. In this situation small firms usually prefer the private to the public limited form. Hence, the new issue market cannot be as important a part of the greater capital market in Bangladesh as in a country of big corporations and industry. The new issue market is only one of the several sources of business finance, and is not necessarily the cheapest source. After the World War II, the economic situation of Japan was full of uncertainty and the average financial asset holdings of the household sector remained at a very low level. Household sector could not afford to have widely diversified portfolios due to high transaction costs, and concentrate their saving into highly divisible, liquid and safe assets in the form of a bank or postal saving deposit. Sophisticated forms of financial transactions appeared not encouraging in general. The situation called for the financial intermediation of the hierarchy solution[12]. At the early stage of the high growth era, the government of Japan adopted the strategy of controlling the financial system by indirect measures, which consisted of various moral suasions given to groups of major financial institutions, in particular big city banks (Hamada and Horiuchi, 1987). This strategy presupposed the existence of the stable function of the hierarchy solution and cooperation among private agents. According to Miyajima (1994) underdeveloped capital markets imply that capital is to be supplied largely by financial institutions (rather than stock exchange), and special ties with a major bank facilitate access to loans by mitigating imperfect information problems between lenders and borrowers. Such ties with a main bank are specially important in capital-intensive industries with much need for capital, and for firms with limited access to non-bank capital (Gerlach, 1992a). Since the hierarchy depends on the long term relationship between lenders and borrowers, the process of financial intermediation dependent on it tends to be more stable than that arranged by the market solution.

The burgeoning literature on Japanese business groups has presented several theories including the anti-takeover theory, externality theory, successive monopoly theory, anti-opportunism theory and cultural theory. The anti-takeover theory suggests that the shareholding interlocks are to make takeovers less likely, either to insulate managers from disciplining by shareholders (Odagiri, 1975; Kobayashi, 1980; Aoki, 1984) or to prevent hostile stock raiders from abrogating a firm's long term contracts (Ramsayer, 1987; Sheard, 1991). The externality theory argues that firms affiliated with one another in order to internalize the gains from activities with potential spillover effects. The activities entailing spillovers can be advertising, using trademarks, research and development (R&D) etc. (Hadley, 1970; Goto, 1982). Firms with the market power and trading partners hold each others shares to encourage one another to set prices or orders for production with the objective to protect common interest instead of individual interest (Caves and Uekusa, 1976; Fung, 1991). This is the contention of successive monopoly theory. Flath (1996), Gilson and Roe (1993) and Berglof and Perotti (1994) argue that the economic purpose of interlocking shareholdings is to deter opportunistic behavior. The firms that hold shares in a trading partner can penalize the partner by unilaterally divesting. Holding stock in a trading partner may favor the partner in bargaining over product market variables while divesting may work reverse. The culturist theory regards the Japanese business group as a coherent system consistent with the Japanese cultural tradition. The Japanese system emphasizing the groupism is regarded as distinct from the Western system emphasizing individualism (Sakai, 1990; Smith, 1959; Murakami, 1984). However, the following discussion is aimed at analyzing the major issues concerning the implications of Japanese experience in the context of a developing country like Bangladesh.

Cultural dialectic and strategic rationality

Culturalist like Sakai (1990), Abegglen (1958), Murakami (1984) and others have argued that the core of the Japanese business organization is groupism. They have drawn such conclusion from historical customs and social values of the Japanese. Sakai has drawn similarity between the ancient Japanese *han* and modern *keiretsu*. In ancient times Japan was divided into small feudal fiefdoms called *han*. Each *han* was controlled by a man known as *daimyo* who lived in a castle town surrounded by the agricultural land that provided his tax base and his power. The *daimyo*'s extended family included people who were related only by marriage and even some were adopted - all were entitled to wear the family crest. *Daimyo* was placed at the top of social hierarchies and common people like farmers, artisans, merchants were placed at the bottom. In between there were different strata of *samurai* who were trusted retainers. The commoners were treated more as property than as human being. *Samurai* were expected to show unconditional loyalty to their *daimyo*. They would not desert their master even when there were works for them elsewhere. Sakai argued that similar concept is at work in modern corporate behavior in the following way:

> The parent company in a manufacturing group thinks of itself as a *daimyo*, the supreme power, the apex of a pyramid in which production flows from the bottom upward and rewards from the top downward . . . The modern corporate *han* are no different: vertical hierarchy is the hard and fast rule. Smaller companies produce for the next level up. No matter how bad times may get, companies can never leave their industrial group to seek employment elsewhere. And if they tried, no one would hire them - nobody likes deserters, even when they come cheap (Sakai, 1990).

Smith (1959) has emphasized this group orientation as culturally conditioned by the collective memory of ancient agrarian village life. Most Japanese land was not actually suited to paddy cultivation in its original form. In order to make the soil suitable for paddy cultivation, collective control over the water supply had to develop in the form of *tameike* (reservoir) and later in the form of large scale irrigation along the rivers. This necessitated mutual help and collective coordination among villagers with respect to water allocation, concentrated labor inputs and timely plantations of seedlings. It is thus argued that the present day Japanese corporate behavior inherits the customs of mutual help, collective coordination and risk sharing experience through generations.

On the other hand, Dore (1973), Koike (1984) and others have presented a different view emphasizing the rationalistic aspects of Japanese corporate practices. They have emphatically viewed the Japanese corporate behavior as strategic, rationalistic and universal. Some of these features have been identified as the rational responses to the imperatives of advanced industrial development. Dore has observed a 'sufficient consistency' in differences between the Japanese and British employment system. In examining the historical development of the Japanese employment system, he has identified some of its features were the result of unconscious habits or of a certain traditional behavior or deliberate adaptations of earlier employment patterns. Some of them have been consciously borrowed from abroad or wholly indigenously developed. The system of seniority pay was developed as a management response to the excessive mobility of skilled workers in the early years of this century. He has also noted that 'it should not be forgotten that many of the modern features of the 'system' were established as a result of union pressure in the period of intense hardship and insecurity after the (Pacific) war.' Ramseyer (1987) has argued that like any other cultural order, the Japanese tradition is an unstable set of conflicting and manipulable norms. Among them, individuals must choose. And generally they choose to their own advantage. Cultural orders constitute a 'symbolic grammar' that individuals can - and will - appropriate for their own gain. No explanation of Japanese behavior, whether of employees or managers, will succeed unless it accounts for both this cultural mutability and this capacity for strategic action. 'From the standpoint of the firm, by forming or joining a group, it can economize on the transaction costs that it would have incurred if the transaction had been done through the market, and at the same time, it can avoid the scale diseconomies or control loss which would have occurred if it had expanded internally and performed that transaction within the firm. If the net benefit of forming or joining a group exceeds that of implementing transactions within the firm or through the market, the firm has the incentive to form or to join a group' (Goto, 1982). Koike (1984) convincingly has asserted that most of the organizational practices at large firms are the natural outcome of rational behavior. His assertions mainly focussed the life term employment, wide range of job experiences, enterprise-based union and so on. Some scholars (Yamamura, 1979; Imai, 1990a) have identified cross shareholding as symbolic. This argument appears to be not tenable. According to Flath (1996), if this is so then the size of the shareholding is not important so long as it passes some threshold of observability which may be quite small. For it is not the shareholding itself but the relationship which it signals that alters the calculations of the firm, its rivals, customers or suppliers. Instead, he argued for the economic purpose of deterring opportunism. The rising volume of cross shareholding since the crash of stock markets in 1965 indicates some strategic behavior. The immediate causes of this rise were the following. When the stock markets crash occurred in 1965, two institutions - *Shoken Hoyu Kumiai* (Securities Holding Union) and *Kyodo Shoken* (Cooperative Securities) - were created to buy and freeze a certain amount of stocks to stabilize the market. After stabilization had been achieved, these stocks were sold through the market. At this time (beginning of 1970s), the Japanese economy was moving toward liberalization of foreign investments, and most firms were fearful of being taken over by foreigners. Therefore, the management of private firms asked other firms to hold their stocks, obviously to obviate the foreign takeover. This is consistent with the strategic and rational behavior. It is now understandable that if the group formation subsequently proved disadvantageous or loss sustaining effort, no one could continue it in spite of their historical tradition. Of course, the efforts for group formation might have been easier for the Japanese business due to their historical orientation.

Our point is not to show that the Japanese culture is irrelevant nor rationality is the only relevant explanation of the Japanese organizational practices. Rather we like to argue that in some cases cultural issues have been overemphasized to the extent strategically rational business practices have not been duly recognized. It is true that the Japanese have long tradition of harmony, loyalty and consensus. But it also can't be denied that some aspects of the Japanese business practices are the natural outcome of their strategic and rational corporate behavior.

'Hierarchy vs. market solution'

Historically, both Bangladesh and Japan have furnished only a fraction of total financing through issue of corporate securities. As we have seen, in highly levered firms of Japan, the close relationship between banks and firms is of paramount importance. Because by purchasing shares and appointing directors in the firm, the main bank obtains information, reviews firm operations, and reduces managers' ability to avoid debt payments. Miyajima (1994) and Kiyonari and Nakamura (1980) have indicated that the bank's motive in establishing close ties with client firms was the protection of outstanding debt[13]. Although Bangladeshi firms are highly levered, the bank-firm relationship is not so close as that of Japan. If the bank-firm relationship is promoted to be closer, it may have its likely positive impact on the prevailing 'default culture' of the borrowing firms. In the preindependence days industrial entrepreneurship in Bangladesh was a close preserve of a few already established business houses, as evidenced by the concentration of industry in the hands of a few Managing Agents[14]. Much of the capital reached Bangladesh industries through the intermediary of these Managing Agents in those days. Several large agencies extended their activities to include up to thirty corporations, usually in several often unrelated industries. Thus there were business groups in Bangladesh like Japan, though on a smaller scale and in different form. Managing agency system has been abolished in Bangladesh after liberation but the business group exists in Japan even today in the form of *kigyoshudan/keiretsu*. In India Managing Agency system was formally abolished in 1970. But still the large industrial houses have managed to retain effective control over their enterprises. They control the key and strategic decision-making areas of investment expansion and diversification, pricing, product planning, and hiring of key personnel - almost all areas of top management and corporate planning (Agarwala, 1986). In other Asian countries, Korea in particular, a number of *zaibatsu*-like business groups exist. In a country like Bangladesh where entrepreneurship and capital are scarce, formation of effective business groups is likely to contribute toward its industrial development. However, in that effort the dangerous aspect of a business group like the 'financial oligarchy' created by *zaibatsu* in Japan needs to be taken into consideration.

A securities market is not the only avenue of external finance for a firm, nor the only means by which prospective investment alternatives may be compared. The question at issue is whether a market improves the allocational machinery over and above the functioning of banks and other institutional lenders. The disposition of investable funds via the securities market is made in accordance with the apparent profit prospects of the companies which compete for share and debenture issues. But relative profit rates (adjusted for risk) may not reflect relative efficiencies between firms because profit rates may be distorted by market imperfections arising from monopoly power, tariff protection, import quotas, credit rationing and so on. If these imperfections did not exist, it might appear that the securities market would allocate investable funds neutrally, in strict accord with expected investment yields. The complexity of allocative effect of the securities market can be understood from the following statement.

> It can be argued that in LDCs only the most creditworthy firms can sell their securities via a capital market that these firms also have prime access to bank

loans, and hence that such firms have greater freedom of choice between different sources of finance (in terms of availability of funds), for example, between bank loans and security issues. Development of capital markets provides no reallocation of resources to such firms. We have to examine instead where the buyers of securities obtain their funds, and how they would have used them alternatively; and how the lending banks derive its loanable funds, and to what use it would have put them alternatively (Wai and Patrick, 1973).

Accordingly, possibilities of unproductive or less efficient uses need to be considered when steps are taken to divert funds from financial institutions to securities markets. In this connection it is noteworthy that 'high rates of interest for lenders and borrowers introduce the dynamism that one wants in development, calling forth new net saving and diverting investment from inferior uses so as to encourage technical improvement' (McKinnon, 1973)[15]. It is difficult to explain the dynamics of investment financing of the Japanese firms using the orthodox hypothesis of share price maximization and high interest rates. It seems necessary to consider the changing power balance between individual investors and banks as one of the possible explanatory factors. In its great growth phase from 1950-70 the financial sector of Japan was notable for its ceilings on deposit rates, which produced real interest rates of zero or fractionally above zero, a household saving ratio which was consistently around 20 percent of disposable income, a private sector which was very highly geared and heavily dependent on bank loans for new financing, and a banking sector which was obliged to hold artificially low yielding securities issued by government and long term credit banks. Bank reserve requirements, though were very low, specially when borrowing by banks is consolidated. In other words, Japan managed to experience high growth with a repressed financial sector. The key to the rate of investment was the high saving rate, which reached 40 percent of GNP in 1972, when households, corporations and governments are included. It is sometimes suggested that the rapid growth may have induced a high level of savings, as consumption growth, for various reasons, tended to lag behind income growth. Moreover, the facilities for savings, and the social and cultural pressures to save, may have assisted the process, as did the absence of tax on interest on small deposits (see for further details Patrick and Rosovsky, 1976). Both theoretical reasoning and historical evidence suggest that the financial intermediation (banking system) can play a positive growth-inducing role. Goldsmith's (1969) calculated values of the financial interrelation ratio (FIR) for 1963 put Japan and Great Britain at the top with ratios of 1.75 and 1.71 respectively. Countries with low FIR are developing countries like India, Venezuela with ratios of 0.35 and 0.39

respectively[16]. Gupta (1984) used statistical tests to investigate the direction of causality between financial and economic development. For a sample of 14 countries his findings indicated that the direction of causality ran from financial to real development, suggesting an activist role for the financial sector. These findings did not appear to be sensitive to any particular characteristics of the countries included in this sample.

Banking system in Bangladesh

In Bangladesh, like other colonial countries, there are also the rudiments of a modern banking system and capital markets. They arose originally out of the requirements of foreign investors who transacted business within the country, usually in connection with foreign trade and transmission of funds to their home country. The English investors normally invested their own resources and plowed back their earnings. They supplied their own capital and introduced the managing agency system to spread their entrepreneurial skills widely and to distribute finance among the enterprises of the agency which required it. However, some of the members of the urban middle class as well as a few of the wealthier rural families, desired to invest on their own, and there was a demand on the part of the rising larger urban financiers and industrialists for speculative investment of otherwise idle funds. Stock exchanges arose to provide a center for such purchases and sales. Historically, British India had a large unorganized money market which met the demands for funds on part of the rural and poor urban population, an almost unrelated modern banking system, the main purpose of which was to supply the short term capital needs of firms whose longer term requirements were largely met from the internal sources of the firm or the ownership group and a security market which contributed to meeting the longer term investment needs of only a few firms (Rosen, 1962). It appears that there was a time when the internal sources and ownership group played a dominant role in providing industrial finance in Indian Subcontinent instead of securities markets. The banking system of Bangladesh has a limited role that distinguishes it from the Japanese and German banking system. We have seen in Chapter 3 that the Japanese banking sector is the largest representing 167 percent of GNP followed by Germany and U.S.A. while that of Bangladesh remained far behind representing only 56 percent of GNP. Relatively large size of the banking sector has influenced the Japanese corporate structure with shared authority at the top, large financial intermediaries that hold concentrated blocks of stock, interaction of bankers and managers in structured settings and multiple intermediaries that split the vote.

Presently, the corporate structure is dominated by family influences in Bangladesh. The family-owned business gathered pace and is particularly strong in the stock market. It is likely that with the bullish sentiment in the stock market, wealthy families tend to diversify their portfolios by holding a range of stocks rather than having a large, concentrated holding in the family business. That may result in divorce of control from ownership gradually. In this transformation process, financial intermediaries may come to the scene with a greater role to play.

Schumpeter assigned a 'delegated monitoring' role to banks. '......the banker must not only know what the transaction is which he is asked to finance and how it is likely to turn out but he must also know the customer, his business and even his private habits, and get, by frequently talking things over with him, a clear picture of the situation (Schumpeter, 1939). Equipped with all information about the borrowing firm, banks are supposed to get ready to bring about changes in the management at the time of need. However, close association between banks and borrowing firms could tend to create problems, since under the present practice in Bangladesh the banks give advice to customers as outsiders rather than insiders and have tended to keep away from the firms facing financial constraints. This is not consistent with the long term relationship between banks and firms. Besides, banks may be lured to use its position and may compel an enterprise for premature liquidation to safeguard its own interest at the cost of others. In Japanese system banks play the role of 'quasi-residuals'. It is found that banks take the burden of the lion share of losses so that creditors do not incur loss. It suggests that banks need to be induced to nurse the sick firms, promoting management changes and seeking liquidation only as a last resort when it will also be one of the residual risk bearers.

Besides, it could be apprehended that institutional involvement may pressurize unduly on company boards resorting to short term outlooks. In this case a clear understanding among different institutions could be established about the long term success of companies instead of a short term. They need to take into account that their current performance for dividends does not put too much pressure on company's cash flows, particularly during bad business condition. Dividends paid by the Japanese companies are usually stable and hardly burdensome on the part of the companies as we have seen in Chapter 5. High dividends are advantageous specially when more reliance on external finance is contemplated, but the low payout ratio of Japanese companies has displayed a remarkable achievement. It follows that institutions need to consider whether a high dividend rate is in the best interests of the companies in which they have long term commitment. Moreover the shareholdings by financial and nonfinancial institutions can be justified in terms of better diversification and professionalism which are difficult for individual.

Business group vs. spreading of stock ownership

From the earlier discussion it can reasonably be claimed that creation of business groups has resulted in chronic shortage of Japanese enterprises' stocks. In fact, if business groups would not exist, the mutually held shares by the member enterprises of the group could be exchanged among general public. Consequently, a wider distribution of share ownership would come about. In Bangladesh, the Company Law Reform Commission has debated to help spread share ownership more widely. Since the sponsors of a firm in Bangladesh need to put up a small percentage of the total project cost (about 20 - 30 percent; sometimes less), it is felt that this fact adds to the justification of spreading stock ownership among the general public. While formation of business groups through cross stockholding favors concentration of stocks among group enterprises, it may adversely affect the securities market development because of the resulting discouragement to investment for the potential investors. The public good nature of managerial monitoring effort leads to its suboptimal provision, a problem which is likely to be more severe when the number of shareholders increases and their average stake in the firm falls (Stiglitz, 1985). As ownership concentration is likely to be inversely proportional to the number of shareholders, diffusely-held firms are likely to be poorly monitored, and to the extent that managers maximize objectives other than profit maximization, their profits would, *ceteris paribus*, tend to be lower than profits of similar firms with a more concentrated ownership structure (Yafeh, 1995). A comparative

Table-7.2
Composition of stock ownership in DSE and TSE

(Figures in % of total)

Category	Dhaka Stock Exchange (DSE)	Tokyo Stock Exchange (TSE)
Government	11.3	0.6
ICB	12.3	-
Bank and Financial Institutions	7.6	43.8
Sponsors/Directors	46.3	-
Individuals and others	22.5	30.4
Business Corporations	-	23.9
Securities Companies	-	1.3

Source: Compiled from DSE Fact Book, 1984-85 and TSE Fact Book, 1995.

picture of shareownership structure in Bangladesh and Japan is presented in Table-7.2 which will give an understanding of the relevant market structures. The statistics in the Table highlight the following points: (i) Individual ownership is very low in Japan. This share is lower in case of Bangladesh. If the share of sponsors/ directors is included in this category, this share becomes quite high, more than 68 percent. (ii) Among different categories of share ownership, the share of sponsors/directors is the highest suggesting a high concentration of ownership in a few hands. In view of the prevailing market condition of Bangladesh it is highly probable that they are not well diversified. (ii) The share ownership by business corporations is around 30 percent in Japan but this phenomenon has not developed in Bangladesh indicating nonexistence of mutual shareholding. (iii) The ownership of banks and financial institutions is also very high in Japan while this share is far lower in Bangladesh. Anyway, the large share of financial institutions and business corporations indicate the cross shareholding.

Of course, the Japanese corporate structure dominated by banking system is likely to induce stagnancy due to lack of incentives to introduce various kinds of financial instruments and contracts that the market would require. With the rapid development of the Japanese economy as well as financial environment the rigidity of the bank-based system has come up. It has been argued that the influence of the bank-based system has suppressed the full-scale development of an efficient capital market in Japan. Business corporations with good performance have begun to go abroad for raising relatively cheap capital. This has created pressure on the system to change. In response to the changing environment the Japanese financial system is in the process of structural change to cope with the situation resulting in increasing volume of share trading by the corporations as noted earlier in this Chapter. All these suggest that the primary objective of corporate stockholding is gradually switching over to investment return from control of other companies only. In other words, corporate stockholdings are turning into institutional investors. It follows that even with smaller equity contribution, the bank-based system associated with cross stockholding is likely to have favorable impact on the initial stages of industrialization process and apprehension for fostering the policy measures toward that end is desirable.

Concluding remarks

Although the analyses can be extended, Japanese evidence has brought into question the prevailing textbook models including Berle-Means corporate governance structure. Investigation of Japanese corporate finance ventilates the following important points. Firstly, the suppression of external markets does not necessarily mean disappearance of their functions. Instead, the location of the allocation function may shift, as it appears to have done in the Japanese case, to internal capital markets within economic groups of firms. Secondly, incentives for high leverage were accompanied in Japan by the development of institutions, such as the main bank relationship, that could accommodate them.

Bangladesh economy is dominated by agricultural activities which are not organized on a corporate basis. Besides, the average size of industrial enterprises is small. For them the market would not be very important since the high cost of small issues and several other factors discourage small firms from taking recourse to the new issue market instead they prefer private to public limited form. Thus, the new issue market appears to become not as important a part of the greater capital market in a country dominated by agriculture and small businesses. On the investors' side, with lower level of income and saving rate, they are reluctant to invest in risky assets rather prefer riskfree assets. These are conceivably conducive for hierarchy solution.

It is likely that the firms in Bangladesh can't readily adopt the Japanese market structure due to some differences in corporate practices in both countries. Japanese corporate practices still have some implications for development approach of developing markets like Bangladesh. Our point is not to suggest that the Japanese corporate practice including cross shareholding is the only way for development with a different tax, legal, financial and other structural factors prevailing there. We like to emphasize that even if the experience of one country proves irrelevant for the other, the study of the differences in corporate practices in different environment is useful as far as it highlights the weaknesses or strengths of different practices. This may provide some different direction and emphasis in a persuasive way for an effective approach of development. Maybe, the experience in a different socioeconomic condition is unlikely to fit the conditions of others. Even if the foreign structures are found not congenial, it may be useful in charting a new course for evolving an effective corporate governance structure. We believe the Japanese experience of industrial structure is neither wholly applicable nor an utterly irrelevant case for the present day developing countries like Bangladesh. In spite of the contrasts in some economic and noneconomic terms, Japanese experience as an Asian country and late comer in the field of industrialization is likely to be more instructive in many respects than that of any Western nation.

Notes

1   In 1984, commercial banks in Japan owned more than 20 percent of the outstanding stock of all firms whereas commercial banks in the U.S.A. have been prevented by law from holding any corporate stock on their

own account. Insurance companies in Japan held more than 17 percent of the outstanding shares of firms, more than three times the amount held by their U.S. counterparts. Holdings by nonfinancial corporations in Japan are more than twice what they are in the U.S. Overall, corporate share holdings in Japan are close to twice what they are in the U.S., where individual share ownership predominates (Prowse, 1992).

2 This figure compares with roughly 50 percent of share ownership by individuals before the war, a figure mainly consisting of share holding by the wealthy *zaibatsu* founding families, with few shares held by other private investors.

3 Cross stockholding was an important aspect of the prewar *zaibatsu* wherein the members of a *zaibatsu* held each other's stocks mutually. In the postwar period two types of cross stockholding is observed. First, business groups developed among the members of the prewar *zaibatsu* groups, although these were dissolved after the World War II, known as *keiretsu / kigyoshudan*. Secondly, cross stockholding is widely practiced among enterprises that have regular business transactions, such as suppliers, distributors, banks and insurers, as token of goodwill and mutual support even without group ties.

4 *Mochiai* literally means to hold mutually, it also implies 'shared interdependence' and 'helping one another' (Gerlach, 1987).

5 Institutional investors held half the stock of the largest American corporations, although in small blocks. However, the blocks were never as concentrated as those found in Japan (See for details Lipton and Rosenblum, 1992).

6 Theoretically, shareholders' meeting should be the corporation's highest decision-making body. But a shareholders' meeting of Japanese corporation is far from ideal. The corporation official in charge of the shareholders' meeting wants to end it as quickly as possible by all means available including employing such shareholders who can mobilize the meeting. Thus all proposals on the agenda are approved in less than 30 minutes. Apparently, this implies that 'management leadership is as solid as a rock' (see for details Okumura, 1986). This is consistent with Fama (1980) who explained shareholders powerlessness as efficient; stockholders should not influence firm decisions because their speciality was bearing risk, not decision making.

7   Low risk debt refers to small probability of change in the value of debt. That is, change in debt value is independent of the firm-specific information revealed to investors. Other things, such as a general shift in interest rates may change debt value. See Myers and Majluf (1984) for details.

8   Taxation on intercorporate dividends may be explained with the following example. Suppose that a firm bought x yen worth of stock in some past year, and α of this amount was financed by borrowing at an interest rate of r and $(1-\alpha)$ by internal funds. In the current year, the company receives dx of dividends, where d is the dividend yield. The amount $dx - r\alpha x = \Delta d$ is taxable when Δd is positive. The amount $r\alpha x$ is preferred as profit because this will simply offset the deduction of interest paid against the purchase of the stock from profits of the firm. Thus the firm clearly prefers (unrealized) capital gains to dividends.

9   The analysis may be extended to the general case by issuing the following symbols: $\lambda_i =$ the total profits of corporation i, $R_i =$ profits of corporation i resulting from ordinary production, $\alpha_i =$ payout ratio of corporation i, $h_{ij} =$ the jth corporation's shareholdings ratio in respect to the ith corporation's stocks, and $t_{ij} = \alpha_i h_{ij}$. $\alpha_1 R_1 + \alpha_2 R_2$ is considered as the total of dividends drawn by the individual shareholders before interlocking stockholdings. Now if both companies increase their capital by way of reciprocal share holding then the profits are: $\lambda_1 = R_1 + \alpha_2 \lambda_2 h_{21} = R_1 + t_{21} \lambda_2$ and $\lambda_2 = R_2 + \alpha_1 \lambda_1 h_{12} = R_2 + t_{12} \lambda_1$. Solving these two equations for λ_1 and λ_2 we get, $\lambda_1 = (R_1 + t_{12})/(1 - t_{12} t_{21})$ and $\lambda_2 = (R_2 + t_{12})/(1 - t_1 t_{21})$. Then P, total amount of dividends paid to individuals follows from: $P = \alpha_1 \lambda_1 (1 - h_{12}) + \alpha_2 \lambda_2 (1 - h_{21}) = 1/(1 - t_{12} t_{21}) [(\alpha_1 - t_{12})(R_1 + t_{21} R_2) + (\alpha_2 - t_{21})(R_2 + t_{12} R_1)]$. Accordingly, $\alpha_1 R_1 + \alpha_2 R_2 - P = 1/(1 - t_{12})[\{(1 - \alpha_2) + t_{21}(1 - \alpha_1)\} t_{12} R_1 + \{(1 - \alpha_1) + t_{12}(1 - \alpha_2)\} t_{21} R_{21}]$. The last equation shows that $(\alpha_1 R_1 + \alpha_2 R_2) > P$ always holds, except $\alpha_1 = \alpha_2 = 1$.

10 Side payment may be defined as an arrangement among different types of security holders whereby the firm's bondholders and stockholders are free to compensate one another for the effects of operating decisions that increase the wealth of one group but not the other. That is, an implicit contract between creditors and equityholders for sharing gains or losses may be reached with the objective to attain maximization of firm value rather than maximizing the value of a particular class of security holders' share in an uncertain business world (For further details see Fama and Miller, 1972).

11 We have in mind the restrictive practices of the *zaibatsu* system in the prewar Japan and group behavior in postwar period.

12 In the hierarchy solution, production of financial information and other activities of financial intermediation, such as risk taking, are integrated in a hierarchy called as a financial intermediary, e.g., a commercial bank. On the other hand, market solution assumes production and distribution of relevant information through market mechanisms. However, 'market vs. hierarchy solution' is compatible with the most conventional use of 'the direct vs. indirect finance' introduced by Gurley and Shaw (1960) (See for details Horiuchi, A., 1989).

13 In addition, banks may also have been interested in attracting deposits of client firms and their employees (Okazaki, 1993; Teranishi, 1993).

14 These agents provided, as their name indicates, the management of the majority of private corporations during British and Pakistani regimes. They acted as an entrepreneur, capitalist, financier and business manager. Thus, to aconsiderable extent they assumed the role of investment banker.

15 Repression theory assumes that the level of financial savings is determined largely by interest rates and accordingly, establishing high time deposit rates (high compared to anticipated inflation) has become a standard part of the policy advice given to LDCs by the experts (See for details Van Wijnbergen, 1982).

16 The financial interrelation ratio, $FIR = (F_n + F_x + F_f)/W$, where F_n, F_x and F_f stand for the market values of domestic nonfinancial, foreign (net), and outstanding financial institutions' instruments, and W for the market value of national wealth. Domestic physical assets and net foreign balance are included in national wealth (Goldsmith, 1969, p.283).

Bibliography

Abegglen, J. (1958), *The Japanese Factory*, Free Press: New York.
Agarwala, P.N.(1986), 'The Development of Managerial Enterprises in India', in Kobayashi, K. and Morikawa, H. (Eds.), *Development of Managerial Enterprises*, University of Tokyo Press: Tokyo.
Aghion, Philippe and Bolton, Patrick (1992), 'An 'Incomplete Contract' Approach to Bankruptcy and the Financial Structure of the Firm', *Review of Economic Studies*, Vol. 59, No.3, pp.473-94.
Agmon, T. and Lessard, D.R.(1977), 'Financial Factors and the International Expansion of Small-country Firms,' in Agmon, T. and Kindleberger, C.P. (Eds.), *Multinationals from Small Countries*, MIT Press: Cambridge, Mass.
Ahmed, M. Farid (1978), 'Institutional Behavior of Finance: A Perspective of Bangladesh Shilpa Bank', *Business Review*, University of Dhaka, Vol. 4, No. 2, pp.59-70.
------------(1985), *Japanese Way of Financing Industries: Its Applicability to Developing Countries, Bangladesh in Particular* (Unpublished Master Thesis), Yokohama National University, March.
------------(1988), 'A Study of Stockholding-Structure in Japanese Business Group', *The Economic Science*, Nagoya University, Vol. 35, No. 3, pp. 205-36.
------------(1992), *Stock Market Behavior in Bangladesh*, Bureau of Business Research, University of Dhaka: Dhaka.
------------(1992), *Valuation of Share and Capital Market Structure*, Unpublished doctoral dissertation, Nagoya University, Nagoya.
------------Khan, Harun-ar-Rashid and Islam, Md. Sadiqul (1993), *Industrial Financing Through Capital Market in Bangladesh: A Study on the Demand Side*, Asia Foundation and Bureau of Economic Research, University

of Dhaka: Dhaka.
Ahmed, Q.K. (1978), 'The Manufacturing Sector of Bangladesh - An Overview', *The Bangladesh Development Studies*, Vol. 6, No. 3, pp.30-65.
Ahmed, Z.; Aqbal, M. and Khan, M.F. (1983), *Money and Banking in Islam*, International Center for Research in Islamic Economics: Jeddah and Institute of Policy Studies: Islamabad.
Akimoto, H. (1991), 'The Stock Market (II)', in Foundation for Advanced Information and Research, Japan (FAIR), *Japan's Financial Markets*, FAIR, pp.193-10.
Alamgir, M. and Berlage, L.J.J.B. (1974), *Bangladesh National Income and Expenditure, 1949/50-1969/70*, Research Monograph No. 1, BIDS: Dhaka.
Alam, K. (1989), 'Developing Capital Market', *The Bangladesh Observer*, 20 October.
------------(1993), 'Privatization: Some Points', *Proceedings of the Regional Seminar on DSE: Link-up Efforts with Global Securities Markets*, Dhaka Stock Exchange and Asia Foundation: Dhaka, April 8 & 9, pp. 47-58.
Alamgir, M.Khan (1985), 'Development Banks in Bangladesh', paper presented in the *Annual Conference of Bangladesh Economic Association*, J.N.University, Dhaka.
Amsden, A.H. (1989), *Asia's Next Giant: South Korea and Late Industrialization*, Oxford University Press: New York.
Ando, A. and Modigliani, F. (1963), 'The Life Cycle Hypothesis of Saving: Aggregate Implication and Tests', *American Economic Review*, Vol. 53, No.1, pp.55-84.
Aoki, M. (1980), 'A Model of the Firm as a Stockholder-Employee Cooperative Game', *The American Economic Review*, Vol. 70, No.4, pp.600-10.
------------(1982), 'Equilibrium Growth of the Hierarchial Firm: Shareholder-Employee Cooperative Game', *The American Economic Review*, Vol.72, No. 5, pp.1097-10.
------------(1984), 'Aspects of the Japanese Firm', in Aoki, M.(Ed.), *The Economic Analysis of the Japanese Firm*, North Holland, Elsevier Science Publishers, B.V.:Amsterdam, pp.3-46.
------------(1984), 'Shareholders' non-unanimity on Investment Financing: Banks vs. Individual Investors', in Aoki, M. (Ed.), *The Economic Analysis of the Japanese Firm*, North Holland, Elsevier Science Publishers, B.V.: Amsterdam, pp.193-24.
Arena, J. (1965), 'Post War Stock Market Changes and Consumer Spending', *Review of Economics and Statistics*, Vol. 47, No. 4, pp.379-91.
Arowolo, Edward A. (1971), 'The Development of Capital Markets in Africa, with Particular Reference to Kenya and Nigeria', *International Monetary Fund Staff Papers*, July, pp. 420-69.

Arrow, K.J. (1974), 'Limited Knowledge and Economic Analysis', *American Economic Review*, Vol. 64, No. 1, pp.1-10.

Asian Development Bank (ADB) (1989), *Report on the Second Round Capital Market Study on Bangladesh,*Manila, November.

-------------(1992), *Asian Development Outlook, Manila.*

Asquith, P. and Mullins, D. (1986), 'Equity Issues and Offering Dilution', *Journal of Financial Economics*, Vol. 15, No. 1-2, pp.61-89.

Ball, R. and Brown, P. (1968), ' An Empirical Evaluation of Accounting Income Numbers', *Journal of Accounting Research*, Vol. 6, No.2, pp.159-78.

Bandon, R. (1983), *The Other Hundred Years War*, Collins: London.

Bangladesh Bank, *Economic Trends* (various issues), Bangladesh Bank: Dhaka.

-------------(1993, 1994), *Schedule Banks Statistics*, Bangladesh Bank: Dhaka.

-------------(1989-90), *Annual Report*, Bangladesh Bank: Dhaka.

-------------(1994), *Bangladesh Bank Bulletin*, July-September, Bangladesh Bank: Dhaka.

-------------(1993), *Index Numbers of Stock Exchange Share Prices*, Quarterly, January-March, Bangladesh Bank: Dhaka.

Bangladesh Bureau of Statistics (1993), Ministry of Planning, Government of Bangladesh, *Statistical Yearbook of Bangladesh*, Bangladesh Bureau of Statistics: Dhaka.

Bank of Japan (BOJ) (1962), *Fukko Kinyu Kinko ni tsuite* (On RFB) in *Nihon Kinyushi Shryo Showa Zokuhen* (Materials on Financial History of Japan, Sequel Volumes of Showa), BOJ (Ed.), Vol. 11, Ministry of Finance(MOF), Government of Japan (in Japanese).

Barnea, A; Haugen, R. and Senbet, L. (1981), 'Market Imperfections Agency Problems and Capital Structure', *Financial Management*, Vol. 10, No. 3, Summer, pp.7-22.

Barrett, M.E.; Price, L.N. and Gehrke, J.A.(1974), 'Japan: Some Background for Security Analysts', Financial Analysts Journal, Vol. 30, No.1, pp.33-44.

Basch, A. and Kybal, M. (1975), *Capital Markets in Latin America*, Praeger Publishers: New York.

Baumol, W. (1965), *The Stock Market and Economic Efficiency*, Fordham University Press: New York.

Beaver, W.H. (1968), 'The Information Content of Annual Earnings Announcement', *Journal of Accounting Research*, Supplement to Vol. 6, pp. 67-92.

-------------Kettler, P. and Scholes, M. (1970), The Association Between Market Determined and Accounting Determined Risk Measures', *The Accounting Review*, Vol. 45, No. 4, pp. 654-82.

Berg, E. (1985), *Divestiture of State-Owned Enterprises*, Report prepared for the World Bank, Mimeo. Washington, November (cited in Killick and Commander, 1988, p. 2).

Berglof, E. and Perotti, E. (1994), 'The Governance Structure of the Japanese Financial *Keiretsu*', *Journal of Financial Economics*, Vol. 36, No. 2, pp. 259-84.

Bhatia, K. (1972), 'Capital Gains and the Aggregate Consumption Function', *American Economic Review*, Vol. 62, No. 13-15, pp. 866-72.

Bhatia, Rattan J. and Khatkhate, Deena R. (1975), 'Financial Intermediation, Savings Mobilization and Entrepreneurship Development: The African Experience', *IMF, Staff Papers*, Vol. 22, No. 1, pp. 132-58.

Bichitra (National Weekly of Bangladesh) (1996), Vol. 28, 29 November (in Bengali).

Black, F. (1976), 'Dividend Puzzle', *The Journal of Portfolio Management*, Vol. 2, No. 1, pp. 5-8.

------------Jensen, M.C. and Scholes, M. (1972), 'The Capital Asset Pricing Model: Some Empirical Tests', in Jensen, M.C. (Ed.), *Studies in the Theory of Capital Markets*, Praeger Publishing: New York.

Blume, M. (1975), 'Betas and Their Regression Tendencies', *Journal of Finance*, Vol. 10, No. 3, pp. 785-95.

Board of Investment (BOI) (1995), *Bangladesh: The Best Investment Choice in South Asia*, BOI, Prime Minister's Office, Government of Bangladesh, January.

Bouin, O. (1992), *Privatization in Developing Countries: Reflections on a Panacea*, OECD Development Center: Paris.

Briston, R.J. (1976), *The Stock Exchange and Investment Analyst*, Unwin University Press: London.

Calamanti, A. (1983), *The Securities Market and Underdevelopment*, Finafrica: Giuffre, Milan.

Calder, Kent E. (1993), *Strategic Capitalism: Private Business and Public Purpose in Japanese Industrial Finance*, Princeton University Press: New Jersey.

Cameron, R. (1953), 'The Credit Mobilier and the Economic Development', *Journal of Political Economy*, Vol. 61, No. 6, pp.461-88.

Cameron, R.(1967), *Banking in the Early Stages of Industrialization*, Oxford University Press: New York.

Carrington, A.S. (1977), 'Diversified Models - An Alternative to the Illusion of Certainty in Accounting Reports', in Baxter, W.T. Davidson (Ed.), *Studies in Accounting*, Institute of Chartered Accountants in England and Wales: London.

Caves, R. and Uekusa, M. (1976), *Industrial Organization in Japan*, The Brookings Institution: Washington D.C.

Chambers, R.J. (1979), 'Usefulness - the Vanishing Premise in Accounting Standards Setting', *Abacus,* Vol. 15, No. 2, pp. 71-92.

Chandler, Alfred (1990), *Scale and Scope: The Dynamics of Industrial Capitalism*, Boston University Press: Boston.

Chen, Nai-fu; Roll, Richard and Ross, Stephen (1986), 'Economic Forces and the Stock Market', *Journal of Business*, Vol. 59, No.3, pp. 386-03.

Chenery, H. B. and Strout, A. M. (1966), 'Foreign Assistance and economic development', *American Economic review*, Vol. 56, No. 4, Part 1, pp. 679-33.

--------------and Syrquin, M. (1975), *Patterns of Development 1950-1970*, Oxford University Press: Oxford.

Chowdhury, O. and Rashid, R. (1986), *Status of National Savings Schemes in Bangladesh, A Rural Finance Project Report*, Robert R. Nathan Associates and S.F. Ahmed & Co.: Dhaka, January.

Christian, James W. and Pagoulatos, E. (1973), 'Domestic Financial Markets in Developing Economies: An Econometric Analysis' *Kyklos,* Vol. 26, No. 1, pp.75-90.

Cook, P. and Kirkpatric, C. (1988), 'Privatization in Less Developed Countries: An Overview', in Cook, P. and Kirkpatric, C. (Eds.), *Privatization in Less Developed Countries*, Wheatsheaf Books: Brighton.

Deakin, Edward B.; Norwood, Gyles R. and Smith, Charles M. (1974), 'The Effect of Published Earnings Information on Tokyo Stock Exchange Trading', *International Journal of Accounting*, Vol. 10, No. 1,pp. 123-36.

De Gregorio, J. and Guidotti, P.E. (1993), 'Financial Development and Economic Growth', mimeo, *International Monetary Fund.*

Dhaka Stock Exchange (DSE) (1984-85), *DSE Factbook*, DSE: Dhaka.

--------------(1986), *DSE Factbook*, DSE: Dhaka.

--------------(1994), *DSE Factbook*, DSE: Dhaka.

--------------*DSE Monthly Reviews* (various issues).

Diamond, D. (1984), 'Financial Intermediation and Delegated Monitoring', *Review of Economic Studies,* Vol. 51, No. 166, pp.393-14.

Dikie, R.B. (1981), 'Development of Third World Securities Markets: An Analysis of General Principles and a Case Study of the Indonesian Market', *Law and Policy in International Business,* Vol. 13, pp.177-22.

Dore, R. (1973), *British Factory - Japanese Factory: The Origins of National Diversity in Industrial Relations*, University of California Press: California.

Drake, P. J. (1977), 'Securities Market in Less Develped Countries', *Journal of Development Studies*, Vol. 13, No. 2, pp.74-91.

--------------(1980), *Money, Finance and Development*, Martin Robertson: Oxford.

--------------(1985), 'Some Reflections on Problems Affecting Securities Markets in Less Developed Countries', *Savings and Development*, Vol. IX, No. 1, pp.5-14.

Dryden, Miles M. (1970), 'Filter Tests of United Kingdom Share Prices', *Applied Economics*, Vol. 7, pp. 265-75.

Easterbrook, Frank H. and Fichel, Daniel R. (1981), 'The proper Role of a Target's Management in Responding to a Tender Offer', *Harvard Law Review*, Vol. 94, No. 6, pp. 1161-204.

Economic Times (1990*)*, Dhaka, 22 December.

Edward, Ben (1995), 'Expect a Ducking in Dhaka', *Euromoney*, February, pp. 18-20.

Emi, K. (1971), 'Capital Formation', in Ohkawa, K. et al. (Eds.), *Estimates of Long Term Economic Statistics of Japan Since 1968*, Tokyo Keizai Shimposha: Tokyo.

Errunza, V.R. (1977), 'Gains from Portfolio Diversification into Less Developed Countries' Securities', *Journal of International Business*, Vol. 8, No. 2, pp. 83-99.

Euromoney (1995), 'What to do with the Bangladesh Banks', *Euromoney*, March, p. 163.

Fama, E.F. (1965), 'The Behavior of Stock Prices', *Journal of Business*, Vol 38, No. 1, pp.34-05.

-------------(1970), 'Efficient Capital Markets: A Review of Theory and Empirical Work', *Journal of Finance*, Vol.25, N0. 2, pp. 383-17.

-------------(1976), *Foundation of Finance: Portfolio Decisions and Security Prices*, Basic Books Inc. Publishers: New York.

-------------(1980), 'Agency Problems and the Theory of the Firm', *Journal of Political Economy*, Vol. 88, No. 2, pp. 288-07.

-------------and Miller, M.H. (1972), *The Theory of Finance*, Holt, Rinehart and Winston: Dryden Press, Hinsdale, IL.

-------------and MacBeth, J. (1973), 'Risk, Return and Equilibrium: Empirical Tests', *Journal of Political Economy*, Vol. 81, No.3 pp. 607-36.

-------------and French, Kenneth R. (1992), 'The Cross Section of Expected Stock Returns', *Journal of Finance*, Vol. 47, No. 2, pp. 427-65.

Farouk, A. (1974), *Economic Development of Bangladesh: Some Lessons from Meiji Japan*, Bureau of Business Research, Unversity of Dhaka: Dhaka.

Flath, D. (1984), 'Debt and Taxes: Japan Compared with the U.S.', *International Journal of Industrial Organization*, Vol. 2, pp. 311-26.

-------------(1996), 'The *Keiretsu* Puzzle', *Journal of the Japanese and International Economies*, Vol. 10, No.2, pp. 101-21.

Friend, I. and Puckett, M. (1964), 'Dividends and Stock Prices', *American Economic Review*, Vol.54, No. 5, pp. 656-82.

Fruin, W.Mark (1992), *The Japanese Enterprise System: Competitive Stra-*

tegies and Cooperative Structures, Clarendon Press: Oxford.

Fry, Maxewell J. (1978), 'Money and Capital or Financial Deepening in Economic Development ?', *Journal of Money, Credit and Banking*, Vol. 10, No. 4, pp. 464-75.

------------(1980), 'Saving, Investment, Growth and the Cost of Financial Repression' *World Development*, Vol. 8, No. 4, pp. 317-327.

------------(1982), 'Models of Financially Repressed Developing Economies', *World Development*, Vol. 10, No. 9, pp. 731-50.

------------(1995), *Money, Interest, and Banking in Economic Development*, John Hopkins University Press: Baltimore.

Fukku Kinyu Kinko (Reconstruction Finance Bank (RFB)) (1950), *Fukkin Yushi no Kaiko* (Retrospect of RFB), RFB, (in Japanese).

Fung, K.C. (1991), 'Characteristics of Japanese Industrial Groups and their Potential Impact on U.S.-Japan Trade', in Baldwin, R. (Ed.), *Empirical Studies on Commercial Policy*, University of Chicago Press for the National Bureau of Economic Research: Chicago, pp. 137-68.

Futatsugi, Y. (1986), *Japanese Enterprise Groups*, Monogram No. 4, The School of Business Administration, Kobe University: Kobe.

Gandhi, D.K., Saunders, A., and Woodward, R.S. (1980), 'Thin Capital Markets: A Case Study of the Kuwaiti Stock Market', *Applied Economics*, Vol. 12, pp. 341-49.

Gerlach, M.(1987), 'Business Alliance and the Strategy of the Japanese Firm', *California Management Review*, Vol. 30, N0. 1, pp. 126-42.

------------(1992a), *Alliance Capitalism: The Social Organization of Japanese Business*, University of California Press: Berkeley CA.

------------(1992b), 'Twilight of the *keiretsu*? A Critical assessment', *Journal of Japanese Studies*, Vol. 18, No. 1, pp. 78-18.

Gerschenkron, A. (1965), *Economic Backwardness in Historical Perspective: A Book of Essays*, Frederick A. Praeger: New York.

Gibney, Frank (1982), *Miracle by Design*, Times Books: New York.

Gilson, Ronald J. and Roe, Mark J. (1993), 'Understanding the Japanese *Keiretsu*: Overlaps Between Corporate Governance and Industrial Organization', *The Yale Law Journal*, Vol. 102, No. 4, pp. 871-06.

Goldsmith, Raymond W. (1966), *The Determinants of Financial Structure*, Organization for Economic Cooperation and Development: Paris.

------------(1969), *Financial Structure and Development*, Yale University Press:New Haven.

Gordon, M.J. (1962), *The Investment, Financing and Valuation of the Corporation*, R.D. Irwin: Homewood.

------------(1971), 'Capital Markets and Economic Development', *International Symposium on Development of Capital Markets*, Rio de Janeiro, September.

Gordon, D.L. (1983), 'Development Finance Companies, State and Privately Owned: A Review', *World Bank Staff Working Paper* No. 578.

Goto, A. (1982), 'Business Groups in a Market Economy', *European Economic Review*, Vol. 19, No. 1, pp. 53-70.

Government of Bangladesh, P.O. No. 26 and 27, 1972.

Gupta, K.L. (1984), *Financial and Economic Growth in Developing Countries*, Croom Helm: London.

Gurley, John G. and Shaw, E.S. (1955), 'Financial Aspects of Economic Development', *American Economic Review*, Vol. 45, No. 4, pp.515-38.

------------(1967), 'Financial Structure and Economic Development', *Economic Development and Cultural Change*, Vol. 15, No. 3, pp.257-68.

Hadley, E. (1970), *Antitrust in Japan*, Princeton Unversity Press, Princeton, NJ.

Hamada, K. and Horiuchi, A. (1987), 'The political Economy of the Japanese Financial Markets', in Yamamura, K. and Yasuba, Y. (Eds.), *The Political Economy of Japan:The Domestic transformation*,Stanford University Press, Stanford, CA. pp.223-60.

Hanke, S. (1987), 'The necessity of Property Rights', in Hanke, S. (Ed.), *Privatisation and Development*, International Center for Economic Growth (ICEG), International Institute for Contemporary Studies: San Fransisco, California.

Hanson, A.M. (1959), *Public Enterprise and Economic Development*, Routledge and Kegan Paul Ltd.: London.

Haque, M.S. (1992), 'Financing Policy, Procedures and Operations of Development Financing Institutions (DFIs) of Bangladesh', in Nabi, K.A.(Ed.), *Development Financing Institutions (DFIs) of Bangladesh: Policy, Performance, Problems and Prospects*, Goeth Institute: Dhaka, pp. 111-37.

Hart, Oliver (1989), 'An Economist's Perspective on the Theory of the Firm', *Columbia Law Review*, Vol. 89, No. 7, pp.1756-74.

Hemming, R. and Monsoor, A.M. (1987), *Privatization and Public Enterprises*, IMF Working Paper.

Hodder, J. and Tschoel, A. (1985), 'Some Aspects of Japanese Corporate Finance', *Journal of Financial and Quantitative Analysis*, Vol. 20, No. 2, pp. 173-92.

Horiuchi, A. (1989), 'Information Properties of the Japanese Financial System', Japan and the World Economy, Vol. 1, No. 3, pp. 255-78.

Horiuchi, A. and Sui, Q. (1993), 'Influence of the Japan Development Bank Loans on Corporate Investment Behavior', *Journal of the Japanese and International Economies*, Vol. 7, No. 4, pp.441-65..

------------and Otaki, M. (1987), 'Finance: Government Intervention and the Importance of Bank Lending' in Hamada et al. (Eds.), *The Macroeconomic*

Analysis of the Japanese Economy, University of Tokyo Press: Tokyo, (in Japanese).

Hoshi, T. (1986), 'A Test of Stock Price Volatility: The Case of Japan', *Fainansu Kenkyu*, No. 5, pp. 1-18.

Ibbotson, R.G. and Sinquefield, R.A. (1976), 'Stocks, Bonds, Bills, and Inflation: Year-by-Year Historical Returns (1926-1974)', *The Journal of Business*, Vol. 49, No. 1, pp. 11-47.

Imai, K. (1990a), 'The Legitimacy of Japan's Corporate Groups', *Japan Echo*, Vol. 17, No. 3, pp. 23-28.

-------------(1990b), 'Japanese Business Groups and the Structural Impediments Initiative', in Yamamura, K. (Ed.), *Japan's Economic Structure: Should It Change?*, Society for Japanese Studies: Seattle.

International Finance Corporation (IFC) (1992), *Annual Report*, IFC:Washington, D.C.

-------------(1994, 1995), *Emerging Stock Market Factbook*, IFC: Washington, D.C.

International monetary Fund (IMF) (1986), *World Economic Outlook*, IMF: Washington D.C.

Investment Corporation of Bangladesh (ICB) (1994-95), *Annual Report*, ICB: Dhaka.

Investment Corporation of Bangladesh (ICB) Unit Fund (1994-95), *Annual Report*, ICB: Dhaka.

Investment Corporation of Bangladesh (ICB) Mutual Funds (1994-95), *Annual Report*, ICB: Dhaka.

Japan Development Bank (JDB) (1976), *Nihon Kaihatsu Ginko Nijiyo-go Nenshi* (A Twenty-five Year History of the JDB) (in Japanese).

Japan Securities Research Institute, *Securities Market in Japan*, Tokyo: various issues.

Jensen, M. and Meckling, H. (1976), 'Theory of the Firm: Managerial Behavior, Agency Costs and Ownership Structure', *Journal of Financial Economics*, Vol. 3, No. 4, pp. 305-60.

-------------and Ruback, R. (1983), 'The Market for Corporate Control: The Scientific Evidence', *Journal of Financial Economics*, Vol. 11, No. 1-4, pp. 5-50.

Johnson, C. (1982), *MITI and the Japanese Economic Miracle*, Stanford University Press: Stanford, Calif.

Kaldor, Nicholas (1972), 'The Irrelevance of Equilibrium Economics', *Economic Journal*, Vol. 82, No. 328, pp. 1237-55.

Kashem, H. Abul (1985), '*Pujir Bazare Noirajya*' (Indiscipline in Capital Market), *The Weekly Bichitra*, 26 July, pp. 32- 37 (in Bengali).

Kato, Kiyoshi and Schallheim, James S. (1985), 'Seasonal and Size Anomalies in the Japanese Stock Market', *Journal of Financial and Quatitative Analysis*, Vol. 20, No. 2, pp. 243-60.

Kemp, T. (1978), *Historical Patterns of Industrialization*, Longman: London.

Kester, W. Carl (1990), *Japanese Takeovers: The Global Contest for Corporate Control*, Harvard Business School Press: Cambridge, MA.

Khan, Harun-or-Rashid; Khalily, M.A.B. and Islam, Md. Sadiqul (1995), *Development of Securities Market in Bangladesh - A Supply Side Study*, Bureau of Economic Research, University of Dhaka and Asia Foundation: Dhaka.

Khan, M. and Reihard, C.M. (1990), 'Private Investment and Economic Growth in Developing Countries', *World development*, Vol. 18, No. 1, pp.19-27.

Kigyo Keiretsu Soran (A General Survey on Enterprise Affiliations) (1986), Toyo Keizai Shimposha: Tokyo (in Japanese).

Killick, T. and Commander, S.(1988), *Privatization in Developing Countries: A Survey of Issues*, Mimeo., Brighton.

King, R.G. and Levine, R. (1993), 'Finance and Growth: Schumpeter Might Be Right', *Quarterly Journal of Economics*, Vol. 108, No.3, pp.717-37.

Kitchen, R. (1987), 'The Role of the Jamaica Stock Exchange in the Capital Market: A Historical Analysis', *Savings and Development*, Vol.11, No. 3, pp. 249-74.

------------(1993), *Finance for the Developing Countries*, Wiley and Sons: New York.

Kiyonari, T. and Nakamura, H. (1980), 'The Establishment of the Big Business System', in Sato, K. (Ed.), *Industry and business in Japan*, Croom Helm: London.

Kobayashi, Y. (1980), *Kigyoshudan no Bunseki* (An Analysis of Corporate Groups), Hokkaido University Press: Hokkaido.

Kohli, K.N. (1987), 'Financing Public Sector Development Expenditure: The Asian Experience', *Asian Development Review*, Vol. 5, No. 2, pp. 20-38.

Koike, K. (1984), 'Skill Formation Systems in the U.S. and Japan: A Comparative Study', in Aoki, M. (Ed.), *The Economic Analysis of the Japanese Firm*, North Holland, Elsevier SciencePublishers, B.V.: Amsterdam, pp.47-76.

Konya, F. (1978), *'Kabushiki Shijo ni Okeru Toshika Kodo to Shijo Koritsu - CAPM no Kensho'*, (Investors' Behavior and Market Efficiency - Test of CAPM), *Keisoku Shitsu* Technical Paper no. 44 (in Japanese).

Krugman, P.R. (1993), 'International Finance and Economic development' in Giovannini, A. (Ed.), *Finance and Development: Issues and Experience*, Cambridge University Press: Cambridge.

Kuroda, I. and Oritani, Y. (1980), 'A Reexamination of the Unique Feature of Japan's Corporate Financial Structure - A Comparison of Corporate

Balance Sheets in Japan and the United States', *Japanese Economic Studies*, Vol. 8, pp. 82-17.

Lal, D. (1983) *The Poverty of Development Economics*, Institute of Economic Affairs: London

Lau, S.C.; Quay, S.R.; and Ramsay, C.M. (1974), 'The Tokyo Stock Exchange and the Capital Asset pricing Model', *The Journal of Finance*, Vol. 29, No. 2, pp. 507-14.

Lesser, B.(1991), 'When Government Fails, Will the Market Do Better/ The Privatisation/Market Liberalization movement in Developing Countries', *Canadian Journal of Developing Studies*, Vol. 12, No. 1, pp. 159-72.

Lev, B. and Yahalomi, B.(1972), 'The Effect of Corporate Financial Statements on Israili Stock Exchange', *Management International Review*, Vol. 12, No. 2-3, pp. 145-49.

Lintner, J. (1956), 'Distribution of Income of Corpoprations among Dividends, Retained Earnings and Taxes', *American Economic Review*, Vol.46, No.2, pp. 97-13.

------------(1965), 'The Valuation of Risk Assets and the Selection of Investments in Stock Portfolios and Capital Budgets', *The Review of Economics and Statistics*, Vol. 47, No. 1, pp. 13-37.

Lipton, M. and Rosenblum, Steven A. (1992), 'A New System of Corporate Governance: The Quenquennial Election of Directors', University of Chicago Law Review, Vol. 58, No. 1, pp. 187-53

Little, I.M.D. and Mirrlees, J.A. (1968), *Manual of Industrial Project Analysis in Developing Countries*, Development Center of the Organization for Economic Cooperation and Development: Paris.

Lloyd, B. (1977), 'The Efficiency of Financial Institutions and Markets',*Investment Analyst*, No. 47, pp. 5-16.

Lockwood, W.W. (1954), *The Economic Development of Japan: Growth and Structural Change, 1868-1938*, Princeton University Press: Princeton.

Loomis, C.J. (1968), 'A Case for Dropping Dividends', *Fortune*, 15 June, pp.179-87.

Lowenstein, L. (1988), *What's Wrong with Wall Street: Short-term Gain and theAbsentee Shareholder,* Addison-wesley Publishing Company:New York.

------------(1991), *Sense and Nonsense in Corporate Finance*, Addison-Wesley Publishing Company: New York.

MacKinlay, A. Craig (1995), 'Multifactor Models do not Explain Deviations from the CAPM', *Journal of Financial Economics*, Vol. 38, No. 1, pp.3-28.

Malkiel, B.G. (1981), *A Random Walk Down Wall Street*, W.W. Norton and Company: New York.

Maniatis, George C. (1971), 'Reliability of the Equities Market to Finance Industrial Development in Greece', *Economic Development and Cultural*

Change, Vol. 19, No. 4, pp. 598-20.

Markowitz, H.M. (1952), 'Portfolio Selection', *Journal of Finance*, Vol. 7, No. 1, pp.77-91.

Maru, J. and Royama, S. (1974), 'Rates of Return in Relation to Risk: An Empirical Analysis of the TSE', *Japan Securities Research Institute Technical Paper No.* 29, January.

Mason, Robert T. (1972), 'The Creation of Risk Aversion by Imperfect Capital Markets', *American Economic Review*, Vol. 62, pp. 77-88..

Mayer, Colin (1994), 'Stock-markets, Financial Institutions, and Corporate Performance', in Dimsdale, N. and Prevezer, M. (Eds.), *Capital Markets and Corporate Governance*, Clarendon Press: Oxford, pp. 179-08.

------------and Alexander, I. (1990), 'Banks and Markets: Corporate Financing in Germany and U.K.', *Journal of Japanese and International Economies*, Vol. 4, No.4, December, pp. 450-75.

Maynard, G. (1970), 'The Economic Irrelevance of Monetary Independence: The Case of Liberia', *Journal of Development Studies*, Vol. 6, No. 2, pp. 101-22.

McDonald, J.(1989), 'The *mochiai* effect: Japanese Corporate Cross-holding', *Journal of Portfolio Management*, Vol. 16, No. 1, pp. 90-95.

McKinnon, Ronald I. (1973), *Money and Capital in Economic Development*, The Brookings Institution: Washington, D.C.

Mehra, R. and Prescott, E. (1985), 'The Equity Premium: A puzzle', *Journal of Monetary Economics*, Vol. 15, No. 2, pp. 145-61.

Meir, G.M. and Baldwin, R.E. (1964), *Economic Development, Theory, History and Policy*, Asia Publishing House: Bombay.

Miller, M.H. and Modigliani, F.(1961), 'Dividend Policy, Growth and the Valuation of Shares', *Journal of Business*, Vol. 34, No. 4, pp. 411-33.

------------(1966), 'Some Estimates of the Cost of Capital to the Electric Utility Industry', *American Economic Review*, Vol. 56, No. 3, pp. 334-91.

------------and Scholes, M. (1972), 'Rates of Return in relation to Risk: A reexamination of Some Recent Findings', in Jensen (Ed.), *Studies in the Theory of Capital Markets*, Praeger Publishing: New York.

Ministry of Commerce, Government of Bangladesh (1938), *Insurance Act (Bangladesh)*, Dhaka.

------------(1994), *Companies Act (Bangladesh)*, Dhaka.

Ministry of Finance, Government of Bangladesh (1947), *Capital Issues (Continuance of Control) Act*, Dhaka.

------------(1969), *Securities and Exchange Ordinance (Bangladesh)*, Dhaka.

------------(1971), *Securities and Exchange Rules (Bangladesh)*, Dhaka.

------------(1987), *Securities and Exchange Rules (Bangladesh)*, Dhaka.

------------(1988-89), *Resume of the Activities of the Financial Institutions in*

  Bangladesh, Dhaka.

----------(1993a), *Securities and Exchange Commission Act (Bangladesh)*, Dhaka

----------(1993b), *Securities and Exchange (Amendment) Act (Bangladesh)*, Dhaka.

----------(1993c), *Bank Company Act (Amended) of Bangladesh*, Dhaka.

----------(1993-94a) *Economic Survey of Bangladesh*, Dhaka.

----------(1993-94b), *Resume of Activities of the Financial Institutions in Bangladesh*, Dhaka.

Ministry of Finance (MOF), Government of Japan (1976), *Showa Zaisei Shi* (Financial History of Showa Era), Vol. 12, Toyo Keizai Shimposha: Tokyo (in Japanese).

Ministry of Industries, Government of Bangladesh (1985), *Report of the Sub-Committee for Industrial Finance*, Dhaka.

----------(1990), *Report of the Committee Constituted by the Government of Bangladesh to Suggest Remedies for Improvement of the Stock Market from its Bearish Condition*, Dhaka.

Ministry of Planning, Government of Bangladesh, *First Five Year Plan* 1973-1978, *Two Year Plan* 1978-80, *Second Five Year Plan* 1980-85, *Third Five Year Plan* 1985-90 and *Fourth Five Year Plan* 1990-95, Planning Commission: Dhaka.

Miyajima, H. (1994), 'The Transformation of Zaibatsu to Postwar Corporate Group: From Hierarchial Integrated Group to Horizontally Integrated Group,' *Journal of Japanese and International Economies*, Vol. 8, No. 3, pp. 293-28.

Modigliani, F. and Pogue, G.A. (1974), 'An Introduction to Risk and Return: Concepts and Evidence', *Financial Analysts Journal*, Vol. 30, No. 3, pp. 69-86.

Mookerjee, R. (1988), 'The Stock Market and the Economy: The Indian Experience', *The Indian Economic Journal*, Vol. 36, No. 2, pp.30-43.

Moore, G.H. (1975), 'Stock Prices and the Business Cycle', *Journal of Portfolio Management*, Vol. 1, No. 3, pp. 59-64.

Morgan, E. Victor (1965), *A History of Money*, Penguin Books: Harmondsworth.

Mossin, J. (1966), 'Equilibrium in a Capital Asset Market', *Econometrica*, Vol. 34, No. 4, October, pp. 768-83.

Murakami, Y. (1984), '*Ie* Society as a Pattern of Civilization', *Journal of Japanese Studies*, Vol. 10, pp. 350-68.

Myers, S. (1977), 'Determinants of Corporate Borrowing', *Journal of Financial Economics*, Vol. 5, No. 2, pp. 147-75.

----------(1984), 'The Capital Structure Puzzle', *Journal of Finance*, Vol.

39, No.3, pp. 575-92.

---------and Rice, E. (1978), 'Measuring Portfolio Performance and Empirical Content of Asset Pricing Models', *Journal of Financial Economics*, Vol. 7, No. 1, pp. 3-28.

---------and Majluf, N. (1984), 'Corporate Financing and Investment Decisions When Firms Have Information Investors Do Not Have', *Journal of Financial Economics*, Vol. 13, No. 2, pp. 187-21.

Myint, H. (1970), 'Dualism and the Internal Integration of the Underdeveloped Economies', *Banca Nazionale del Lavoro Quarterly Review*, Vol. 22, No. 2, pp. 128-56.

Myrdal, Gunnar (1968), *Asian Drama: An Inquiry into the Poverty of Nations*, Penguin: Harmondsworth.

Nabi, Ahmed (1992), *Development Financing Institutions of Bangladesh: Policy, Performance, Problems and Prospects*, Goeth Institute: Dhaka.

Nakatani, I. (1984), 'The Economic Role of Financial Corporate Grouping', in Aoki, M. (Ed.), *The Economic Analysis of the Japanese Firm*, Elsevier Science Publishers, B.V.: North-Holland, pp. 227-58.

---------(1990), 'Opening up Fortress Japan', *Japan Echo*, Vol. 17, No. 3, pp. 8-11.

Nankani, H. (1990), 'Lessons of Privatisation in Developing Countries', *Finance and development*, Vol. 1, pp. 43-45.

Ndulu, B. (1991), 'Growth and Adjustment in Sub-Sahara Africa', in Chhibber, A. and Please, S. (Eds.), *Economic Reform in SubSaharan Africa*, World Bank, washington, D.C.

Ness, Walter L. Jr. (1974), 'Financial Markets Innovation as a Development Strategy: Initial results from the Brazilian Experience,' *Economic development and Cultural Change*, Vol. 22, No. 3, April, pp. 453-72.

Nichols, Nancy A. (1993), 'Efficient? Chaotic? What's New Finance?', *Harvard Business Review*, Vol. 71, March-April, pp. 50-60.

Nihon Keizai Shimbun (The Japan Economic Journal) (1984), '*Mein Banku no Nai Yowami*' (The Weakness of Not Having a Main Bank), 29 February, Tokyo (in Japanese).

---------(1987), *Nihon Keizai Shimbun*, 28 February, Tokyo (in Japanese).

Noland, M. (1990), 'Indicative Planning in Japan: Discussion', *Journal of Comparative Economics*, Vol. 14, No. 4, pp. 648-56.

Nurkse, R. (1952), *Problems of Capital Formation in Underdeveloped Countries*, Basil Blackwell: Oxford.

Nyong, M.O.(1994), 'Potential Effect of Privatisation on Economic Growth in Africa: An Alternative Framework', *The Singapore Economic Review*, Vol. 38, No. 2, pp. 177-90.

Odagiri, H. (1975), *'Kigyo Shudan no Riron'* (A Theory of Industrial Groups),

Kikan Riron Keizaigaku, Vol. 26, pp. 144-154.

OECD (1972), *The Industrial Policy of Japan*, OECD: Paris.

Ogura, S. and Yoshino, N. (1984), 'Taxation and Fiscal Investment and Loan Program', in Komya et al. (Eds.) *The Japanese Industrial Policy*, University of Tokyo Press, Tokyo, (in Japanese).

Oka, Juntaro (1991), 'The Stock Market' in Foundation for Advanced Information and Research, Japan (FAIR), *Japan's Financial Markets*, FAIR, pp.184-10.

Okazaki, T. (1993), *Nohon no Kigyo Shisutemu no Rekishiteki Genryu* (The Historical Origins of the Japanese Corporate System), University of Tokyo Research Institute for the Japanese Economy, Discussion Paper 93-J-7 (in Japanese).

-------------and Ueda, K. (1995), 'The Performance of Development Banks: The Case of the Reconstruction Finance Bank', *Journal of the Japanese and International Economies*, Vol. 9, No. 4, pp. 486-05.

Okumura, H. (1976), *Nihon no Rokudai Kigyo Shudan* (Six Major Business Group in Japan), Daiyamondosha: Tokyo (in Japanese).

-------------(1981),'*Kaisha to Kabunushi no Kankei*' (The Relationship Between the Firm and its Shareholders), *Shoken Keizai*, Vol. 138, pp. 132-51 (in Japanese).

-------------(1982), 'Interfirm Relations in an Enterprise Group: The Case of Mitsubishi', *Japanese Economic Studies*, Vol. 2, No. 2, pp.53-82.

-------------(1986), *Nihon no Kabushikikaisha* (Japanese Corporations), Toyo Keizai Shimposha: Tokyo.

Osano, H. and Tsutsui, Y. (1985), 'Implicit Contracts in the Japanese Bank Loan Market', *Journal of Financial and Quantitative Analysis*, Vol. 20, No. 2, pp. 221-29.

Otsuka, Muneharu (1983), 'Information Content of Accounting Information Announcement - Tokyo Stock Exchange Case', *Waseda Business and Economic Studies*, No. 19, pp. 33-58.

Ouchi, William (1982), *Theory Z*, Addition-Wesley: Reading, Mass.

Papaneck, G.F. (1967), *Pakistan's Development: Social Goals and Private Incentives*, Harvard University Press: Cambridge, Mass, .

Parkinson, J.M. (1984), 'The Nairobi Stock Exchange in the Context of Development of Kenya', *Savings and Development*, Vol. VIII, No. 4, pp. 363-72.

Parry, M. and Khan, F. (1984), *A Survey of Published Accounts in Bangladesh*, The Institute of Chartered Accountants of Bangladesh and The United Nations Department of Technical Cooperation for Development, Dhaka.

Patrick, H.T. (1966), 'Financial Development and Economic Growth in Developing Countries', *Economic Development and Cultural Change*, Vol. 14,

No. 2, pp. 174-89.

Patrick, H.T. and Rosovsky, H. (Eds.) (1976), *Asia's New Giant: How the Japanese Economy Works*, Brookings Institution: Washington D.C.

Pettit, R. (1972), 'Dividend Announcements, Security Performance and Capital Market Efficiency', *Journal of Finance*, 27, No. 5, pp. 993-08.

Porter, Michael (1992), *Remarks at the U.S. Securities and Exchange Commission Forum on Corporate Governance and American Economic Competitiveness: The Role of Shareholders, Directors and management*, March 20, (quoted in Gilson and Roe, 1993).

Porter, R. C. (1966), 'The Promotion of 'Banking Habit' and Economic Development', *Journal of Development Studies*, Vol.2, No. 4, pp. 346-66.

Prindle, A.R. (1981), *Japanese Finance: A Guide to Banking in Japan*, John Wiley and Sons: New York.

Prowse, S.D. (1990), 'Institutional Investment Patterns and Corporate Financial Behavior in the U.S. and Japan', *Journal of Financial Economics*, Vol. 27, No. 1, pp. 43-66.

-------------(1992), 'The Structure of Corporate Ownership in Japan', *Journal of Finance*, Vol. 47, No. 3, July, pp. 1121-40.

Rahman, M. (1990), 'Industry and Investment', *The Bangladesh Observer*, 7 January, Dhaka.

Ramseyer, J.M. (1987), 'Takeovers in Japan: Opportunism, Ideaology and Corporate Control', *UCLA Law Review*, Vol. 35, No. 1, pp. 1-64.

Reitz, T. (1988), 'The Equity Premium: A Solution', *Journal of Monetary Economics*, Vol. 22, No.1, pp. 117-33.

Robbins, S.M. (1980), *A Securities Market Development Program for Bangladesh (unpublished)*, International Finance Corporation, Washington, D.C.

Roe, M.J. (1993), 'Some Differences in Corporate Structure in Germany, Japan and the United States', *The Yale Law Journal*, Vol. 102, No. 8, pp.1927-03.

Roll, R. (1977), 'A Critique of Asset Pricing Theory's Test', *Journal of Financial Economics*, Vol. 4, No. 1, pp. 129-76.

Rosen, G. (1958), 'Capital Markets and the Industrialization of Underdeveloped Economies', *Indian Economic Journal*, Vol. 10, No. 3, pp.172-94.

-------------(1962), *Some aspects of Industrial Finance in India*, Asia publishing House: Bombay.

Rosovsky, M. (1962), 'Capital Formation in Prewar Japan', *Shakai Keizaigaku*, Vol. 28, No. 2, pp. 25-46.

Ross, S.A. (1976), 'The Arbitrage Theory of Capital Asset Pricing', *Journal of Economic Theory*, Vol 13, No. 3, pp. 341-60.

Royama, Shoichi (1992), 'On the Financial Reform in Japan', in Japan Securities Research Institute (JSRI), *Capital Markets and Financial Services in Japan: Regulation and Practice*, JSRI: Tokyo, pp. 2-7.

Rubinstein, M.E. (1975), 'Securities Market Efficiency in an Arrow-Debreu Economy', *American Economic Review*, Vol. 65, No. 5, pp. 812-24.

Sakai, K. (1990), 'The Feudal World of Japanese Manufacturing', *Harvard Business review*, Vol. 68, No. 6, pp. 38-49.

Sakakibara, S. (1986), *Gendai Zaimu Riron* (Modern Finance Theory), Chikura Shobo: Tokyo.

Samuels, J.M. (1981), 'Inefficient Capital Markets and Their Implications', in Derkinderen, F.G.J. and Crum, R.L. (Eds.), *Risk, Capital Costs and Project Financing Decisions*, Martinus Nijhoff: Boston/The Hague/London, pp.129-48.

-------------and Yacout, N. (1981), 'Stock Exchanges in Developing Countries', *Savings and Development*, Vol. V, No. 4, pp. 217-32.

Sato, K. (1990), 'Indicative Planning in Japan', *Journal of Contemporary Economics*, Vol. 14, No. 4, pp. 625-46.

Schumpeter, J.A. (1939), *Business Cycles*, McGraw-Hill: New York.

-------------(1983), *The Theory of Economic Development*, Harvard University Press, Cambridge, Mass.

Scott, J. (1986), *Capitalist Property and Financial Power - A Comparative Study of Britain, the United States and Japan*, Wheatsheaf Books: Brighton.

Securities and Exchange Commission of Bangladesh (SEC) (1993-94), *Annual Report*, 1993-94, Dhaka.

-------------(1994-95), *Annual Report*, 1994-95, Dhaka.

-------------Quarterly Review - various issues.

Senda, Jun-ichi (1991), 'Changes in the Japanese Financial System' in Foundation for Advanced Information and Research, Japan (FAIR), *Japan's Financial Markets*, FAIR, pp. 4-13.

Seok, M.C. and Park, I. (1992), *Report on the Dhaka Stock Exchange (unpublished)*, The Asia Foundation, Dhaka, January.

Shafique, M. (1986), 'ICB Karjakram Behoto Hosse Keno?' (Why are ICB Activities Hampering?), *The Weekly Bichitra*, Dhaka 19 September, pp. 16-17 (in Bengali).

Sharma, J.L.(1983), 'Efficient Capital Markets and Random Character of Stock Price Behavior in a Developing Economy', *Indian Journal of Economics*, Vol. 63, No. 251, pp. 395-17.

-------------and Kennedy, Robert E.(1977), 'A Comparative Analysis of Stock Price Behavior on the Bombay, London, and New York Stock Exchanges', *Journal of Financial and Quantitative Analysis*, Vol.12, No.3, pp.391-13.

Sharpe, W.F. (1964), 'Capital Asset Prices: A Theory of Market Equilibrium Under Conditions of Risk', *Journal of Finance*, Vol. 19, No.3, pp. 425-42.

-------------and Cooper, G.M. (1972), 'Risk-Return Class of New York Stock

Exchange Common Stocks, 1931-67', *Financial Analysts Journal*, Vol. 28, No. 2, pp. 46-54.

Shaw, Edward S. (1973), *Financial Deepening in Economic Development*, Oxford University Press: New York.

Sheard, P. (1986), *Corporate Organization and Structural Adjustment in Japan*, Working paper, Australian National University.

------------(1991), 'The Economics of Interlocking Shareholding in Japan', *Ricerche Economiche*, Vol. 45, No. 2-3, pp. 421-48.

Shiller, Robert J. (1992), *The Report of the Twentieth Century Fund Task Force on Market Speculation and Corporate Governance*, The Twentieth Century Fund Press: New York.

Smith, T. (1955), *Political and Industrial Development in Japan: Government Enterprises, 1868-1880*, Stanford University Press: Stanford.

------------(1959), *The Agrarian Origin of Modern Japan*, Stanford University Press: Stanford.

Sobhan, Rehman (1974), 'Nationalized Industries in Bangladesh: Background and Problems', in Robinson, E.A.G. and Griffin, K. (Eds.), The Economic Development of Bangladesh Within a Socialist Framework, Macmillan: Basingstoke, pp. 181-200.

------------and Mahmood, S.A. (1981), 'Repayment of Loans to Specialized Financial Institutions in Bangladesh: Issues and Constraints', *The Bangladesh Development Studies*, Winter, pp. 71-98.

------------(1990), *Debt Default to the Development Financial Institutions: The Crisis of State-sponsored Entrepreneurship in Bangladesh*, University Press Ltd.: Dhaka.

Staubus, G.A. (1961), *A Theory of Accounting to Investors*, Texas Scholars Book Company: Texas.

Stigler, G.J. (1966), *The Theory of Price*, Macmillan: New York.

Stiglitz, J. (1985), ' Credit Markets and the Control of Capital', *Journal of Money, Credit and Banking*, Vol. 17, No. 2, pp. 133-52.

Suzuki, H. (1992), '*Zaibatsu kara Kigyo-shudan, Kigyo Keiretsu e*' (From the Zaibatsu to the Corporate Groups), in *Tochi Seido Shigaku* (Journal of Agrarian History), Vol. 135, pp. 1-18.

Tailor, J. (1983), *Shadows of the Rising Sun*, William Marrow and Company: New York.

Tanbi, V. (1987), 'The Public Sector in the Market Economics of Developing Asia', *Asian Development Review*, Vol. 5, No. 2, pp. 51-65.

Task Force on the International Competitiveness of U.S. Financial Institutions of the House Committee on Banking, Finance and Urban Affairs, Report of the Subcommittee on Financial Institutions Supervision, Regulation and Insurance (1990), Report No. 7, 101st cong., 2nd session, (quoted in Gilson and Roe, 1993).

Tatewaki, Kazuo (1991), *Banking and Finance in Japan: An Introduction to the Tokyo Market*, Routledge: London.

Teranishi, J. (1993), Emergence and Establishment of the Financial System in Postwar Japan: Government Intervention, Indirect Financing and the Corporate Monitoring System, Paper prepared for the World Bank Project Strategies for Rapid Growth: Public Policy and the Asian Miracle.

Tobin, J. (1958), 'Liquidity Preference as Behavior Towards Risk', *Review of Economic Studies*, Vol.25, No. 67, pp. 65-86.

------------(1965), 'The Theory of Portfolio Selection', in Hahn, F. and Brechling, F. (Eds.), *The Theory of Interest Rates*, McMillian, Chapter 1.

Tokyo Stock Exchange (1986), *Tokyo Stock Exchange Fact Book*, Tokyo Stock Exchange: Tokyo.

------------(1995), *Tokyo Stock Exchange Factbook*, Tokyo Stock Exchange: Tokyo.

------------*Monthly Statistics Report* -various issues.

Toyo Keizai Shimposha (1978), '*Ginko Obaya Kasu Ruison 320 sha no Kigyo Shindan*' (Treatment to the Banks: A Corporate Diagnosis of the 320 Firms with Accumulated Losses), *Tokei Nenpo*, Vol. 38, No. 4, (in Japanese).

Tokyo University *Henshu Iinkai* (Ed.) (1971), *Okuma Shigenobu Kankei Monjo* (Writings connected with Okuma Shigenobu, Vol. IV, (in Japanese).

Trezise, Philip H. and Suzuki, Y.(1976), 'Politics, Government and Economic Growth in Japan', in Patrick, H. and Rosovsky, H. (Eds.) *Asia's New Giant: How the Japanese Economy Works*, The Brookings Institution, Washington, D.C.

Ueno, H. (1978), *Nihon no Keizai Seido* (Economic System In Japan), *Nihon Keizai Shimbun-sha*: Tokyo (in Japanese).

United Nations (1950), *Domestic Financing of Economic Development*, United Nations: New York.

Van de Walle, N. (1989), Privatisation in Developing Countries: A Review of the Issues, *World Development*, Vol. 17, No. 5, 601-15.

van Loo, F. (1977), 'The Effect of Foreign Direct Investment on Investment in Canada', *Review of Economics and Statistics*, Vol. 59, No. 4, November, pp. 474-81.

Van Wijnbergen, S.(1982), 'Interest Rate Management in Developing Countries, Theory and Simulation Results for Korea', *World Bank Staff Working Paper* No, 593.

Varley, J.W. (1992), *Returns and Risks to Long Term Capital, Occasional paper-3 (unpublished)*, Financial Sector Reform Project, Bangladesh Bank, Dhaka, September.

Vasicek, O. (1973), 'A Note on Using Cross-Sectional Information in Bayesian

Estimation of Security Betas', *Journal of Finance*, Vol. 8, No. 5, pp. 1233-39.

Vernon-Wortzel, H. and Wortzel, L.(1989), 'Privatisation: Not the Only Answer', *World Development*, Vol. 17, No. 5, pp. 633-41.

Vogel, Ezra (1979), *Japan as Number One,* Harvard University Press: Cambridge.

von Furstenberg, G.M. and Malkiel, B.G., (1977), ' The Government and Capital Formation: A Survey of Recent Issues', *Journal of Economic Literature*, Vol. 15, No. 3, pp.835-78.

Wade, R. (1992), 'East Asia's Economic Success: Conflicting Perspectives, Partial Insights, Shaky Evidence', *World Politics*, Vol. 44, No.2, pp. 270-320.

Wai, U.T.(1972), *Financial Intermediaries and National Savings In Developing Countries*, Praeger Publishers:New York.

-------------and Patrick, H. T. (1973), 'Stock and Bond Issues and Capital Markets in Less Developed Countries', *IMF Staff Papers*, July.

-------------and Wong, Chorng-huey (1982), 'Determinants of Private Investment in Developing Countries', *The Journal of Development Studies*, Vol. 19, No.1, pp.19-36.

Wallich, H.C. and Wallich, M.I.(1976), 'Banking and Finance', in Patrick, H. and Rosovsky, H. (Eds.), *Asia's New Giant: How the JapaneseEconomy Works*, The Brookings Institutions: Washigtonton, D.C., pp. 153-48.

Washington SyCip (1967), ' Professional Practice in Developing Nations'; *The Journal of Accountancy*, Vol. 123, pp. 41-45.

Washio Toru (1974), *Keiretsu Yushi (ge)*(Group Finance, Part II), *Ginko Kenkyu*, Vol.357, pp. 78-83 (in Japanese).

Weil, P. (1989), 'The Equity Premium Puzzle and the Riskfree Rate Puzzle', *Journal of Monetary Economics*, Vol. 24, No. 3, November, pp. 401-22.

Weisskopf, T.E. (1972), 'The Impact of Foreign Capital Inflow on Domestic Savings in Underdeveloped Countries', *Journal of International economics*, Vol. 2, pp. 25-38.

Williams, D. (1966), 'The Growth of Capital and Securities Markets', *Finance and Development*, Vol. 3, No. 3, pp. 212-221.

Williumson, O. (1975), *Markets and Hierarchies*, The Free Press: New York.

Wilson, D. (1984), Privatisation of Asia, *Banker*, Vol. 134, No. 703, pp. 47-65.

Wolf, Marvin (1983), *The Japanese Conspiracy*, Empire Books: New York.

World Bank (1978), *Bangladesh - Report on Domestic Financial Resource Mobilization*, Report No. 1919-BD, Washington, D.C., 26 April.

-------------(1981), *Accelerated Development in Sub-Saharan Africa: An Agenda for Action*, Washigton, D.C.

-------------(1989a), *Bangladesh Manufacturing Public Enterprise Reform,*

Washington, D.C.

----------(1989b), *World Development Report 1989*, Washington, D.C.

----------(1991), *Developing the Private Sector: The World Bank's Experience and Approach*, Washington, D.C.

----------(1992), *Bangladesh: Selected Issues in External Competitiveness and Economic Efficiency*, Washington, D.C.

----------(1993), *The East Asian Miracle*, Oxford University Press: New York.

----------(1994a), *Bangladesh Privatization and Adjustment*, Washington, D.C.

----------(1994b), *Bangladesh: From Stabilization to Growth*, Washinton, D.C.

Yafeh, Y. (1995), 'Corporate Ownership, Profitability and Bank-Firm Ties: Evidence from the American Occupation Reforms in Japan', *Journal of the Japanese and International Economies*, Vol. 9, No. 2, pp. 154-73.

Yalawar, Y.B. (1988),'Bombay Stock Exchange: Rates of Return and efficiency', *The Indian Economic Journal*, Vol. 35, No. 4, pp. 69-121.

Yamamura, K. (1979), 'Behind the made in Japan Label', in Hyoe, M. and Hirschmeier, J. (Eds.), *Political Economics in Contemporary Japan*, Japan Culture Institute: Tokyo.

Yoder, R., Borkholder, P. and Friesen, B. (1991), 'Privatisation and Development: The Empirical Evidence', *The Journal of Developing Areas*, Vol. 25, No. 3, pp. 425-34.

Yonezawa, Y. and Konya, F. (1982), 'The Japanese Market and Economic Environment', *Journal of Portfolio Management*, Vol. 9, No. 1, pp.36-45.

----------and Maru Junko (1984), *Nihon no Kabushiki Shijo* (The Stock Market of Japan), Toyo Keizai Shimposha: Tokyo (in Japanese).

Zarnowitz, V. and Boschan, C. (1975), 'Cyclical Indicators: An Evaluation of New Leading Indexes', *Business Condition Digest*, pp. v - xix.